D1190539

WORKING PAPERS IN THE THEORY OF ACTION

WORKING PAPERS

IN THE

THEORY OF ACTION

BY

TALCOTT PARSONS,

ROBERT F. BALES

AND

EDWARD A. SHILS

THE FREE PRESS, *New York*

COLLIER-MACMILLAN LIMITED, *London*

CONTENTS

WORKING PAPERS IN THE THEORY OF ACTION

PREFACE

THE PRESENT PUBLICATION SHOULD NOT BE CONSIDERED IN THE USUAL sense as a book, but exactly what its title, *Working Papers,* implies. It constitutes, with perhaps the one exception of the first paper in the collection, a set of working drafts written as the theoretical ideas in them developed and not yet either reworked to constitute a logically well-integrated whole or, except fragmentarily, empirically tested. We have welcomed the suggestion of the Free Press to publish these papers in the present form because we hope to benefit from the discussion they will provoke among theoretically minded members of the interested professional groups. Such discussion should, we feel, hasten the process of theoretical development and enable us later to produce a more integrated and finished result, and do it earlier than would otherwise be possible.

As working papers, the contents of this publication make no attempt to present the background which would make them readily comprehensible to the reader who is unfamiliar with our previous work—to do this would require a good deal of space and would not be in accord with the purpose of the publication. The most important background will be found in three previous publications: Bales, *Interaction Process Analysis,* (Addison Wesley Press, 1950); Parsons and Shils (eds.), *Toward a General Theory of Action,* (Harvard University Press, 1951), especially Part II by Parsons and Shils, "Values, Motives and Systems of Action"; and Parsons, *The Social System,* (Free Press, 1951). Nor have we attempted to revise the earlier papers in the light of later developments. With the addition of a few editorial notes they are left exactly as originally written and are printed here in the order in which they were written. We reserve the attempt at a single consistent presentation for a later occasion.

The circumstances leading up to the present collaborative publication are briefly as follows. All three authors have been closely associated over a period of years. Bales' approach to the analysis of interaction in small groups grew out of the same tradition of sociological theory as Parsons' and Shils' consideration of the more macroscopic levels of the structure and functioning of social systems. Though not formally a collaborator in the volume *Toward a General Theory of Action,* Bales participated actively in many of the discussions on which that publication was based and contributed much to them.

9

Further intensive discussions were carried on between Parsons and Bales in connection with the subsequent writing of Parsons' *The Social System,* especially the chapters on the processes of socialization and on deviant behavior and social control. Furthermore, in the spring term of 1950-51 we participated with Charles Morris and several other colleagues in an informal discussion group on the theory of symbolism in relation to action, which greatly stimulated our thinking. We owe a particularly great debt to Professor Morris.

The first paper in the series, "The Superego and the Theory of Social Systems,"* is included because it constitutes a transition between Parsons' previous publications and the more recent phase in which the present authors have collaborated. It was written in May, 1951, for a meeting of the American Psychiatric Association, and the subject to which it was addressed was chosen as appropriate to this occasion. It was, however, concerned with very general problems of theory. It is hoped that its inclusion here will help the reader to understand the path of development by which the main ideas presented in the subsequent papers came to be worked out.

In the early fall of 1951, partly in connection with theory construction for an empirical research project on social mobility, Parsons took up the theme of symbolism again by writing the paper on that subject which appears as Chapter II of the present publication. This was done in continual consultation with Bales. The new light on the significance of the pattern variable scheme which came out of the venture made it increasingly clear that there was an intimate relation between this and Bales' scheme of categories for the analysis of interaction process. It was the sudden insight that Bales' four system-problems and a particular new combination of four of the pattern variables (excluding self- vs. collectivity-orientation) were essentially the same thing and that they could be regarded as alternative formulations of the dimensions of a four-dimensional space which constituted the big step toward consolidation of the two schemes. It was essentially this insight, which came almost immediately after the completion of the paper on symbolism, which led us to formulate the first collaborative paper, Chapter III of this publication. This was written in November, 1951.

With this consolidation, it became almost immediately clear

*Already published in *Psychiatry,* February, 1952. We are indebted to the editors of this journal for their kind permission to reprint the paper here.

that the pattern variable scheme, the four system-problems, the twelve categories of interaction process, the typology of deviant orientations developed in Parsons' *The Social System,* and the corresponding paradigm of the processes of social control could all be brought together in a single analytical scheme along the lines outlined in our paper on the four dimensions.

These insights, which came with great rapidity following the initial "break through," left us, however, with many complex theoretical problems unsolved. The second collaborative paper, Chapter V, essentially documents a next stage of progress in work on these problems as a result of several months of effort in following up the implication of the earlier theoretical consolidation.

The main outline of this paper was worked out by Parsons and Bales in April and May, 1952. It had been possible, however, to draft only an introductory section before Bales' departure for Europe to teach in the Salzburg Seminar. In the meantime, it had been arranged for Shils to come to Cambridge in the early summer to resume his previous collaboration with Parsons on general theoretical work. They undertook the further development of the draft planned by Parsons and Bales. It turned out that quite extensive developments occurred before the present tentative closure was reached. A first draft of this paper was written by Parsons and Shils. On Bales' return from Europe, however, the three authors have worked over the problems together and the version appearing in print represents an extensive revision of this draft.

Chapter V develops the earlier leads in two main directions. The first is the use of the four-dimensional scheme in the analysis of action-process as such, which culminates in a clarification of the analysis of phase movement of the process in both its motivational and its symbolic-cultural aspects. The second main direction is the articulation of the dimensional scheme with the analysis of the structure of systems, especially social systems, as this has been developed in previous work, particularly *The Social System* and, on a more microscopic level, in *Interaction Process Analysis.* The two directions of extension are brought together above all by a careful working out of microscopic-macroscopic levels of system reference and how they articulate with each other. Indeed we regard this as perhaps the most important single key to theoretical clarification in this field.

It is important to emphasize that the theoretical work documented in this set of papers has proceeded concomitantly and in the closest connection with each of our empirical research interests. Certain empirical results of Bales' work on small groups were indeed the source of some of the major insights which we state in more general form in the earlier papers. The interaction level of analysis provided us throughout with a stable, empirical point of reference, which helped us untangle some of the very slippery semantic problems connected with the fact that the conceptual scheme with which we are dealing is applicable through a microscopic-macroscopic range of action systems. Bales' paper, which appears as Chapter IV of the collection was written in May, 1952, for this collection. We hope it may aid the reader to see more concretely the empirical relevance of some of the most abstract ideas of the general theory, particularly those dealing with the problem of an equilibrating system, and perhaps even to share with us some of the excitement we feel in having at hand a way of producing data that link so directly with the most abstract level of theory. Shils also has been working on primary groups and on other problems in the analysis of social structure.

At the same time much of Parsons' share of the work has been closely connected with the project in the field of social mobility which he has been carrying on in collaboration with Samuel A. Stouffer and Florence Kluckhohn with the help of a small staff and the members of a graduate research seminar. In this connection, the attempt to delineate the structure of occupational roles as a reference system has driven us deeper into the analysis of the social system as a whole than we had thought would be necessary. A brief account of the approach to the classification of occupational roles developed in this way is included in Chapter V of the Papers. Fuller exposition and treatment of data is reserved for future publications in connection with the mobility project.

It is not possible adequately to acknowledge our indebtedness to many others in connection with this work. All of it has been carried on in a situation of continuing discussions with many colleagues and students and, as we have noted, is most intimately connected with our empirical research and hence our collaborators in this work. Without their contribution our specific job could not have been accomplished.

T. P.
R. F. B.
E. A. S.

Cambridge, Massachusetts
October 1952

CHAPTER 1

THE SUPEREGO AND THE
THEORY OF SOCIAL SYSTEMS*

IN THE BROADEST SENSE, PERHAPS, THE CONTRIBUTION OF PSYCHOA-
nalysis to the social sciences has consisted of an enormous deepen-
ing and enrichment of our understanding of human motivation.
This enrichment has been such a pervasive influence that it would
be almost impossible to trace its many ramifications. In the present
paper I have chosen to say something about one particular aspect
of this influence, that exerted through the psychoanalytic concept
of the superego, because of its peculiarly direct relevance to the
central theoretical interests of my own social-science discipline,
sociological theory. This concept, indeed, forms one of the most
important points at which it is possible to establish direct relations
between psychoanalysis and sociology, and it is in this connection
that I wish to discuss it.

Psychoanalysis, in common with other traditions of psychological thought, has naturally concentrated on the study of the personality of the individual as the focus of its frame of reference.
Sociology, on the other hand, has equally naturally been primarily
concerned with the patterning of the behavior of a plurality of individuals as constituting what, increasingly, we tend to call a social

*The substance of the present paper was read at the meeting of the Psycho-
analytic Section of the American Psychiatric Association, Cincinnati, Ohio,
May 7, 1951. The theme of the meeting at which it was read was "The Contribution of Psychoanalysis to the Social Sciences." It was published in *Psychiatry*, Vol. XV, No. 1, Feb. 1952.

14 *Working Papers in the Theory of Action*

system. Because of historical differences of perspective and points of departure, the conceptual schemes arrived at from these two starting points have in general not been fully congruent with each other, and this fact has occasioned a good deal of misunderstanding. However, recent theoretical work [1] shows that, in accord with convergent trends of thought, it is possible to bring the main theoretical trends of these disciplines together under a common frame of reference, that which some sociologists have called the "theory of action." It is in the perspective of this attempt at theoretical unification that I wish to approach the analysis of the concept of the supergo.

One of the principal reasons for the selection of this concept lies in the fact that it has been, historically, at the center of an actual process of convergence. In part at least, it is precisely because of this fact that Freud's discovery of the internalization of moral values as an essential part of the structure of the personality itself constituted such a crucial landmark in the development of the sciences of human behavior. Though there are several other somewhat similar formulations to be found in the literature of roughly the same period, the formulation most dramatically convergent with Freud's theory of the superego was that of the social role of moral norms made by the French sociologist Emile Durkheim—a theory which has constituted one of the cornerstones of the subsequent development of sociological theory.

Durkheim's insights into this subject slightly antedated those of Freud. [2] Durkheim started from the insight that the individual, as

[1] Cf. Talcott Parsons and Edward A. Shils (eds.), *Toward a General Theory of Action;* Cambridge, Harvard Univ. Press, 1951. Also Talcott Parsons, *The Social System;* Glencoe, Ill., Free Press, 1951.

[2] Durkheim's insights were first clearly stated in a paper, "Détermination du Fait moral," published in the *Revue de Métaphysique et de Morale* in 1906, and were much further developed in *Les formes élémentaires de la vie religieuse,* his last book (Paris, F. Alcan, 1912).

The earlier paper was reprinted in the volume, *Sociologie et Philosophie,* edited by Charles Bouglé (Paris, F. Alcan, 1929). Its theme is further elaborated in the posthumously published lectures, delivered at the Sorbonne in 1906, which carry the title, *L'Education morale* (Paris, F. Alcan, 1925).

Strongly influenced by Durkheim is the work of the Swiss psychologist, Jean Piaget, who has developed his view on the psychological side. See especially his *The Moral Judgment of the Child* (Glencoe, Ill., Free Press, 1948). I presume that the psychiatric reader is familiar with the relevant works of Freud. However, two of the most important discussions of the superego are found in *The Ego and the Id* (London, Hogarth Press, 1949) and the *New Introductory Lectures on Psychoanalysis* (New York, Norton, 1933).

a member of society, is not wholly free to make his own moral decisions but is in some sense "constrained" to accept the orientations common to the society of which he is a member. He went through a series of attempts at interpretation of the nature of this constraint, coming in the end to concentrate on two primary features of the phenomenon: first, that moral rules "constrain" behavior most fundamentally by moral authority rather than by any external coercion; and, secondly, that the effectiveness of moral authority could not be explained without assuming that, as we would now say, the value patterns were internalized as part of personality. Durkheim, as a result of certain terminological peculiarities which need not be gone into here, tended to identify "society" as such with the system of moral norms. In this very special sense of the term society, it is significant that he set forth the explicit formula that "society exists only in the minds of individuals."

In Durkheim's work there are only suggestions relative to the psychological mechanisms of internalization and the place of internalized moral values in the structure of personality itself. But this does not detract from the massive phenomenon of the convergence of the fundamental insights of Freud and Durkheim, insights not only as to the fundamental importance of moral values in human behavior, but of the internalization of these values. This convergence, from two quite distinct and independent starting points, deserves to be ranked as one of the truly fundamental landmarks of the development of modern social science. It may be likened to the convergence between the results of the experimental study of plant breeding by Mendel and of the microscopic study of cell division—a convergence which resulted in the discovery of the chromosomes as bearers of the genes. Only when the two quite distinct bodies of scientific knowledge could be put together did the modern science of genetics emerge.

The convergence of Freud's and Durkheim's thinking may serve to set the problem of this paper, which is, How can the fundamental phenomenon of the internalization of moral norms be analyzed in such a way as to maximize the generality of implications of the formulation, both for the theory of personality and for the theory of the social system? For if it is possible to state the essentials of the problem in a sufficiently generalized way, the analysis should prove to be equally relevant in both directions. It should thereby contribute to the integration of the psychanalytic theory of personality and of the sociological theory of the social system, and thus to the further development of a conceptual scheme which is essentially common to both.

16 *Working Papers in the Theory of Action*

The essential starting point of an attempt to link these two bodies of theory is the analysis of certain fundamental features of the *inter*action of two or more persons, the process of interaction itself being conceived as a system. Once the essentials of such an interactive system have been made clear, the implications of the analysis can be followed out in *both* directions: the study of the structure and functioning of the personality as a system, in relation to the other personalities; and the study of the functioning of the social system as a system. It may be surmised that the difficulty of bringing the two strands of thought together in the past has stemmed from the fact that this analysis has not been carried through; and this has not been done because it has "fallen between two stools." On the one hand, Freud and his followers, by concentrating on the single personality, have failed to consider adequately the implications of the individual's interaction with other personalities *to form a system*. On the other hand, Durkheim and the other sociologists have failed, in their concentration on the social system as a system to consider systematically the implications of the fact that it is *the interaction of personalities* which constitutes the social system with which they have been dealing, and that, therefore, adequate analysis of motivational process in such a system must reckon with the problems of personality. This circumstance would seem to account for the fact that this subject has ben so seriously neglected.

It may first be pointed out that two interacting persons must be conceived to be objects to each other in two *primary* respects, and in a third respect which is in a sense derived from the first two. These are (1) cognitive perception and conceptualization, the answer to the question of *what the object is*, and (2) cathexis—attachment or aversion—the answer to the question of *what the object means* in an emotional sense. The third mode by which a person orients himself to an object is by evaluation—the integration of cognitive and cathectic meanings of the object to form a system, including the stability of such a system over time. It may be maintained that no stable relation between two or more objects is possible without all three of these modes of orientation being present for *both* parties to the reationship.[3]

Consideration of the conditions on which such a stable, mutually oriented system of interaction depends leads to the conclusion that

[3] Further development of this analytical starting point and of the reasons for assuming it will be found in Parsons and Shils (eds.), *Toward a General Theory of Action* (reference footnote 1). See esp., the "General Statement," and Part II, "Values, Motives, and Systems of Action." The reader may also wish to consult Parsons, *The Social System* (reference footnote 1).

on the human level this mutuality of interaction must be mediated and stabilized by a *common culture*—that is, by a commonly shared system of symbols, the meanings of which are understood on both sides with an approximation to agreement. The existence of such symbol systems, especially though not exclusively as involved in language, is common to every known human society. However the going symbol systems of the society may have developed in the first place, they are involved in the socialization of every child. It may be presumed that the prominence of common symbol systems is both a consequence and a condition of the extreme plasticity and sensitivity of the human organism, which in turn are essential conditions of its capacity to learn and, concomitantly, to mislearn. These features of the human organism introduce an element of extreme potential instability into the process of human interaction, which requires stabilizing mechanisms if the interactive system, as a system, is to function.

The elements of the common culture have significance with reference to all three of the modes of orientation of action. Some of them are primarily of cognitive significance; others are primarily of cathectic significance, expressive of emotional meanings or affect; and still others are primarily of evaluative significance. Normative regulation for the establishing of standards is characteristic of all of culture; thus there is a right way of symbolizing any orientation of action in any given culture. This is indeed essential to communication itself: the conventions of the language must be observed if there is to be effective communication.

That a person's cathexis of a human object—that is, what the object means to the person emotionally—is contingent on the responsiveness of that object is a fact familiar to psychoanalytic theory. It may be regarded as almost a truism that it is difficult if not impossible in the long run to love without being loved in return. It is more difficult to see that there is an almost direct parallelism in this respect betwen cathexis and cognition. After all, a person's cathexis of an inanimate object, such as a food object, is not directly dependent on the responsiveness of the object; it is surely anthropomorphism to suggest that a steak likes to be eaten in the same sense in which a hungry man likes to eat the steak. Similarly the cognition of the inanimate object by a person is not directly dependent on the object's reciprocal cognition of the person. But where the object is another person, the two, as ego and alter, constitute an *inter*active system. The question is what, in a cognitive sense, *is* alter from the point of view of ego, and vice versa. Clearly the answer to this question must involve the place—or "status," as sociologists call it—of ego and alter in the structure of the inter-active system. Thus when I say a person is my mother, or my friend, or my student, I am characterizing that person as a participant in a system of social interaction in which I also am involved.

Thus not only the cathectic attitudes, but also the cognitive images, of persons relative to each other are functions of their inter-action in the system of social relations; in a fundamental sense the same order of relationship applies in both cases.

Thus a social system is a function of the common culture, which not only forms the basis of the intercommunication of its members, but which defines, and so in one sense determines, the relative sta-tuses of its members. There is, within surprizingly broad limits, no intrinsic significance of persons to each other independent of their actual interaction. In so far as these relative statuses are defined and regulated in terms of a common culture, the following apparently paradoxical statement holds true: what persons *are* can only be understood in terms of a set of beliefs and sentiments which define what they *ought to be*. This proposition is true only in a very broad way, but is none the less crucial to the understanding of social systems.

It is in this context that the central significance of moral stand-ards in the common culture of systems of social interaction must be understood. Moral standards constitute, as the focus of the evalua-tive aspect of the common culture, the core of the stabilizing mechanisims of the system of social interaction. These mecha-nisims function, moreover, to stabilize not only attitudes—that is, the emotional meanings of persons to each other—but also cate-gorizations—the cognitive definitions of what persons are in a socially significant sense.

If the approach taken above is correct, the place of the superego as part of the structure of the personality must be understood in terms of the relation between personality and the total common cul-ture, by virtue of which a stable system of social interaction on the human levels becomes possible. Freud's insight was profoundly cor-rect when he focused on the element of moral standards. This is, indeed, central and crucial, but it does seem that Freud's view was too narrow. The inescapable conclusion is that not only moral standards, but *all the components of the common culture* are inter-nalized as part of the personality structure. Moral standards, indeed, cannot in this respect be dissociated from the *content* of the orien-tation patterns which they regulate; as I have pointed out, the

content of both cathectic-attitudes and cognitive-status definitions
have cultural, hence normative significance. This content is cultural
and learned. Neither what the human object *is*, in the most significant respects, nor what it *means* emotionally, can be understood
as given independently of the nature of the interactive process itself;
and the significance of moral norms themselves very largely relates
to this fact.

It would seem that Freud's insight in this field was seriously
impeded by the extent to which he thought in terms of a frame of
reference relating a personality to its situation or environment without specific reference to the analysis of the social interaction of
persons as a system. This perspective, which was overwhelmingly
dominant in his day, accounts for two features of his theory. In
the first place, the cognitive definition of the object world does not
seem to have been problematical to Freud. He subsumed it all under "external reality," in relation to which "ego-functions" constitute
a process of adaptation. He failed to take explicitly into account the
fact that the frame of reference in terms of which objects are cognized, and therefore adapted to, is cultural and thus cannot be taken
for granted as given, but must be internalized as a condition of the
development of mature ego-functioning. In this respect it seems to
be correct to say that Freud introduced an unreal separation between the superego and the ego—the lines between them are in fact
difficult to define in his theory. In the light of the foregoing considerations the distinction which Freud makes between the superego and the ego—that the former is internalized, by identification
and that the latter seems to consist of responses to external reality
rather than of internalized culture—is not tenable. These responses
are, to be sure, *learned* responses; but internalization is a special
kind of learning which Freud seemed to confine to the superego.

If this argument raises questions about cognitive function and
therefore about the theory of the ego, there are implications, *ipso
facto*, for the superego. The essential point seems to be that Freud's
view seems to imply that the object, as cognitively significant, is
given independently of the actor's internalized culture, and that
superego standards are then applied to it. This fails to take account
of the extent to which the constitution of the object and its moral
appraisal are part and parcel of the *same* fundamental cultural patterns; it gives the superego an appearance of arbitrariness and dissociation from the rest of the personality—particularly from the ego
—which is not wholly in accord with the facts.

The second problem of Freud's theory concerns the relation

of cathexis or affect to the superego. In a sense, this is the obverse of its relation to cognition. The question here is perhaps analogous to that of the transmission of light in physics: how can the object's cathectic significance be mediated in the absence of direct biological contact? Indeed, embarrassment over this problem may be one source of the stressing of sexuality in Freudian theory, since sexuality generally involves such direct contact.

To Freud, the object tends, even if human, to be an inert something on which a "charge" of cathectic significance has been placed. The process is regarded as expressive of the actor's instincts or libido, but the element of mutuality tends to be treated as accessory and almost arbitrary. This is associated with the fact that, while Freud, especially in his *Interpretation of Dreams,* made an enormous contribution to the theory of expressive or cathectic symbolism, there is a very striking limitation of the extension of this theory. The basis of this may be said to be that Freud tended to confine his consideration of symbolism in the emotional context to its directly expressive functions and failed to go on to develop the analysis of its communicative functions. The dream symbol remained for him the prototype of affective symbolism. It is perhaps largely because of this fact that Freud did not emphasize the common culture aspect of such symbolism, but tended to attempt to trace its origins back to intrinsic meanings which were independent of the interactive process and its common culture. More generally the tenor of the analysis of affect was to emphasize a fundamental isolation of the individual in his lonely struggle with his id.[4]

This whole way of looking at the problem of cathexis seems to have a set of consequences parallel to those outlined above concerning cognition; it tends to dissociate the superego from the sources of affect. This derives from the fact that Freud apparently did not appreciate the presence and significance of a common culture of expressive-affective symbolism and the consequent necessity for thinking of the emotional component of interaction as mediated by this aspect of the common culture. Thus, the aspect of the superego which is concerned with the regulation of emotional reactions must be considered as defining the regulative principles of this interactive system. It is an integral *part* of the symbolism of emotional expression, not something over, above, and apart from it.

The general purport of this criticism is that Freud, with his

---

[4] This view has certainly been modified in subsequent psychoanalytic thinking, but it is the major framework within which Freud introduced the concept of the superego.

formulation of the concept of the superego, made only a beginning at an analysis of the role of the common culture in personality. The structure of his theoretical scheme prevented him from seeing the possibilities for extending the same fundamental analysis from the internalization of moral standards—which he applied to the superego—to the internalization of the cognitive frame of reference for interpersonal relations and for the common system of expressive symbolism; and similarly it prevented him from seeing the extent to which these three elements of the common culture are integrated with each other.

This very abstract analysis may become somewhat more understandable if examples are given of what is meant by the cognitive reference or categorization system, and by the system of expressive symbolism, considering both as parts of the internalized common culture.

One of the most striking cases of the first is that of sex categorization—that is, the learning of sex role. Freud speaks of the original "bi-sexuality" of the child. The presumption is that he postulated a constitutionally given duality of orientation. In terms of the present approach, there is at least an alternative hypothesis possible which should be explored.[5] This hypothesis is that some of the principal facts which Freud interpreted as manifestations of constitutional bisexuality can be explained by the fact that the categorization of human persons—including the actor's categorization of himself taken as a point of reference—into two sexes is not, except in its somatic points of reference, biologically given but, in psychological significance, must be learned by the child. It is fundamental that children of both sexes start life with essentially the same relation to the mother, a fact on which Freud himself rightly laid great stress. It may then be suggested that the process by which the boy learns to differentiate himself in terms of sex from the mother and in this sense "identify" with the father, while the girl learns to identify with the mother, is a learning process. One major part of the process of growing up is the internalization of one's own sex role as a critical part of the self-image. It may well be that this way of looking at the process will have the advantage of making the assumption of constitutional bisexuality at least partly superfluous as an explanation of the individual's sex identification. In any case it has the great advantage of linking the

---

[5] This is in no way meant to suggest that there is *no* element of constitutional bisexuality, but only that *some* things Freud attributed to it may be explicable on other grounds.

determination of sex categorization directly with the role structure
of the social system in a theoretical as well as an empirical sense.
Every sociologist will appreciate this since he is familiar with the
crucial significance of sex role differentiation and constitution for
social structure.

An example of the second role, that of common expressive symbolism, may be found in terms of the process by which a reciprocal
love attitude between mother and child is built up. Freud quite
rightly, it seems, points to the origin of the child's love attitude as
found in his dependency on the mother for the most elementary
sources of gratification, such as food, elementary comforts, and
safety. Gradually, in the process of interaction, a system of expectations of the continuation and repetition of these gratifications
comes to be built up in the child; and these expectations are bound
together as a result of the fact that a variety of such gratifications
comes from the single source, the mother.

In this process, one may assume that well before the development of language there begins to occur a process of generalization,
so that certain acts of the mother are interpreted as *signs* that gratifying performances can be expected—for example, the child becomes able to interpret her approaching footsteps or the tone of her
voice. It is suggested that one of the main reasons why the erotic
component of the child's relation to the mother is so important lies
in the fact that, since bodily contact is an essential aspect of child
care, erotic gratifications readily take on a symbolic significance.
The erotic element has the extremely important property that it is
relatively diffuse, being awakened by any sort of affectionate bodily
contact. This diffuseness makes it particularly suitable as a vehicle
of symbolic meanings. By this process, then, gradually, there is a
transition from the child's focus on erotic stimulation as such, to
his focus on the mother's *attitude* which is expressed by the eroti-
cally pleasurable stimulation. Only when this transition has taken
place can one correctly speak of the child's having become dependent on the *love* of the mother and not merely on the specific
pleasures the mother dispenses to him. Only when this level is
reached, can the love attitude serve as a motivation to the acceptance of disciplines, since it can then remain stable—even though
many specific gratifications which have previously been involved in
the relationship are eliminated from it.

The essential point for present purposes is that, in its affective
aspect, the child's interaction with the mother is not *only* a process
of mutual gratification of needs, but is on the child's part a process

of learning of the symbolic significance of a complicated system of acts on the part of the mother—of what they signify about what she feels and of how they are interdependent with and thus in part consequences of his own acts. That is to say, there is developed a complex language of emotional communication between them. Only when the child has learned this language on a relatively complex level, can he be said to have learned to love his mother or to be dependent on her love for him. There is, thus, a transition from "pleasure dependence" to "love dependence." One primary aspect of learning to love and to be loved is the internalization of a common culture of expressive symbolism which makes it possible for the child to express *and communicate* his feelings and to understand the mother's feelings toward him.

It would seem that only when a sufficiently developed cognitive reference system and a system of expressive symbolism have been internalized is the foundation laid for the development of a superego; for only then can the child be said to be capable of understanding, in both the cognitive and the emotional senses, the meaning of the prescriptions and prohibitions which are laid upon him. The child must mature to the point where he can begin to play a *responsible* role in a system of social interaction, where he can understand that what people feel is a function of his and their conformity with mutually held standards of conduct. Only when he has become dependent on his mother's love can he develop meaningful anxiety, in that then he might jeopardize his security in that love by not living up to her expectations of being a good boy.

The above considerations have important implications for the nature of the process of identification in so far as that is the principal mechanism by which the superego is acquired. If this analysis is correct, the crucial problem concerns the process of internalization of the common culture, including all three of its major components —the cognitive reference system, the system of expressive symbolism, and the system of moral standards.

In the first place, it would seem to be clear that *only* cultural symbol systems can be internalized. An object can be cathected, cognized, and appraised, but it cannot as such be taken into the personality; the only sense in which the latter terminology is appropriate is in calling attention to the fact that the common culture is indeed part of the personality of the object, but it is only an aspect, not the whole of it. Two persons can be said to be identified with each other in so far as they *share* important components of common culture. But since roles in the social system are differentiated, it should be noted that it is always important to specify *what* elements of culture are common.

Secondly, it is important to point out that the learning of the common culture may lead to the assumption either of a role identical with that of the object of identification or of a role differentiated from that object's role. Thus in the case of the boy vis-à-vis his mother, the learning of his sex categorization enables him to understand and accept the fact that with respect to sex he is different from her. The standards of proper behavior for both sexes are shared by the members of both, but their *application* is differentiated. The usage of the term identification has often been ambiguous, since it has been used to imply a likeness both of standards and of application. From the present point of view it is quite correct to speak of a boy learning his sex role by identification with the mother—in that he learns the sex categorization partly from her—and by the fact that he and she belong to different sex categories, which has important implications for *his* behavior. This is different from identification with his father in the sense that he learns that, with respect to sex, he is classed with his father and not with his mother.

Thirdly, there seems to be excellent evidence that while identification cannot mean coming *to be the object,* it is, as internalization of common culture, dependent on *positive cathexis of the object.* The considerations reviewed above give some suggestions as to why this should be true. Internalization of a culture pattern is not merely knowing it as an object of the external world; it is incorporating it into the actual structure of the personality as such. This means that the culture pattern must be integrated with the affective system of the personality.

Culture, however, is a system of generalized symbols and their meanings. In order for the integration with affect, which constitutes internalization, to take place, the individual's own affective organization must achieve levels of generalization of a high order. The principal mechanism by which this is accomplished appears to be through the building up of attachments to other persons—that is, by emotional communication with others so that the individual is sensitized to the *attitudes* of the others, not merely to their specific acts with their intrinsic gratification-deprivation significance. In other words, the process of forming attachments is *in itself* inherently a process of the generalization of affect. But this generalization in turn actually is in one major aspect the process of symbolization of emotional meanings—that is, it is a process of the acquisition of a culture. The intrinsic difficulty of creation of cultural patterns is so great that the child can only acquire complex cultural generalization through interaction with others who already possess it. Cathexis of an object as a focal aspect of identification is then another name for the development of *motivation* for the internalization of cultural patterns, at least for one crucially important phase of this process.

The conditions of socialization of a person are such that the gratifications which derive from his cathexis of objects cannot be secured unless, along with generalization of emotional meanings and their communication, he also develops a cognitive categorization of objects, including himself, and a system of moral norms which regulate the relations between himself and the object (a superego). This way of looking at the process of identification serves perhaps to help clear up a confusing feature of Freud's method of treatment. Freud, it will be remembered, denies that the very young child is capable of object cathexis, and speaks of identification, in contrast with object cathexis, as "the earliest form of emotional tie with an object." He then speaks of identification with the father in the oedipus situation as a reversion to the more "primitive" form of relation to an object.

I would agree that the child's early attachment to the mother and his later cathexis of her are not the same thing. It seems probable that the earliest attachment is, as it were, precultural, while true object cathexis involves the internalization of a cultural symbol system. But it seems extremely doubtful whether the relation to the father in the oedipus situation can be correctly described as a reversion to a presymbolic level. It is impossible to go into this problem fully here; but it may be suggested that the oedipus situation might be better interpreted as the strain imposed on the child by forcing him to take a major further step in growing up, in the process of which the father becomes the focus of his ambivalent feelings precisely because the child dare not jeopardize his love relation to the mother. Although regressive patterns of reaction would be expected under such a strain, these are not the core of the process of identification; however important, they are secondary phenomena.

If the foregoing account of the internalized content of personality and of the processes of identification points in the right direction, it would seem to imply the necessity for certain modifications of Freud's structural theory of personality. The first point is that it is not only the superego which is internalized—that is, taken over by identification from cathected social objects—but that there are involved other important components which presumably must be included in the ego—namely, the system of cognitive categorizations of the object world and the system of expressive symbolism.

If this is correct, it would seem to necessitate, secondly, an important modification of Freud's conception of the ego. The element of *organization*, which is the essential property of the ego, would then not be derived from the "reality-principle"—that is, from adaptative responses to the external world alone. Instead it would be derived from *two* fundamental sources: the external world as an environment; and the common culture which is acquired from objects of identification. Both are, to be sure, acquired from outside, but the latter component of the ego is, in origin and character, more like the superego than it is like the lessons of experience.

Third, there are similar problems concerning the borderline between the ego and the id. A clue to what may be needed here is given in Freud's own frequent references to what have here been called "expressive symbols," as representatives to the ego of the impulses of the id. It seems to be a necessary implication of the above analysis that these symbolized and symbolically organized emotions are not only representatives *to* the ego; they should also be considered as integral *parts of* the ego. This may be felt to be a relatively radical conclusion—namely, that emotions, or affect on the normal human adult level, should be regarded as a *symbolically generalized* system, that it is never "id-impluse" as such. Affect is not a direct expression of drive-motivation, but involves it only as it is organized and integrated with both the reality experience of the individual and the cultural patterns which he has learned through the processes of identification.

More generally, the view of personality developed in this paper seems to be broadly in line with the recent increasing emphasis in psychoanalytic theory itself on the psychology of the ego, and the problems of its integration and functioning as a system. Freud's structural theory was certainly fundamentally on the right track in that it clearly formulated the three major points of reference of personality theory—the needs of the organism, the external situation, and the patterns of the culture. In view of the intellectual traditions within which Freud's own theoretical development took place, it was in the nature of the case that the cultural element, as he formulated it in the concept of the superego, should have been the last of the three to be developed and the most difficult to fit in.

In the light of the development of the more general theory of action, however, the cultural element must, as I have attempted to show, certainly occupy a very central place. For if the ego and the id in Freud's formulations are taken alone, there is no adequate bridge from the theory of personality to the theoretical analysis of culture and of the social system. The superego provides exactly such a bridge because it is not explicable on any other basis than that of acquisition from other human beings, and through the process of social interaction.

Essentially what this paper has done has been to examine the concept of the superego in the light of the maturing bodies of theory in the fields of culture and of the social system; and it has attempted to follow through the implications of the appearance of the superego in Freud's thinking for the theory of personality itself. The result has been the suggestion of certain modifications in Freud's own theory of personality.[6]

[6] Perhaps the nature of these modifications will be made clearer to the reader by the following revision of Freud's famous diagram of the personality as a system, which he introduced in *The Ego and the Id* (reference footnote 2; p. 29), and which appears in the *New Introductory Lectures* (reference footnote 2; p. 111 in revised form.) Freud's two versions differ in that only the latter includes the superego. Hence my comparison will be made with this version.

First, in Freud's diagram the superego is placed on one side of the ego. Here it is treated as the focus of the internalized cultural system, and hence put in a central place.

Second, my suggested new diagram follows Freud in treating the superego as essentially part of the ego, but extends this conception to include as part of the ego all three components of the internalized culture.

Third, a distinction is introduced which Freud does not take account of at all; namely, that between cultural elements as internalized in the personality, and as objects of the situation, as follows:

Cultural Objects	*Internalized Subject and Social Objects*
1. Cognitive reference System	Internalized self-object images
2. Common moral standards	Superego
3. Expressive symbolism	Symbolically organized affect

I think of self as oriented *both* to alter and to the nonsocial situation, which includes both physical and cultural objects. Both orientations include cognition *and* cathexis, and both are subject to evaluative appraisal; but only in the case of alter as an object are these orientations *mutual*.

In this sense the paper has contained a good deal of criticism of Freud, which may appear to be out of place in a paper dealing with the contributions of psychoanalysis to social science. It is, however, emphatically not the intent of the author to have this appear as primarily a critical paper. It has been necessary to emphasize the critical aspect at certain points, since the psychiatric or psychoanalytic reader is not likely to be adequately familiar with the developments in sociological theory which are so importantly related to the concept of the superego. The essential intent, however, is to contribute to the development of a common foundation for the theoretical analysis of human behavior which can serve to unify all of the sciences which take this as their subject matter. The massive and fundamental fact is that Freud formulated the concept of the superego and fitted it into his general analysis of human motivation. This and the parallel formulations in the field of sociology are the solid foundations on which we must build. I believe it can truthfully be said that we are now in a position to bring the theory of personality and the theory of the social system within essentially the same general conceptual scheme. Freud's contribution of the concept of the superego has been one of the important factors making this possible.

According to my view, the ego thus includes all three elements of the common culture and repression cuts across all three. Furthermore, there is no reason why large parts of the common culture, repressed or not, should not belong to the unconscious.

It seems to be implied by the position taken here that the integration of personality *as a system* should be regarded as the function of the ego; but, following Freud, it is equally important, as has been said above, that the ego faces three ways, as it were, and is subject to pressures from all three directions—that is, from the individual's own organism (id), from the external situation, and from the internalized symbol systems of the culture. I am indebted to Dr. James Olds for help in drawing the diagram.

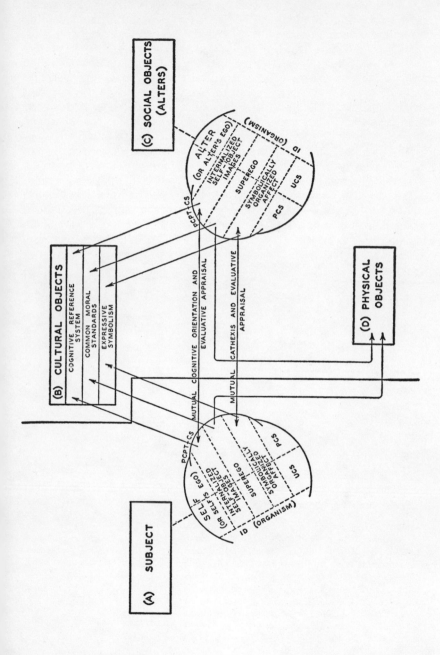

CHAPTER 2

THE THEORY OF SYMBOLISM

IN RELATION TO ACTION

BY TALCOTT PARSONS

THE STARTING POINT OF THIS PAPER IS THE FACT THAT THE DISCI-plines comprising the theory of action have notably failed to evolve a coherent treatment of the *content* as distinguished from the meanings, of expressive symbolism. The intention is to suggest an approach to this problem and indicate its relevance to that of generalization as this concept has been central to the interests of learning theory.

The level on which our direct theoretical concern with the problem focuses is that of culturally patterned social interaction. In this connection we have attempted to make clear (*Social System*, Chapter IX and passim) that the particular motivationally-intended act must, in general, be regarded as possessing symbolic significance in an expressive sense relative to the *attitude* which it is interpreted both by alter and by ego, to "manifest". Thus such symbolic acts are to be regarded on this level of cultural interaction as the prototypes of expressive symbols. Other objects acquire symbolic significance in the expressive sense by association with symbolic acts. Our problem here is twofold. It is first, to analyze more specifically the way in which an attitude in this sense, and its relations to the acts which "express" it, are built up out of the more elementary components of action, with special reference to the more general theory of symbolism and its relations to the action frame of reference. Secondly, we are concerned, on the background of such an analysis, to consider the problems of the patterns of generalization of expressive symbolism which will throw some light on the organization of its *content*, and not merely its "subjective" references.

We may start by following Morris (and certainly many others) in the statement that a symbol, as a special member of the larger class of signs, is, in action terms, a situational object, or event, or aspect of it which is in certain respects *associated with* the action process. The word "associated" indicates that the symbolic object or event is not, in the particular context in question, the *main* intrinsically significant goal-object or object of cathexis, though in another context such objects or events may be symbolic objects. In this as in so many other connections, it is vital to keep points of reference straight.

Seen in this light a symbol is, as it were, to be thought of as "suspended between" the motivational drive or need-disposition of the actor and the goal-object or state, that is the relations to the object(s) of cathexis which are motivationally primary in the relevant action process. It is inevitably "associated" *with both*. In addition of course as Morris points out, we must consider the actor to whom the symbol is significant as a cognitive point of reference, the "interpreter".[1]

It follows that a symbol *always* has *both* "cognitive" and "expressive" meanings. The distinction between cognitive and expressive symbolism which is so fundamental to the theory of action is a difference of relative *primacy of significance* of the two orders of meaning, not of separately distinct "kinds", if that is taken to mean that the components of the two types are entirely separate from each other. In the cognitive type, in the present interpretation, the *primary* meaning-reference is to the situational object-world; while in the expressive type, the *primary* reference is to the actor's own "motivations" or "intentions", to what Morris calls his "disposition to respond". But in spite of the primacy of one of the two meaning-references, the other is in the nature of the case *always* also involved. For example in the clearest cases of cognitive primacy, where the dominant *interest* of the actor is in the solution of a cognitive problem, we may say that the motivational, or for our later purposes "attitudinal", meaning of the symbolic complex will be characterized by the "disposition to know" without primary reference to other need-disposition components of the actor's motivational system. Treating a symbol in such a way *in*

[1] As a general reference in this field see Charles Morris, *Signs, Language and Behavior*. Prentice-Hall, New York, 1946.

action is to say, not only that in terms of cultural standards it must be "appropriate" *to the relevant object or objects,* but it must also at the same time, as an expressive symbol, *express the appropriate attitude.* Conversely, where the primacy of meaning is on the expressive side, the symbol must not only be appropriate as an expression of the attitude which is its primary "referent" but it must also be appropriate to the "situation", that is to the context in which the expressive activity takes place; it must, that is, be part of a symbolically, in this sense "meaningfully", integrated object system, remembering that the symbol is always *itself a situational object.* This is one aspect of what we mean by the integration of the action system on the level of "meaning".

Sign behavior of any sort (involving either "signals" or symbols in Morris' sense) implies a certain differentiation of the most elementary form of action system, and also the extension of action process in time, in such a way that the concept of expectation (and memory) becomes relevant. In the most elementary paradigm, cognition and cathexis are not differentiable except analytically. The action process *as such* is the consummatory act or process of gratification. The object is both cognized as "suitable for a gratifying relationship" and cathected, in the same undifferentiated act.

But with further differentiations of the action system, the situation itself becomes differentiated, relative to both cognitive and cathectic bases of interest. In the expressively relevant case there is a differentiation between what may be called *primary* objects of cathexis and other objects. The criterion of a primary object of cathexis is that a specific relation to it is the condition of a consummatory process of gratification. Other objects (i.e. events, qualities and performances of objects) may then acquire significance as *signs* relative to the cathectic or expressive, as well as the cognitive, *meaning* of the primary object of cathexis. Thus, to take a very simple example, the eating of food may be treated as a consummatory act. The smelling of food cooking is not as such a consummatory act in the same sense. The object of the olfactory perception is not a primary object of cathexis but, for our purposes, a sign. It acquires a "pleasurable" connotation because of its association with the gratificatory meaning of the consummatory act. It *not only means* in cognitive terms the probability that food will soon be available to eat, but perception of the sign *itself* evokes the "affective tone" aroused by the primary object of cathexis itself, or at least some of it, and of the same "quality". Similarly, by classical Pavlovian conditioning other situa-

tional objects or events may acquire the same sign-meaning, even
if they are not "intrinsically" connected with the consummatory
act.

What is ordinarily called cognitive symbolism involves treatment of the actor *only* in his capacity as "knower" or "interpreter", and beyond that involves an association between sign
and principal object or "referent". The *motivation* of the interpreter is "held constant" in a particular way and is usually
implicit. Furthermore, this motivation is of a special quality known
in our version of the theory of action as "affective neutrality",
so that it is not readily associated with the affective tonings generally dealt with in the analysis of cathexes. In the case of expressive primacy in the sign relationship of significance, on the other
hand, it is *not possible* to hold this factor constant. Hence the
problem becomes more complex than in the cognitive case. It
must involve, on the one hand, the basis of association between
the principal object and the sign object, by virtue of which the
sign can come to "stand for" the principal object. On the other
hand, it must *also* involve a *meaning reference* to the expressive,
or gratificatory significance of the principal object which is "generalized" to the sign object.

We must say, then that, not only must the sign object be
associated with and thus in some sense mean or stand for the
principal object in the cognitive aspect, that is that the two
objects must have "something in common" by virtue of which
they are associated, i.e. "belong together", but the sign object
must also be *cathected* in a secondary sense, so that it is of
motivational significance to the actor to establish a specific relation to it, a relation which is in some sense and to some degree
"gratifying". [2] We have, then, as one set of components of the
symbolic relationship the association of situational objects, as the
other set of components the "transfer of cathexis" to, or perhaps
better the "sharing of the cathexis of the principal object *with*"
the sign object.

This extremely elementary account of the fundamental structure of the sign-relationship in action in terms of its expressive
aspect above all fails to give an account of two ways in which
these elementary components come to be organized in systems
of a higher order of complexity. These are, respectively, their involvement in the interaction of two or more actors, and the organization of the orientations of one actor in relation to a plurality

[2] Essentially the same considerations apply if the relation is deprivational.

of objects of cathectic significance, so that his orientations constitute an organized system and not a set of random "responses" to unrelated stimuli. *Both* are inevitably involved in systems of action on the human cultural level, and hence there is a certain arbitrariness in which is taken up first. But because of our central concern with interaction we will start with this.

The mutual interdependence of actors for essential gratifications is not in need of comment. We will simply assume that some acts or qualities of alter, or direct and immediate instrumental consequences of such acts, constitute consummatory processes of gratification of ego, *something* about alter is in this sense a *primary* object of cathexis for ego; the same of course will be true in reverse.

The first essential point is the *contingency* of ego's gratification in this case on alter's action, and the second the *interpretation* by ego of that contingency, and, of course, vice versa on both points. Contingency can, in the first place, be meaningful only if action is oriented to expectations and thus in some sense an uncertainty element is involved in the expectation system. Ego's gratification must, that is, be dependent on what alter *may or may not do;* if it were quite certain what he would do the types of meaning problem we have in mind could never arise. It may be a matter of alter's physical presence or absence at certain places and times, or of various performances in the presence of or in relation to ego. But the essential point is that whether or not alter "does" something, or "how" he does it, makes a gratificational *difference* to ego, and that in ego's expectation system there is the *possibility* at least that alter will fail to do it or will do it the wrong way.

We may say that in the presence of uncertainty in this sense ego will in the nature of the case be both cognitively and affectively "interested in" *signs* which may indicate which of the possibilities inherent in the situation is more likely to eventuate. And so far as the differences between the possibilities are interpreted to be contingent on something alter does, the interest naturally focuses on signs of what alter is most likely to do.

This leads to the second point, namely the interpretation by ego of the *meaning* of what alter does, both in the primary cathexis context, and in the sign context. In the former case the "problem of meaning" is posed first by the *difference* between alternative specific relations between ego and alter, or the direct consequences of such relations, seen in its gratificational significance; in the latter case it is the *indication of* the probability or possibility of a difference which poses the problem. But sign process already implies *some* generalization. An object is no longer always significant to ego *only* in terms of its possibilities for direct consummatory gratification or deprivation, but *also* as signifying various probabilities of gratification or deprivation from objects other than itself. But if this generalization exists for ego, it must also exist for alter, and the question arises of how their respective generalizations mesh with each other. In other words are the meanings of signs, in their expressive significance, each "private" to each actor, or is there such a thing as a *common* meaning; if so what are the conditions on which it depends?

With respect to the cognitive aspect, the problem is fairly well understood, and cognition is always a *component* of the concrete expressive sign or symbol. The essential point is that the "perception" of the same sign should "point to" the same property or properties of the same designated object or class of objects, given "context" etc. The expressive case involves the further complications we have alluded to, namely the sign object is not *only* cognitively associated with the designatum or referent, but the cathectic significance of the primary object of cathexis is *generalized to the sign object*, which thereby acquires a secondary cathexis. Hence, on this level the condition of a sign object having a common significance for both ego and alter is that it should have primary or secondary cathexis by both in such a way that each may "feel" its significance to the other. It must arouse either the *same* feelings, that is expectations of gratification or deprivation, or *at least complementary* feelings in both, it must that is be cathected by both in ways which are integrated with the motivational system of each vis-a-vis that of the other.

We may now introduce another generalization or postulate. This is that two or more objects which are cathected with the same *quality* of cathectic significance, which in expressive terms have the same order of meaning for ego, will tend to become symbolically associated with each other. Then the cathexis of the sign object will tend to be generalized to cathexis of persons associated with it. If the sign object is, as is the most important case for us, itself a performance, then the cathexis of the performance will tend to be *generalized to alter* so far as the latter is interpreted as the actor, i.e. as the social object who is interpreted to be "responsible" for the cathected sign-performance.

The mutuality of the interactive process is crucial here. In so far, that is, as one of his own performances is an "expression" of ego's motivation, as it becomes susceptible to interpretation by himself or alter as an expressive sign or symbol relative to that motivation, he may in a certain sense be said to be "externalizing" his motivation. There are two senses in which this is true. First, he "operates" on the situation to bring it more into accord with his motivational need-dispositions. This is the goal-striving aspect of performance. But secondly, at the same time and by precisely the same acts, he "signifies" his motivations, he "gives them expression" in the sense that to himself and to alter he gives a "visible sign" of what he wants or does not want, strives for or seeks to avoid. Seen in this light then, the condition of a set of *common* expressive symbols is that the generalization of cathectic significance should extend in *both* directions, to the motivational systems of *both* ego and alter, in such a way that the meanings are congruent with each other.

Any given actor, as we well know, appears in the interaction process in a dual capacity. On the one hand he is the orienting, motivated entity, "he who acts", who wants things, makes choices, etc. On the other hand he is the *object* of orientation, both to himself and to alter. Then one aspect of the actor *as object*, that is of what we call a social object, must *always* be as the author of performances, and thus as he who has the motivations of which the performances are interpreted to be expressive signs. Furthermore, relative to the same social object, there must be a way of discriminating *what* performances, and properties of them, are in fact adequate signs of given types of motivation, and what are irrelevant to this significance-context, and what qualities are the relevant "performance capacities" and what are not. The social object then, both as object of primary cathexis and as author of expressive signs must be divided into aspects relevant to motivational interpretation and those not so relevant. This is the familiar pattern variable of ascription-achievement, seen in its more elementary quality-performance context.[3]

The interpretation of a performance, or of its consequence as expressive of the author's motivation, as therefore a sign, is another way of saying that this performance is related to the author's "intentions". In other words to say that an act of alter may be interpreted as an expressive sign relative to alter's motiva-

---

[3] The terms quality-performance are generally used in these papers because of their more general connotations.

tion, and to say that alter "intended to do it" and|or to bring
about a relevant consequence, *are two ways of saying the same
thing.*

In interaction then, every performance has a double aspect,
relative to which there may be a difference of primacy. On the
one hand it is an act oriented to the optimization of ego's gratification-deprivation balance; this may be called its "intrinsic" significance. On the other hand it is a sign, which may be oriented
to communication to alter (or to ego himself) which in the more
highly developed cases, *symbolizes* the motivational intent of the
author. In interaction the relation of the two aspects is very close,
since only by communicating to alter, can ego presumably influence alter's own motivations in the direction favorable to his
gratifications. Hence the primary intrinsic significance of a given
performance may be to communicate to alter; in this case intrinsic
and symbolic significance coincide.

It must not be forgotten that when we speak of communication here there is always a cognitive component, but the distinctive
feature of expressive symbolism is its communication of "affect" or of "feeling". Because the expressive sign, particularly the
sign-performance, has cathectic as well as cognitive meaning for
both ego and alter, its "interpretation" by ego is not only its cognitive "understanding", but is the "arousal" in ego of the feeling
corresponding to the motivation of alter in performing the act.
It is crucial that *what* is communicated is *not only understanding
of motives* in the cognitive sense, but is *mutuality of affective
meanings.* Only so far as this is the case can we properly speak
of *expressive* symbolism. But since the sign is an object, and there
is always cognition as part of the action process, the sign object
is always *also* interpreted in cognitive terms for its cognitive
meaning relative to its author as an object, which must in the
nature of the case *include* his motives. It is very easy to become
confused on this point.

A further point needs to be made. A set of expressive signs
or symbols in this sense comes to be organized as a system. As
such, a principal condition of its serving the communicative function in either its cognitive or its expressive aspect is necessarily
that the interacting actors are oriented to conformity with normative standards. The "conventions" of the symbolic system must
be observed if there is to be effective communication, just as in
the case of language. It is not possible by arbitrary whim to give
an expressive act "any old meaning" and still be understood.

Meanings have become established in the interaction process, and attempts to redefine them are disturbing to the stability of interaction. Thus when two boys are "roughhousing" we would say that a blow beyond a certain level of intensity is established as an "aggressive act" whereas short of this it may be friendly "fooling around". The boy who exceeds the limit may, if he hits his partner too hard, get him "mad" even if he did not intend to (though concretely there may be of course an unconscious aggressive motive), because he has violated the established convention of the expressive meaning of an act. The normal response to such a shift of meaning is the *imputation of intention* to the actor, thus, "in hitting me so hard you must have *intended* to hurt me". In so far as the expressive-communicative functions of symbolic processes have primacy, the generalization of the normative requirements of a system of expressive symbols constitutes appreciative standards.

We shall see that this organization of expressive symbols, according to appreciative standards on a cultural level, is not merely "external" to the actor but becomes, by "internalization", a constitutive part of his own personality structure.

We may now turn to the problem of the organization of expressive symbols in the orientation system of the individual actor. From one point of view this may be looked at as the problem of what constitutes the cathexis of *an object*. Freud quite correctly pointed out that object cathexis in the sense of a "love" relationship could not be regarded as a primitive phenomenon, but developed only as a result of a complex process.

It is generally agreed that there are elementary gratifications of "primary" drives. Thus no human infant or other animal can survive without food, and food-deprivation beyond certain limits certainly constitutes "distress" independently of any learning process. But, in terms of the above elementary paradigm of expressive symbolism, it is not the "mother" which is the significant object of the most elementary hunger drive, but in the first place the food-object itself, e.g. the milk, and then the nipple as the immediate source of the milk. The infant also has other primary drives, that is, gets into states where some readjustment of its relation to the situation becomes imperative, as in relation to warmth, safety, etc. But, as is well recognized, there is no reason to believe that the object world which comprises the objects of cathexis for these drives is "structured" for the infant in the adult way. The infant does not "love his mother" because she is the principal source of these primary gratifications, because in the relevant sense, *the mother* as an object does not yet exist for the infant.

Reconstruction of the process by which she becomes such an object is hazardous, but we may put our theoretical argument in such terms. Gratification of primary drives occurs in a time coordinate. Therefore, consummatory acts are preceded by events which may readily come to serve as signs of the coming gratification, and of course this always occurs in a context. The mother as *agent* of these gratifications is an obvious generalization from the sequence of events leading to the consummatory acts, and from the context in which they occur. According to the principles stated above, we may presume then that various acts of the mother preparatory to feeding, so far as they are observable to the infant, and features of the mother as organism during feeding, e.g. the breast, her arms holding the baby, etc., come to be *signs* which acquire a secondary cathexis relative to the primary food objects.

The same will be true with reference to other gratification processes with respect to which the infant is "dependent" on the mother as we ordinarily say. The processes of generalization of which we speak will then not only tend to build up a sign-symbol complex relative to each primary gratification need, and the processes and objects which come to be symbolically associated with the consummatory acts, but there will tend to be some kind of integration of the complex *relative to the common authorship of the meaningful acts,* and relative to the fact that the qualities observable, of the acts and of the organism of the mother, hang together as belonging to *one* object. Then the mother as a single object is not only she who feeds, but also who cleans, warms, etc.

It follows from the treatment of affective generalization above that, so far as there is a common tone of gratification to the various acts and qualities and their symbols, regardless of the diversity of particular original primary objects of cathexis, they can form a complex of mutually symbolic components. Feeding, then, is symbolically associated with cleaning and protection and vice versa.

When we speak of an attachment to "the mother" as distinguished from a need or wish to be fed, to be warmed, etc. we presumably mean in this sense a generalized expectation *system* of associated gratifications, and the cathexis of symbolic qualities and performances associated with gratification, which is organized relative to an object of the situation, the mother. An *attitude* toward the mother as a single object then must be regarded psychologically as a composite, an organized *system,* by virtue of which the various discrete qualities and performances of the mother are symbolically generalized relative to each other. On this level, there is a sense in which the distinction we made above between the primary object of cathexis and the symbolic or sign object, ceases within the organized complex, to be significant except for special purposes of analysis. We are dealing with a system which as a system, we may presume, has boundary-maintaining properties. There is a sense in which the system is cathected *as a system,* and its components in their capacity as components of the system.

It also follows from the analysis of the relevant aspects of interaction above that a primary axis of the organization of this system of mutually symbolic performances and qualities of the mother-object will be the ways in which the performances are interpreted as expressions of the *intentions* of the mother, and other qualities are associated with these intentions. Only when such a set of symbols relative to what are interpreted to be her intentions has been built up can there be a highly generalized communication system on expressive levels between mother and child.

We must now remember that such a symbol system must have a normative aspect. Not only must the "meaning" of the symbols be learned but both communication and contingent gratifications are dependent on their *proper* use, that is, on maintaining conformity with the *standards of the system.* It is, indeed, this orientation to standards which appears to be the primary source of the boundary-maintaining properties of the system. Action, that is, is *controlled* relative to certain pattern properties of the system.

This normative component is not only a condition of the functioning of the system as a system, but it is also the source of a fundamentally important element of flexibility in such systems. Symbolic generalization means cathexis of *all* the object-components of the system as evoking the same affective tone-quality. Within limits imposed by the intrinsic gratification needs of ego, then, there is the possibility of substitution of one object for the other, and indeed of the extrusion of some objects from the system, and the inclusion of new ones in it. To a degree, which empirically must not be taken for granted, new objects, or transfers of cathexis within the system, may be the "equivalents" of the original cathexes. The system, that is, can maintain stability through processes of change in its "object content" and the distribution of cathexes among the component object elements. Hence this mode of organization of expressive symbols can have a fundamental function in the socialization process, because it is by inclusion of new objects in the symbolic integration of the expressive system, that learning to cathect new objects becomes possible and, conversely, old objects can be renounced and new ones substituted without undue disturbance, so long as the cathectic system itself is not disorganized. This would seem to be a very fundamental aspect of the normal mechanism of substitution, while disturbances of the equilibrium of such a system constitute essential aspects of the mechanisms of displacement and projection.

To have the properties which we have attributed to the cathexis of what in this sense is a "complex" object, that is one in relation to which there exist a plurality of primary cathexes, and a complex of expressive symbolism, the system of expressive meanings must be organized or "patterned" in a double sense. In the first place, the symbolic objects relative to their expressive meanings *cannot be a random assortment,* but must constitute a symbolically meaningful system. In the second place, these "patterns" must have a normative aspect, they must, that is, to an important degree be patterns of *value-orientation.*

If these considerations are kept directly in mind it appears that by this path we have simultaneously reached an interpretation of what we mean by the *internalization* of patterns of value-orientation and of what we mean by the *attitude* of a social object as the primary focus of the cathectic significance of that object in personality and in the interaction process. These are, indeed, essentially two aspects of the same thing.

By internalization of a pattern of value-orientation we *mean* that, in orientation to a given aspect or "sector" of the situation there has been built up a system of mutually symbolic object-significances such that the *relations* between the symbolically significant objects on the one hand, and between the cathectic meanings of the objects on the other hand, follow patterns of organization which are at the same time both structurally constitutive and normative. A pattern is internalized, that is, so far as it generalizes the relations either between objects which in the expressive sense are mutually symbolic objects or between the cathectic meanings of these objects or both. Such a pattern is the *pattern of organization* of a cathected *system* of symbolically significant elementary objects and their expressive meanings. Such generalization means that the *particular* object cannot be segregated from the system of which it is a part, that therefore new objects must "fit" the pattern of the system, and old objects have a certain element of "equivalence" along the "pattern-gradients" of the system. *Internalization of a pattern therefore means only that the meanings of cathected objects are organized in systems which are patterned,* and thus cannot be treated discretely, and that there is an element of flexibility according to which the intrinsic properties of discrete objects may be less important than the "fitting" of any object into the patterned system. It clearly means that the actor will be "disposed" to cathect objects which fit the patterns already established in the system, and to avoid objects or to cathect them negatively, which are incompatible with the organization of the system, which threaten to disturb its organization. In other words, internalization of patterns is a way of speaking of the fact that the cathectic orientation system of an actor has achieved a relative stability of organization as a boundary-maintaining system, on the level of expressive-symbolic processes.

But there is also an implication beyond this, namely that "conformity" with the pattern has become endowed with affective significance through the process which we have called the symbolic generalization of affect. This means that non-conformity through altering the symbolic meanings of expressive acts and of the non-social objects symbolically associated with them, will be a disturbance of the equilibrium of the system, which will set up tendencies to re-establish that equilibrium. The mechanisms of learning, defense and adjustment are beyond certain levels of complication to be understood in this context as ways in which the reorganization of such systems can take place. Of course such an attitudinal system is a sub-system of the total personality organization, and its relations to other sub-systems must be taken into account. One criterion of internalization then is that there will be a disturbing effect for the actor of upsetting the equilibrium of the cathected symbolic system. Its maintenance has become *emotionally* important and this maintenance always involves conformity with pattern.

The attitudinal aspect of the phenomenon we have been discussing constitutes simply the organization of cathexes *relative to the structure of objects in the situation.* We have illustrated this above by the case of the building up of an attitude toward the mother on the part of the child. An attitude in this sense then is the dispositional aspect of a need-disposition or complex of them; it is the symbolically generalized organization of cathexes relative to *complex* objects, which are not themselves original "primary" objects of cathexis but require *both* a learned organization of cognitive orientation toward the object world, *and* a learned organization of cathectic components relative to such learned objects.

In our intellectual tradition, in spite of a good deal of philosophical sophistication on the problem of the "fallacy of misplaced concreteness" we have a strong "realistic" bias, and tend to assume that an object simply "is" what it purports to be. However serious the problem in relation to non-social objects, in relation to *social* objects such a bias is doubly dangerous. For we have several times brought out that, within the limits of variability of the structure of interactive action systems, the social object *is* what it is defined to be, it is *constituted* in its cognitive properties by the mutual orientations of interacting actors, and by the internalization of the relevant patterns of orientation. Thus, to be a "mother" in the *social status-role sense*, is not merely to be the female biological parent of a given child, but is to play a certain role in the social system. *What* the object *is* in these aspects, is not merely the "significance of what it does" as defined by the value-patterns of the culture. This is the core of the meaning of W. I. Thomas' famous dictum that a "situation defined as real is real in its consequences" and of Durkheim's theorem that "collective representations" themselves *constitute* the "reality" of society by virtue of which, relative to personality and environmental factors society is a "reality sui generis."

Thus a social attitude, i.e. toward alters in the interactive process, involves the *cognitive constitution of the object*, or class of objects, but it *also* involves the *cathectic organization* to which we have referred, according to which the various components of the complex object are symbolically integrated with each other as *expressive* symbols, each of which can evoke the emotional reaction appropriate to the object as a whole as a complex *system*.

It has become clear that our analysis of the problem of expressive symbolism has led us directly to certain of the problems of the *organization* of systems of action. This brings us back to the more general theory developed in *Values, Motives and Systems of Action* and in *The Social System*.

Essentially what we have done is to show the way in which

the theory of symbolism fits into that more general theory. If this interpretation is correct, it has two important orders of implications. First, the concepts which have been found to be so important for the analysis of the general problems of the structure of systems of action *must* have their relevance for the analysis of symbolic processes in action. Secondly, seeing these concepts in their relation to symbolic processes should contribute importantly to our interpretation of their nature and general place in the theory of action.

We have attempted to show that the patterns of organization of mutually symbolic meanings *must be patterns of value-orientation* and that these patterns are essentially of two orders, (1) those which concern the relations of association between "principal objects" and sign-objects, and (2) those which concern the organization of cathectic meanings relative to complex objects.

If this is correct, then these patterns of value-orientation must be the same as those which have proved capable of conceptualization in terms of the pattern variables, and the distinction between the two fundamental orders of organizational patterning of symbol systems, must be that formulated in terms of the symmetrical asymmetry of the pattern variable system. And indeed, when the problems are seen in this light, there develops a most gratifying illumination, both of the structure of symbolic systems in action, and of the significance of the pattern variables themselves.

We may start with the problem of symbolic association between principal objects and sign-objects. Primarily cognitive symbol-systems are, we must remember, a special case for the more general theory of symbolism. All symbol systems have a cognitive aspect, and it is this which must be formulated in the "laws of association" of designatum and symbolic object. It is suggestive that the specific cognitive symbol need not in any way resemble the object to which it refers. Thus the "word" *table* does not, either as a sound combination in speech, or as a visual symbol in written form, in any *physical* way resemble an example of the class of objects to which it refers. But the patterns of *order* by which *systems* of cognitive symbols are built up must be "congruent" with the patterns of order in the object-systems to which they refer. The element of "arbitrariness" in the choice of the particular symbol cannot, thus, extend to the ways in which such symbols are combined in systems. In general we say that cognitive symbols are ordered in terms of the *common properties* of objects, and of their *interrelations* so far as these can be stated as general or universal propositions *indepen-*

dent of the particular relations of the objects to ego as a point of reference. This type of symbol system is that central to modern rational knowledge—however arbitrary the devices by which it *names* objects, there are definite patterns by which it *associates* objects, their properties and relationships. These are the patterns which in our scheme we call *universalistic*.

The universalistic mode of associative patterning is essential when we are dealing with content from the point of view of the *validity of propostions*, which is the dominant methodological interest of modern science and philosophy. But in terms of significance for action there is a second basis of association of objects and their properties which cuts across the first one, namely their *particular relationship* to a given actor, individual or collective, taken as a point of reference. Objects then may, regardless, or at least independently, of their universalistically conceived properties and interrelationships, "belong" together because of the common property of belonging in the *same relational* system relative to a given actor, e.g. several otherwise diverse physical objects have the common property of being "ego's possessions". This is, in our terms, the *particularistic* basis or aspect of the organization of objects in systems in relation to action and its interests, and it cuts across the universalistic one. Objects which are classed together or associated with each other in universalistic terms, may be segregated in particularistic terms and vice versa.

Particularism is thus a principle of the *ordering of objects* and their properties and relationships to one another in systems, and is just as applicable to the ordering of symbol-referent relationships and of symbols themselves to each other, as to the ordering of the "intrinsic" relationships of objects in relation to action systems independently of their symbolic significances. We may say then, that when objects are symbolically associated with each other, there must be universalistic considerations of choice involved, and there must be particularistic considerations, and there must be some sort of evaluative decision of primacy between them in different contexts. In some contexts a universalistically defined common property shared by the principal object and the sign object, may be the "appropriate" basis of association, in others, a particularistic common relation to ego. Thus in a very simple example, the resemblance of a food object to those previously eaten and liked, predisposes the actor to the arousal of hunger needs. But at the same time, the question of "whose" food it is may also be relevant. Only when actual or potential possession is as a particularistic criterion added to universalistic properties, does it become a fully "appropriate" object for hunger gratification. It has to be both "the right kind" of food and "my food". Or, to take another particularistic basis of food preference, a child may be predisposed to accept food offered it by its own mother, that is chosen by the criterion of a particularistically related agency of availability of the object, while it would reject the same food if offered by another person.

In the terminology of learning theory, these universalistic and particularistic modes of association of objects are two different "gradients of generalization". The actor extends his attention, and includes in the same class as objects of his attention and motivation, objects which "belong together" by virtue of some criterion. He tends to treat objects which, by the relevant criterion, do belong together in the same or similar ways. What the concepts of universalism and particularism do is to distinguish two different *types of criterion* by which generalization may take place from the point of view of a given actor. In order to understand the generalization process it is necessary to know *which* of these types of criterion is relevant to the actor's generalization.

The relevance of this pattern variable to generalization is not confined to the case of symbolic associations, but of course includes it, and does so whether the primacy in symbolic significance is cognitive or expressive, because symbolic association is always in one aspect *classing objects together*. But there is an important difference between the two types of primacy in symbolic relationships. In the cognitive case the problem of validity is the focus of the relation to normative standards, while in the expressive case the corresponding standard is that expressive or appreciative "adequacy". This means that the "intrinsic" interrelationships of objects and their properties *need not* play a prominent part in expressive symbolization. The properties by which objects are associated may, from the cognitive point of view, be of altogether "superficial" significance, and yet the complex may still serve expressive-symbolic functions perfectly adequately. Thus in Christian religious ritual there seems little doubt that the resemblance of red wine and blood in both being liquids of about the same color, is essential to the symbolic association of the wine with the "blood of Christ". To the biochemist of course the differences between wine and blood are far more important than their similarities. But as a basis of symbolic association the resemblances are sufficient. The "superficiality" of the resemblances from the point of view of certain cognitive interests should not, however, lead to the view that for symbolic association to occur *it does not matter* whether there are *any* resemblances or not. Such a conclusion clearly would not follow, because the question is that of the significance of resemblances *in a given functional context.* That the resemblances in question are "trivial" in a scientific cognitive context says *nothing* one way or the other about their significance or adequacy in a particular kind of expressive-symbolic context. It also says nothing about how far symbolic association can dispense with gradients of generalization at all. The whole analysis of this paper suggests that these are indeed highly important and their study will prove to be illuminating, when they are seen in the proper context.

The distinction of universalitic and particularistic gradients of generalization does not, however, exhaust the bases of the association of objects, and hence of sign-referent associations. For we have continually emphasized, precisely with respect to *objects,* the fundamental importance in the theory of action of the question of *intentions* of actors, and this is, for the reasons outlined above, particularly important with reference to expressive symbolism. For an act of alter which is interpreted by ego as "intentional"—and in terms of the common culture by alter also—is necessarily and *in itself* an expressive symbol whatever its intrinsic significance may be. On the other hand a property or quality of alter as a social object which is not interpreted as an expression of his intentions, becomes an expressive symbol only by specific processes of association, and may not have the same order of significance. Hence the basic discrimination between objects, including events, which are interpreted to be the consequences of motivational intentions, and those which are not, must *always* be involved in the bases of association of objects with each other, that is of their being classed together. What corresponds to the common properties of objects classed together apart from this factor, is, where intentions are involved, either the *common authorship* of the events constituting the action, or of the objects interpreted to result from it, or the common characteristics of sub-systems of the motivations of more than one actor. Objects then are associated by virtue of being expressions of the motivation of the *same actor,* a particularistic basis, or as being expressions of the same *kind* of motivation, e.g. friendliness or aggressiveness, on the part of a plurality of actors (a universalistic basis). On the other hand of course objects may be classed together independently of their being the expressions of the intentions of *any* actors, again on either universalistic or particularistic basis.

This, of course, is the pattern variable of ascription-achievement in its application as the basic distinction of quality and performance. It also obviously has its application to the problem of generalization. We thus have not merely two possible bases of classing objects together, but four, in that these two pattern variable distinctions cross-cut each other yielding a four-fold table of possibilities.

This is, of course the basic frame of reference for the structure of the object world, and particularly of actors as social objects. It therefore serves to order the possibilities of status-categorization in the social system. Spelled out in considerable detail of sub-classification this classificatory scheme is to be found on pp. 142-43 of *The Social System*. What is new here is merely the insight that the *same* fundamental frame of reference is involved in the association of objects in the symbolic relationship, that since sign-referent relations are relations between objects, the same frame of reference must underlie the organization of symbols and their object-referents in systems which underlies the organization of social objects themselves in systems. For this part of our problem, then, the object-object relationship, the two status-categorization pattern variables give us the basis of an orderly treatment; they constitute the frame of reference for a theory of the *content* of symbolic systems, both cognitive and expressive. The problem of generalization in the psychological sense is furthermore seen to be an aspect of the same general problem area. Objects can only symbolize each other if they are somehow classified together, and what these pattern variables do is to formulate the *possible bases of classification* which can serve as gradients for generalization. A few of the implications of this fact for the analysis and classification of the mechanisms of learning, defense and adjustment will be taken up below.

But so far we have dealt with only half the problem, the half which is explicit in the cases of cognitive primacy. The other half is the problem of the generalization of cathexis involved in the organization of discrete primary objects of cathexis, and of expressive symbols which have received a secondary cathexis relative to them, into *ordered systems*.

Here the "attitudinal" pattern variables have the place which corresponds to that of the object-categorization variables in relation to object-object association. The keynote is the proposition that cathexes come to be *organized relative to the structure of the object world*. There are the correlative processes of the *construction* of "complex objects" by the cognitive definition of the situation, and the generalization of cathexes from elementary or primary objects and elementary sign-objects to these complex objects, as boundary-maintaining systems.

The pattern variable of diffuseness-specificity defines the alternative possibilities of organizing cathexes relative to the concrete object-unit as a unit, e.g. the person as a social object, or on the other hand, relative to a "functional" interest-type or basis. The child learns to "love the mother" in a diffuse relationship without specific reference to any *one* of the many gratifications of which she is the source. On the other hand he is pleased by the appearance of the ice cream truck on the street because it is the source of a particular object or type of object of gratification of a particular "interest". There may be a diffuse "penumbra" of cathexis of the driver of the truck, but primarily the driver is "the man who has the ice cream". This can of course generalize to soda fountain clerks, and indeed to all dispensers of desired food-objects, and still remain specific in the pattern-variable sense. The specific mode of the organization of cathexes then, *cuts across* the situation as a system of discrete concrete objects, and classes all which have a particular *type of cathectic significance* together, ignoring other aspects and gratification potentialities of the same objects.

The other attitudinal pattern variable is that of affectivity vs. affective neutrality. This, as we know, concerns not the scope of cathectic significance of the object, but the *kind* of cathectic significance with reference to one fundamental orientation-decision, namely whether or not to seize opportunities for gratification at a given moment in a given situation. The general significance of course arises from the exigencies of the organization of cathexes in systems. The seizure of all presented opportunities for gratification would be incompatible with stable organization. Thus to take a familiar example, mutual erotic gratification is a potentiality as between any two normal adults of opposite sex. But if the erotic component is fundamentally integrated, including necessarily symbolically, with the other components in a diffuse love attachment to a particular object, indiscriminate seizure of erotic gratification opportunities with other available objects comes into serious conflict with the *meaning* of erotic gratification in the love-relationship complex. One aspect of the disturbing effect of this conflict is the reaction of jealousy on the part of the "injured" partner to the love relationship. However, it is realistically impossible for example for married persons not to have contacts with persons of opposite sex which present potential opportunities for erotic gratification. The attitude of affective neutrality is, in such a context, the emotional capacity to inhibit the potentially activated need-disposition.

In the present context of the relevance of expressive symbolism in the affective mode of cathectic organization of attitudes, the permissiveness for gratification *means* symbolically integration of the particular gratification in a stable symbolic system, so that taking advantage of the opportunity is not disturbing to the equilibrium of the system. Affective neutrality on the other hand means symbolically that the gratification in question would not fit in the relevant part of the actor's stable cathectic system.

These two pattern variables, then, in their cross-classification, yield four major modes of the organization of the attitudinal systems of actors. They divide up the object world in a fourfold way, on the one hand into diffusely cathected complex objects, and into classes of specifically cathected objects, secondly into objects and occasions where there is permissiveness for direct gratification and into "prohibited" objects and occasions, where "disipline" is called for. Perhaps the most fundamental point is that these orders of the cathectic significance of objects are *not intrinsic* to the "nature" of the objects in a cognitive-situational sense. For every aspect of an object which is formulated in terms of the status-categorization pattern variables, there is in the nature of action *an open alternative* or set of alternatives as to what cathectic meaning that object is going to acquire for a particular actor in a particular kind of relation to the object. Thus the person of opposite sex may be "intrinsically" a possible sex partner, but this fact does not determine whether or not he or she actually becomes cathected as an erotic object; this must be determined by the organization of the attitudinal system of ego. Describing the orientation as one of affective neutrality is a way of stating the fact that this potentiality of cathexis is not realized in this particular case. This is the fundamental sense in which the structure of the object world and the structure of attitudes relative to it must be treated as independently variable relative to each other.

The case of affective neutrality brings up an important problem concerning the *patterning* of expressive-symbolic systems. In the case of affectivity, the permission for gratification means that the stability of organization of the symbolic system is not threatened by the particular gratificatory act, or its prospect. For this reason affective activity is not as such specifically oriented to the maintenance of, or conformity with pattern. The question of conformity, that is, is not at issue. In the case of affective neutrality on the other hand, there is by definition a potential conflict between the particular gratification interest and the stability of the cathectic system. Orientation in this situation can take the form of the feeling of "obligation" to maintain conformity with the pattern, so there is a sense in which we may say that affective neutrality constitutes "cathexis of the pattern". This is, however, an elliptical statement. A pattern is, as internalized in this sense, *not an object*, and strictly speaking only objects can be cathected. The full statement would be to the effect that, the organized system of object-cathexes is structured in such a way that taking advantage of the gratification opportunity in question would create a disturbance in the system. Therefore the actor is motivated not to act in this way, his interest in the stability of his cathectic orientation system is greater than his interest in the potential object. So far as the "pattern is internalized" the "decision" is spontaneous without sense of conflict and this is what is meant by cathexis of the pattern, namely there is not sufficient motivation to act in ways incompatible with the pattern. Organization of cathexes *always* involves patterning in symbolic systems in this sense. Therefore there is always an affectively neutral aspect of every attitude structure; it is always *selective* in its permissiveness for potential gratifications.

Finally, the above discussion gives us an excellent basis for interpreting certain phases of the significance of the fifth pattern variable, that of self-vs. collectivity-orientation, and of the reasons why it occupies a special place in the system, and should not be directly classed with either the status-categorization pair or the attitudinal pair. The most fundamental reason is that it conceptualizes the *convergence* of the two fundamental orientation components in the structure of the social system itself. There are two aspects of this. The first is the constitution of the collectivity as an object. All other classes of objects have bases which are outside of and analytically independent of the system of interaction itself. Physical objects, by definition, are independent of interaction process however essential they may be to it, and however often they may be "products" of past action or interaction. Culture, again, in its object significance, is "separable" through embodiment in physical symbols from the system of action; this is fundamental to communication and diffusion of culture. Furthermore the personality is "grounded" in the biological organism, and its functional problems are inseparable from those of the organism. But a collectivity has *any existence at all only as itself an organized system of inter-action,* this is the *sole* basis of its constitution as an object. It is obviously dependent on physical objects, on inherited culture, and on the biological characteristics of the individual actors, but these objects do not themselves, apart from the organization of systems of social interaction, *ever* constitute collectivities. Therefore the collectivity as object is not independent, but is created and sustained *solely* by the attitudes of its members. This after all is the basic insight of Durkheim's later work.

The second aspect is the obverse, namely that in so far as they constitute collectivities, there is a special relation between attitudes and the complex object of cathexis. The object itself is nothing but the *mode of integration* of the cathectic-symbolic systems of the members. But by no means all of the cathectic-symbolic orientations of individual actors are in this sense directly constitutive of the collectivities of which they are members. It is therefore essential that there should be a fundamental conceptualization in the theory of action of the distinction between those attitudinal components which are and those which are not constitutive of collectivities. We mean *constitutive,* not merely "conditions of the existence or effective functioning of collectivities". The distinction is *fundamental.* This is the ultimate basis of the importance of sociological theory as science. Put a little differently, the concept collectivity-orientation is the focus of the basic phenomenon of the institutional integration of motivation.

The most important implication of these considerations for the present context is to see clearly that the fact that collectivities as objects are constituted out of the attitudes of their members, *must* mean that what they *are* is special types of integrates of symbolic meaning-complexes in our sense. This is what Durkheim meant by his famous dictum that "society *exists only* in the minds of individuals." If we are to understand the bases on which collectivities are built up, we must understand expressive symbolism.

We have now covered the most essential analytical ground of this paper. What we have done is essentially to integrate the theory of symbolism with the general theory of action much more closely than before, and to work out certain implications of this integration for a series of theoretical problems in the action field. In particular we have shown the fundamental importance of the expressive aspect of symbolic systems, and how the development of systems of expressive symbolization is the primary *mode of organization* of the cathectic components of the motivational orientation of action. It is by symbolic organization of these components that the phenomenon we call internalization of patterns comes about. We have

furthermore attempted to show that the pattern variables constitute precisely the organization patterns of these symbolic systems.
They state the ways in which, on the object-categorization and the
attitudinal sides respectively, symbolic relationships can be *generalized*. This fact lies at the basis of the significance of the pattern
variables in the theory of action.

In conclusion we will attempt to indicate the empirical relevance of this analysis for a few problem areas in the theory of action.
First we may take the problem of "symbolic action" in such a sense
as that found in religious ritual. The primary feature of such action
from one point of view is that it is "useless" in a double sense, in
that first it is not instrumentally contributory to any empirical goal
—e.g. funeral ceremonial does not restore the deceased to life, help
dispose of the corpse, or make provision for "taking over" his instrumental functions,—and also secondly in that it does not directly
gratify any "primary" cathectic need. Thus again bereavement may
activate guilt feelings relative to the deceased, but funeral ceremonial does not permit "making restitution" in any direct way, or
"making it up to him".

The cathectic significance of such symbolic action is made clear
however, in terms of its relation to the systems of expressive symbolism which we have discussed. *Direct* gratification of an activated
need complex may be blocked, partly by the nature of the situation as in the fact that death removes the object from the situational field, and partly by the normative structure of the social
system so that, for example the direct acting out of hostility against
members of the in-group is inadmissable. Then the relevant emotional reactions are expressed through acts which belong *in the
same symbolic system*. The acts and symbolically associated objects
are associated with the primary center of the "disturbance" along
the relevant gradients of generalization. In *one* sense, then, symbolic action is "substitute gratification" or even in a sense "phan-
tasy gratification". But such a formula must be interpreted with
great caution. We have tried to make clear that once an attitudinal
system has become fully organized through internalization of patterns, the maintenance of the pattern integrity of the *system itself*
becomes the primary focus. The "primary cathexis" ceases to have
its original independent significance. Hence in a very real sense
opportunity to express emotion "symbolically" is not a "second rate"
substitute but can be the "real thing". Its exact significance must
be judged in the context of the total action system of which it is a

part. It may be that only genetically viewed should it be regarded as a "substitute". [4]

But in any case the theory of expressive symbolism put forward above should give us criteria of what *kinds* of symbolic action will be "functionally adequate". These criteria are of two sorts. First on the attitudinal side, the emotional tone of the action must be such as to express the appropriate attitudinal reactions. Secondly, the selection of symbols must be consistent in object-categorization patterning with the definition of the primary objects of cathexis that is the activating situation in this case. Thus in a very obvious sense the use of family symbolism in the Catholic Church makes it possible readily to generalize sentiments generated in the family into the religious sphere; the priest as "father" can act as a substitute father even though he does not perform the instrumental functions of a real father. Similarly of course with "Mary, Mother of God". The accent here of course is on the motherhood. The selection of symbolic objects, including acts, must be regarded as a resultant of the interaction of several variables. The occasion for ritual action will focus the reaction tendencies on particular need-disposition components. As we noted, for various reasons the most direct and in need-terms "first priority" path of discharge may be blocked. But the cathectic-symbolic system is so organized that the impulse is transferred to another "circuit" where the channels are free. But it must be a circuit which is satisfactorily integrated with the first priority need-disposition.

Secondly, we may say something about the mechanisms of learning, defense and adjustment, though this is so big a field that only a few suggestions can be made here. First let us take the mechanism of substitution as a learning mechanism. Essentially we may say this is the name for the process of extension of the expressive-symbolic system to include a new object. Or, perhaps we should say that this is one principal aspect, the other being the process of renunciation of an old object, i.e. of certain cathectic significances of it. For the extension aspect, we can see, the most fundamental requirement of successful substitution will be the symbolic appropriateness of the new object, its congruence with the pattern structure of the symbolic complex. It must, that is, be the *right kind of object*, in the appropriate ways. This *may* be a matter of its "intrinsic" capacity to gratify, as in the case of food, but we all know how fundamental

---

[4] This problem is clearly central to the interpretation of the place of infantile gratifications in the adult personality.

the symbolic aspect even of food preferences and aversions becomes. Indeed one can almost say that no matter *how* important this intrinsic aspect may be, unless the object can be integrated in the symbolic system, it cannot be successfully cathected.

The renunciation aspect of substitution should be distinguished from the extension aspect. Here it is a question of what the occasion for renunciation is. It may be simply situational change, as the lack of availability of accustomed foods in a foreign country. On the other hand it may require inhibition because the old object is a continuing part of the situation. Here again one should distinguish between the case where the inhibition is required because for some reason the *particular* object is no longer suitable, and that where the renunciation is a necessary part of a process of reorganization of the *pattern structure* of the cathectic system. The renunciation of infantile objects of attachment is clearly a case of the latter; the continuation of the mother-attachment unchanged is incompatible with the new demands of being more "grown up", for example because it includes a dependency component which would block independence. Here we should probably not speak of simple substitution.

Displacement we may here interpret as substitution along a gradient of symbolic generalization, where the new object is clearly a "second best", where that is, there is a fundamental motivational reason for preferring a primary object, but its cathexis is incompatible with conflicting motivational needs. The familiar example of hostility in relation to in-group solidarity will illustrate the point. It is not motivationally nearly as satisfactory to hate the scapegoat, as it would be to hate one's own kind, but it is better to hate the scapegoat than not to have any expression of the aggressive impulses, and the symbolic relationship means that there is partial equivalence, and some genuine gratification. Displacement may, it is clear, occur along any one of the gradients of symbolic associative generalization. The general requirement of symbolic pattern-congruence should, where we know displacement has occurred, give us very important clues as to the focus of the displaced affect. Thus in Anti-semitism the sharpness of the emphasis on the business practices and "character" of the Jew would lead us to suspect that the "adequacy" problem was more importantly at the root of anti-semitism than was the more particularistic security problem. The Jew is not an appropriate symbol for failure of diffuse love, but rather for a sense of failure in universalistically patterned performance spheres.

Whereas displacement may be regarded as the name for the

most-generalized process of symbolic substitution of a less satisfactory object for the "really" desired one, projection is a more
specialized mechanism; in fact, it is a special case of displacement.
Here *motivational intention* is the primary focus, and the element
which is displaced, is the *authorship* of expressively significant action.[5] The occurrence of projection then immediately allows us to
infer that there is a fundamental conflict in the actor's personality
relative to his *own responsibility* for prohibited actions, projection
that is would seem to be impossible without a powerful guilt factor
in the personality. It clearly means that performance-responsibility
is a focus of strain.

Finally, a few words may be said about possibilities of the use
of this scheme in the analysis of so-called "psycho-somatic" phenomena. Clearly what we have spoken of as performance always
operates through "behavior" of the organism, through alterations
in the state of the organism which in turn alter its relations to its
environment. Therefore it follows that every performance, every
in our sense intentional or motivated act, includes a "somatic"
change which in one aspect is *itself an expressive symbol*. Every
change in the state of the organism then, which implements a
motivated action, or which is by the paths of association we have
analyzed, associated with such action can be cathected as an expressive symbol. The physiological processess of eating, of moving
the body, of uttering speech sounds, etc. are in the nature of the
case always in one aspect expressive symbols.

There is a structure of this expressive symbol aspect of bodily
function which has a "normal" integration with the cathectic orientation system of the actor, which includes or rather *is* the organization of his feelings about the "normality" of his bodily states.
But obviously the same considerations which we discussed above
about "symbolic action" apply to the possibilities of "using" bodily
states and changes in them as substitute expressive symbolization
channels when for any reason what are felt to be normal channels
of expression are blocked. Many of these substitutions may be
regarded as completely normal and are continually occurring, and
certainly have much to do with the physiological aspects of emotion. An excellent example would be the bodily changes occurring
in fear situations. On occasion, however, when there are conflict elements in the personality, displacements onto bodily states can constitute appropriate partial resolutions of the conflict just as displace-

[5] It thus involves not only attitudes *toward* the object but categorization
of it.

4

ments onto other objects can. This may be particularly true when more direct and overt "acting out" is particularly anxiety-provoking. Such motivated bodily changes must of course conform with the conditions of "voluntary" control of organic processes so far as these are known, but then in turn of course they can have further physiological consequences which are not voluntarily controlled. Food-intake is certainly voluntarily controlled in the usual sense. But the physiological consequences of persistent deficiency of vitamin intake certainly in general are not. This seems to be the essential principle.

The relevance of the theory of expressive symbolism to the psycho-somatic field, thus, starts with the proposition just stated that *any* bodily change can be an expressive symbol if it can be an object of perception, and can either itself be motivationally controlled, or symbolically associated with intentional action. Then aspects of the "body image" will have this sort of significance and there will be various cathexes of the sub-objects of the body organized into various attitudinal complexes. The ways these body parts and bodily processes are symbolically integrated into the actor's motivational system, then should provide us with ways of understanding why this particular somatic phenomenon acquired the kind of significance it did for the actor, and why he controlled it the way he did, if he did. Then the physiological analysis of consequences can take over. But without some sort of application of the theory of action along the lines indicated, these phenomena must remain simply mysterious and inexplicable.

Appendix to Paper on Symbolism[6]

The above analysis of the problems of symbolism has led up inevitably to a reconsideration of the systematic relationships between the pattern variables. It has been clear for a long time that they did not constitute simply a catalogue, but in some sense a system. This first appeared in the "symmetrical asymmetry" which related universalism-particularism and ascription-achievement above all to the object-situation, and specificity-diffuseness and affectivity-neutrality to the organization of motivation. It has be-

[6] This appendix was written a few days after completion of the above paper. It would be possible to incorporate its content into a revised version of the paper, but since it documents the transition from the present paper to Chapter III which follows, it seemed better to publish it unchanged. It was written only a day or two before the basic insight of Chapter III.

come gradually clearer that this polarity was deeply grounded, and the above discussion has already gone a long way to make clear in just what this grounding consisted. A further very important step has also been taken in showing just why the fifth pattern variable, self-vs. collectivity orientation did not belong with either of the pairs, but occupied a place by itself. This rests, we have shown, on the fact that of all classes of objects, the collectivity alone does not inherently focus on components independent of the system of interaction itself, but is itself directly constituted *by* that system, is thus a mode of integration *of* it.

It now appears, that there is a further extremely important systematic relationship between the "primary" pairs themselves. The whole discussion of symbolism took its departure from the conception that a sign-object *always* has *both* cognitive and expressive meanings. The relationship between the pattern variables in question now appears to be a generalization of this insight. Action is, as we have said many times before, a *relational* system, and *every* act must organize *all the primary components* of that relational system. The fact that every symbol has both cognitive and expressive meanings is a special case of a more general principle, which again has been stated many times before, but its significance for the pattern variables not seen. This may be brought out by the restatement, that every patterning of organization of a system of action *must have both* its "cognitive" aspect, that is a reference to the situational components of the action system, and its "expressive" aspect, that is reference to the motivation components of the system. But integration of a system depends on these two aspects being brought into certain kinds of relation to each other. The "coordinates" relative to which this can take place, that is process in the system be defined and analyzed, must allow reference in both directions.

But let us take this up concretely in relation to the pattern variables themselves. Universalism-particularism, we have seen, distinguishes two different "gradients" along which cognitive-instrumental relations to objects can be organized. Particularism, for example brings out the fact of common belongingness in a single relational system relative to ego. This has its counterpart in the diffuse alternative of the specificity-diffuseness variable. Here the important point is the organization of cathexes, of expressive interests in terms of their relation to the concrete object as such, so that the pattern of their organization must make a place for an indefinite variety of *types* of interest. This is the expressive counterpart of cognitive particularism. Cognitively ego sees the situation particularistically when he organizes it relative to *his* motivational interests with all their motivational variety; expressively he cathects the situation "diffusely" when he organizes it relative to the *particular object of* cathexis. The pattern *principle* is the same in both cases, because in both cases it is organization of action components relative to a particular object. But the two must be distinguished, since every actor unit is *both* object and orienting actor, in the interaction process, and there is independent variability between them. The fact that there must be two, not one pattern variable foci which in this special sense are "particularistic", is a consequence of the fact that the object-significance of the actor must be distinguished from the motivational orientation aspect. It is probably also a consequence of the "double contingency". Whatever term we use for the more general "principle" there must be two "fields of application" because the same unit must be seen in two independently variable ways. This is inherent in the frame of reference.

There is a corresponding relation between universalism on the one hand and specificity on the other. Universalism designates the organization of systems of objects cognitively by *common attributes* independent of the particular relational system of ego. They must be attributes which have the same property of commonness both to ego and to alter. There must be "abstraction" from the specific perspective. Similarly in the case of specificity, there is "abstraction" from the totality of possible cathectic significance of the object, to focus on a specific basis of motivational interest, ignoring other potentialities for cathecting the object. But by the same token, all objects gratifying to the same interest are brought together, not "classed" together in the cognitive sense, but "treated as equivalent" in a motivational context. They have equivalent expressive meanings in our terminology.

Again, then, we have a common "principle" underlying both the cognitive and the expressive aspects of the orientation structure, in this case the principle that the "basis of significance" should be independent of the particularity of a single object and its relational system.

The corresponding relationship for the other two pairs, namely, ascription-achievement and affectivity-neutrality is a little more difficult to see, but when properly seen, very clear. Perhaps the main keynote is to be found in the fact on which we insisted above that a performance in interaction is *always* and in the nature of the case an expressive sign. It is always a visible sign expressing the author's "intentions". But it is a *sign* in the cognitive context, as something to be observed and interpreted. In the *expressive* context, it is an expression of affect, it is "acting out" a need-disposition, then and there in the immediate situation. It can only be an expressive symbol to ego because it is an expression of affect to alter and vice versa. If affect is inhibited, if it cannot be expressed, quite clearly with respect to the affect in question the action cannot be an expressive symbol to alter. In other words again we find that the corresponding alternatives of the two pattern variable are cases of a common "principle" which in this case is to the effect that cognizance must be taken of the motivational significance of events for action, in the one case, cognitively by interpreting the motivational meaning of an act, in the other case expressively, by permitting the motivation to get through into action.

Qualities and affective neutrality are related in the corresponding way. The qualities of an object, as distinguished from its performances, are those features of it which are irrelevant to the motivation of an actor—if it is a social object, they are qualities of himself as actor, if not, of any actor—and must be considered independently of such significance. On the expressive side, the corresponding pattern is the holding back, i.e. the inhibition of need-dispositions from "discharge" into action. Obviously no feature of the motivational system can be unrelated to motivation. But components of the motivational system may very well, in the particular situation, be withheld from direct motivational significance. They are not, that is, directly motivating the specific act in question. This is what we mean by affective neutrality; a potential motive fails to operate in the given specific situation. The functional necessity of this for the personality as a system has been quite sufficiently shown at various points. The common principle here is clearly "irrelevance" to the motivation of the *specific* act or action-sequence in question. That this can be only a *relative* irrelevance, and that the immediately expressed need-disposition is dynamically connected with others in a system, goes without saying.

An important conclusion may be drawn. The pattern variable scheme started with five pairs of concepts. One pair, namely the self-collectivity pair, was shown to be in the presently relevant sense of derivative significance, though that fact is of very fundamental theoretical importance. Now we have shown that the other four pairs, by a relationship which cross-cuts the pairing itself, in *one* sense and on *one* level, reduce to *only two* pairs. This statement should certainly not be interpreted to mean that the cognitive-expressive distinction has lost its significance, but only that, taking account of it in a systematic way, we can then see certain relationships between underlying concepts which were not previously visible.

When we do this, it emerges, that the major "axis" of the pattern variable system as a system boils down to the question of primacy—within the motivation—object frame of reference—as between *two pairs* of alternatives of organization of action-components on the *most* fundamental level. The fact that these are still pairs must be kept clearly in mind. The pairs are, first that between the element of generalization in the more usual sense, that is "common features regardless of specific relations to a particular actor-object", and conversely the focus on particular objects, as objects on the one hand, or as foci of the organization of motivational interests on the other hand. The second is the pair revolving about the significance of what we have variously called motivation, affect, "acting out" etc. on the one hand, and those aspects of or factors in the system which on the other hand are interpreted to be independent of this reference.

In other words, the cognitive-expressive distinction gives us one fundamental coordinate of the frame of reference. But cross-cutting this is the interplay of the two pairs of alternatives, each of which clearly involves *both* cognitive and expressive references. Many problems clearly are not solved by this analysis so far. But there can be little doubt that we are dealing with a genuine *system*. Certain outlines of it seem to be fairly clear, but many things are also obscure.

CHAPTER 3

THE DIMENSIONS
OF ACTION-SPACE

BY TALCOTT PARSONS
AND ROBERT F. BALES

We have long believed that the theory of human social behavior, what technically we call the theory of action, has been in
a process of converging toward a general theoretical scheme which
was applicable in at least certain essentials all the way from the
smallest samples of experimentally controlled animal behavior to
the analysis of large-scale social processes. To cite only works in
which we have been personally involved, *The Structure of Social
Action, Interaction Process Analysis,* and the recently published
volumes *Toward a General Theory of Action* and *The Social System,* have all been dominated by this perspective. In the recent
history of this trend of thought, there has been an impressive
amount of convergence of elements of theory derived from a variety of sources. The purpose of this paper is to document a still further and very recent step[1] in this larger process which we believe
brings us perceptibly nearer to being able to treat social interaction
in a generalized manner.

There are five main pieces of work which, though previously
known to be connected in a broad way, have recently been
brought into much clearer and sharper relations to each other than
before. These include (1) a set of categories for the direct observation and classification of social interaction, (2) a set of pattern

[1] As noted in the introduction this paper was written in November, 1951.
It has only undergone editorial corrections and no substantial revisions since
that time.

63

variables for the classification of dilemmas of choice in action, (3) a paradigm for the classification of aspects of deviant behavior in institutionalized social systems, (4) a corresponding paradigm for the classification of aspects of social control, and (5) some recent work on the nature of symbolism and its relation to interaction. We may begin with a brief sketch of each of these five in order to orient the reader to the main discussion.

(1) First, basing himself on broad foundations of sociological theory, one of us has been at work for some years on an intensive analysis of the processes of interaction in small groups. This study has included the development both of methods of empirical observation and of theoretical analysis. This approach has been published in preliminary form in the book *Interaction Process Analysis.*[2] Our present interest is not in the empirical methods, but in the theoretical scheme involved. The essential approach was to think of the small group as a functioning social system. It was held that such a system would have four main "functional problems" which were described, respectively, as those of *adaptation* to conditions of the external situation, of *instrumental* control over parts of the situation in the performance of goal oriented tasks, of the management and *expression* of sentiments and tensions of the members, and of preserving the social *integration* of members with each other as a solidary collectivity. In relation to this complex of system-problems, a classification of types of action was worked out, falling in twelve categories as given in Fig. 1. It will be seen that they fall into four groups of three each, and further that the total set is symmetrically arranged according to several principles, two of which may be mentioned here. In the first place each of the twelve types is classified according to whether its significance is "positive" or "negative" from the point of view of what the occurrence of the act indicates about the state of solution of the particular system problem it deals with. This is the distinction between those above (1-6) and those below (7-12) the central line. In the second place each half is divided into those which are most directly relevant to the problems of adaptation and instrumental control (4-9) and those primarily relevant to the problems of expression of emotional reactions and tensions and maintenance of group integration (1-3, 10-12).

This set of categories has been extensively used in the empirical observation and analysis of small group interaction situations. That

2 By Robert F. Bales. Cambridge, Mass. Addison—Wesley Press. 1950.

Figure 1.

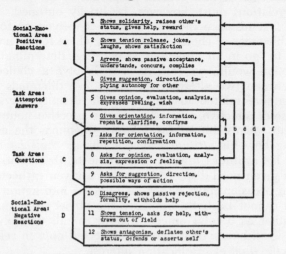

it was grounded in general sociological theory was evident from the first, but its precise relation to certain other conceptual schemes had not been fully worked out.

(2) The other author has for a considerable period been greatly concerned with a set of concepts he has come to call "pattern variables". In the monograph Values, Motives and Systems of Action (with Edward Shils)[3] this scheme was shown to constitute, at its particular level of abstraction, a complete system, which was grounded in the fundamental frame of reference of the theory of action, and which at the same time could be used as a basis of classification, not only of the structural elements of social systems but of the value-orientation patterns of culture and of the need-dispositions of personality.

This scheme was further developed and applied in *The Social System,* indeed it was there used as the main framework for the analysis of the structure of social systems. The basic definitions and classifications of these concepts are given in these works. We will not stop to discuss them here, but will refer the reader to these

[3] This monograph appears as Part II of the volume *Toward a General Theory of Action,* Parsons and Shils, Editors. Harvard University Press, 1951. The pattern variable scheme is most fully developed in Chapter I pp. 76 ff, but is used throughout the monograph. It is also more briefly outlined in Parsons, *The Social System,* Chapter II, pp. 58 ff (The Free Press, 1951) and used throughout that work.

two publications. Certain general properties of these concepts and their interrelations must, however, be briefly outlined.

In the first instance they have been conceived as formulating the main dilemmas of choice in situations where it was not possible for action to "go in all directions at once". A determinate orientation of action would, we felt, have to involve a choice in each respect between two alternatives. These five dilemmas of choice are furthermore related to each other in definite ways. Two of them, those of affective expression versus affective neutrality, and of specificity versus diffuseness, concern dilemmas the actor faces in deciding how his *attitudes toward objects shall be organized,* especially his attitudes toward social objects, that is other actors.

Thus a given need-disposition toward a given cathected object, on a given occasion must either be released into action or be inhibited, it cannot be both. Similarly the object itself may be cathected either as a total object in terms of all possibly relevant cathectic significances, or it may be cathected only in relation to a given specific *type* of gratification interest.

A second pair of dilemmas, those of universalism versus particularism and of ascribed quality versus performance,[4] concern on the other hand, dilemmas the actor faces in deciding how *objects themselves shall be organized* in relation to each other and in relation to the motivational interests of the actor. Thus an object may be significant in a given action process either because of its generalized properties independent of the specific relation to ego, the actor, or on the other hand, it may be significant precisely because of particular properties specifically deriving from its relation as an object to *him.* In the first case its significance is universalistic, in the second, particularistic. Similarly, an object may be significant for qualities ascribed to it independent of its performance as an actor, or it may be significant rather in terms of the way it performs or achieves in relation to some goal or interest.

The fifth pattern variable, that of self-vs. collectivity-orientation, is not paired with any other, and does not as such belong either to the attitudinal side of the classification or to the situational or object-categorization side. This is because it is concerned with problems internal to the *system* of interaction rather than with problems internal to each act considered in isolation. It concerns

[4] The terms for this pair used in the works cited are ascription versus achievement. It seems preferable here to adopt the more general terms of quality versus performance. This usage will be followed throughout the rest of this publication.

whether the individual actor's orientation in some particular area of activity should be directly constitutive of his solidarity with others in a collectivity, or whether it may remain or become independent of this within certain limits. For the most general purposes of the analysis of systems of action, then, this fifth pattern variable may be neglected.[5]

This scheme of pattern variables, as noted, has proved to be capable of providing a framework for the generalized analysis of the structural aspects of systems of action, both social systems and personalities, and has been extensively used in this respect. It has also been shown to be directly derived from the most general frame of reference of action, as shown in Figure 2, taken from *Values, Motives, and Systems of Action.*

(3) and (4) In the work of the same author a second major conceptual scheme has developed in the last two years, partly documented in *The Social System.*[6] This is what has been called

[5] We shall return to the problem of the status of this pattern variable in Chapter 5 below.

[6] Chapters VI and VII. For convenience of reference the following schematic representation of the pattern-variable scheme may be presented. It was published in each of the two previous works, *Toward a General Theory of Action* and *The Social System.*

Figure 2

Grouping of Pattern Variables

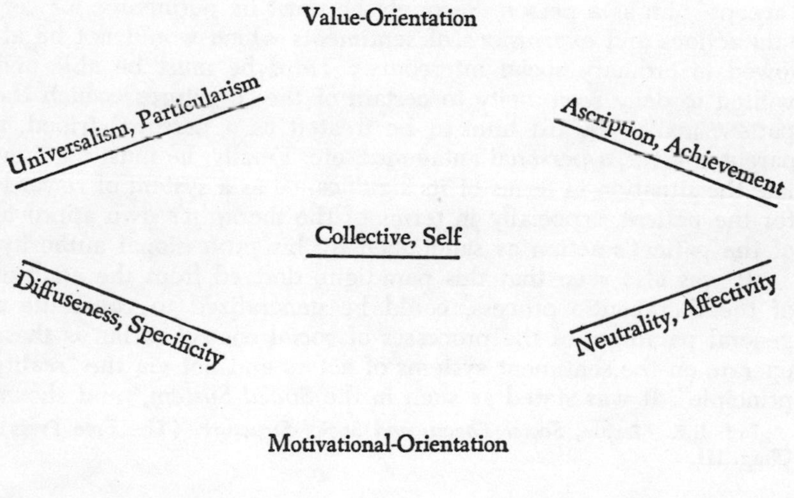

Value-Orientation

Universalism, Particularism

Ascription, Achievement

Collective, Self

Diffuseness, Specificity

Neutrality, Affectivity

Motivational-Orientation

the "paradigm of motivational process". It has started with the assumption that a process of interaction which has been stabilized about conformity with a normative pattern structure, will tend to continue in a stable state unless it is disturbed. Concretely, however, there will always be tendencies to deviance, and conversely these tendencies will tend to be counteracted by re-equilibrating processes, on the part of the same actor or of others.

(3) It was furthermore maintained that neither the tendencies toward deviance nor those toward re-equilibration, that is toward "social control", could occur in random directions or forms. Deviance was shown to involve four basic directions, according to whether the need was to express alienation from the normative pattern—including the repudiation of attachment to alter as an object—or to maintain compulsive conformity with the normative pattern and attachment to alter, and according to whether the mode of action was actively or passively inclined. This yielded four directional types, those of aggressiveness and withdrawal on the alienative side, and of compulsive performance and compulsive acceptance, on the side of compulsive conformity. It was furthermore shown that this paradigm, independently derived, is essentially the same as that previously put forward by Merton for the analysis of social structure and anomie.[7]

(4) In the analysis of social control special attention was paid to the processes of psychotherapy. Here it was felt that four fundamental conditions of successful psychotherapy could be stated. The psychotherapist must first be "supportive" of his patient, he must "accept" him as a person. Secondly he must be permissive for certain actions and expressions of sentiments which would not be allowed in ordinary social intercourse. Third he must be able and willing to deny reciprocity to certain of the "overtures" which the patient makes toward him, to be treated as a personal friend, a parent, a lover, a personal antagonist, etc. Finally, he must manipulate the situation in terms of its significance as a system of rewards for the patient, especially in terms of the therapist's own approval of the patient's action as sanctioned by his professional authority.

It was also seen that this paradigm, derived from the analysis of the therapeutic process, could be generalized to constitute a general paradigm of the processes of social control so far as these operate on the sentiment systems of actors and not via the "reality principle". It was stated as such in the *Social System,*[8] and shown

[7] cf. R.K. Merton, *Social Theory and Social Structure.* (The Free Press). Chap. III.

that *structurally* this paradigm of social control corresponded directly with that for deviance. In sum it was felt that on the paradigmatic level a complete scheme for the analysis of the motivational balance of a social system had been worked out and, furthermore, that this paradigm was independent of the structures of the particular complementary roles in which it operated. The dynamic interconnections between the variables involved in the paradigm could not, however, as yet be formulated, nor could its relations to role structure, formulated in pattern variable terms, be adequately worked out.

(5) Finally, both of us have long been greatly concerned with the place of the theory of symbolism in the theory of action in general and of social systems in particular. The work of Mead, of Cooley, of Morris in particular, but of course of various others, had given us important leads. Work eventuating in the monograph *Values, Motives and Systems of Action* led to substantial clarification in this field, especially in showing the extent to which culture must be considered to constitute systems of common symbols and their meaning-references.

Still, we have not felt that the analysis of the symbolic process was adequately integrated with the general theory of action. Finally, further clarification in this area has been achieved in very recent work[9] which has contributed greatly to the general synthesis we wish to describe in this paper. Perhaps the most important points are as follows. First it has become clear that the distinction between cognitive and expressive symbols, which is essential for many purposes, cannot be regarded as a radical distinction of "kind" but is one of relative *primacy* of common components. *Every* symbol, that is, has *both* cognitive and expressive meanings, it both "refers to" situational objects and events and it "expresses" the attitudes of an actor or actors.

Secondly, *every* overt performance of an actor in the process of interaction is in one aspect an expressive symbol. This implies that an interaction process can be organized and stabilized only in terms of a set of "conventions" defining common meanings of the mutual interactions in their capacity as expressive symbols. All interaction, whether verbal or not, in one fundamental aspect involves the "speaking" of a symbolic language, conveying both cognitive and expressive meanings.

[8] Appendix to Chapter VII.

[9] The paper included in this collection as Chapter II above.

Third the interaction process can not be stabilized unless on both the attitudinal and the object sides of the organization of action, there is a building up by the participants of *complexes* of attitudes, symbolic acts, and objects with symbolic reference to each other, by virtue of which elementary objects of cathexis, secondary objects of interest and motivational interest-components themselves come to be organized in systems. It is the *patterning* of these symbolic references which constitutes the "structure" of a system of action in the strictest sense. Furthermore it becomes clear that what we mean by the "internalization" of a culture pattern[10] is simply the fact of the *organization* of these elementary motivational and object components in terms of mutual symbolic reference. Speaking of the "cathexis of a pattern" then is an elliptical way of speaking of the actor's emotional "investment" in the maintenance of a certain kind of patterning of this system of orientation, of the ways in which his own motivational components and the relation of the object system to him are organized.

This further clarification of the involvement of symbolism in action has paved the way for our seeing much more clearly than before that the pattern variables are deeply involved in what has here been called the mutual symbolic organization of action components. The requirements for stability of such organization are such that there must be particular *relations* between the attitudinal and the situational components of a system of action. These types of relations, it appeared, could be formulated in terms of the combinations of *one* pattern-variable component from the *attitudinal* side of the system with *one* corresponding component from the situational or *object-categorization* side. This way of looking at the pattern variables, by a classification completely cross-cutting the ones which had figured in the many previous analyses of structural problems, opened the way to the present new synthesis of the theoretical components of systems of action.

II

The essential relations which we wish to discuss are, with the exception of the involvement of symbolism, schematically represented in Figure 3. This shows that it is possible to regard the categories of interaction process developed by Bales and the motivational paradigm developed by Parsons, as, in all essentials,

---

[10] Equally, of course, its "institutionalization."

different ways of conceptualizing the same thing. The mode of organization of the scheme revolves about the "functional problems of social systems" put forward by Bales, and the pattern variables of Parsons and Shils, put together in a specific combination; the two in this context turning out to mean essentially the same thing. These statements require considerable elucidation.

The fundamental conception underlying both original schemes is that a process of ongoing social interaction can be usefully described by comparison with a hypothetical system in a state of moving equilibrium. If no new elements at all were introduced into the system, the interaction process would, according to the "law of inertia" stated in *The Social System*,[11] continue unchanged. But such a static equilibrium is, theoretically considered, a limiting case. Actually new elements are continually being introduced, elements which may be classified under three headings. First new information by perception and cognition of the situation is being introduced, from the members of the group or from outside, and this new information influences the orientations of the members. Second, the personalities of the members are only in part directly constitutive of the group process, and new elements particularly in the form of value judgments, and emotional reactions, are being introduced into the interactive system through the processes of interdependence between the social system constituted by the group interaction and the personality systems of the members. Third, the situation in which the group and each of its members operate may be changing in various respects and there have to be processes of adaptation to and attempts to control these changes.

A new element introduced into the system in some way disturbs the expectations of one or more of the members—unless as may happen it has been completely "discounted" in advance. If the system is to regain equilibrium there must be a process of adjustment to this disturbance, to the new situation. This process of disturbance and adjustment is conceived as "oscillating" about an equilibrium state of the system, a moving equilibrium. The action of one of the members, or a situational event perceived by one or more of the members, introduces a new element, which is a disturbance; this evokes a "reaction" which may be opposite in direction in the sense that it tends to restore the equilibrium or may be similar in direction in that it tends further to disturb equilibrium. The complexity of interdependence of the elements of the system

[11] Chapter VI, pp. 204-5.

is such that very seldom will one reaction completely restore equilibrium. Even in relatively stable systems there may be a long series of such action-reaction processes which, however, will tend to narrow in range, leading toward a stable state. This tendency toward an asymptotic approach to a stable state will, however, be continually interrupted by the introduction of a whole series of new elements into the system, not only the initial one.

The two sets of categories or paradigms which, though independently arrived at have here been brought together in a single schema, do *not* attempt to formulate the patterns of succession of different modes of action and reaction in the system,[12] but essentially formulate the *dimensions* along which "movement" or process in the system in the interplay of action and reaction, takes place. In order to show this it is necessary to explain more fully from just what point of view each of the sets of categories has been originally formulated and hence what modifications are necessary in order to make them directly comparable. In the schematic table of Fig. 3 the original terminology has been preserved. In certain respects, it is important to note, these terms designate special cases rather than the most general one.

Bales' categories were formulated for purposes of direct microscopic observation of the interaction process in small groups. They constitute a scheme for classification of what an actor does in terms of the smallest feasible unit of observation. The terms in the table are abbreviations of these action types, the actor "*shows* solidarity", "*makes* a suggestion", "*asks for* orientation" etc. In each case the act is classified according to what the observer judges to be the *primary* feature of the concrete act. It has been fully recognized that this need not be the exclusively significant one, but it has not seemed operationally feasible to attempt to identify and record more than one such feature for each observational unit.

The most significant features of Bales' categories from the present point of view are their *classification* relative to the positive-negative polarity, and relative to the four system-problems mentioned above of integration, expression, instrumentality and adaptation. The symmetrical arrangement of the categories, into the "task-oriented" sections (the middle ones in Bales' arrangement) and the "social-emotional" sections (the outside ones) is, along with the polarity and the internal differentiation within each section, as we shall see, fundamentally important.

12 This problem is taken up in Chapters IV and V below.

The other sets of categories coming from Parsons' and Shils' recent work were arrived at from a different point of view. They were formulated for a more macroscopic analysis and also consisted of two sections which were independently worked out and then put together.

The difference of level from Bales' categories consists essentially in the fact that Bales was concerned with the microscopic level of study of the interaction *process* as such. While of course the broad role structure of the social system stood in the background, framing the orientations of the small group members,[13] there was an explicit attempt to abstract from institutionalized role structure. Parsons, on the other hand, was directly concerned with the analysis of deviance and social control *relative to institutionalized patterns* of social structure as such. Furthermore while Parsons' typology of deviance is phrased in such a way as to apply to any deviant role in the system, the typology of elements of social control is phrased from the point of view of the institutionalized role of the doctor or therapist and then generalized to other role systems; it formulates the "successful" rather than the "unsuccessful" (or deviant) pattern. It is thus the least "generalized" of the various classifications included in the table. These differences in degree of abstraction and direction of concrete application help to account for the fact that Bales' twelve categories make certain distinctions not made by Parsons' eight, and also for the one asymmetry in the comparison of the "active" and "passive" character of the action types.[14]

The first section of Parsons' scheme is the "deviance" paradigm. Once it had become clear how important in social systems was the internalization of normative patterns of the common culture, there has gradually developed the conception of an interaction system stabilized about conformity with a given set of normative patterns. According to the law of inertia such a system should continue unchanged unless disturbances were introduced. But *whatever the source of the disturbance*, the upsetting of the equilibrium of the system would have to take place in one of a small number of definable directions. The problem then was to define what were, in terms of the nature of the stabilized system itself, the most important of these directions.

[13] This problem is of course relevant to the cross-cultural generalization of Bales' findings.

[14] These problems will be taken up again in Chapter V below.

Figure 3. Corresponding Elements in Parsons' and Bales' Typologies of Interaction

"Supportive" Aspect (above double line)

Bales' Categories Negative Movements	Parsons' Types of Deviance	Parsons' Categories Components of successful social control	Bales' Categories Positive Movements	Dimensions as related to Pattern Variables
12) Shows Antagonism (Active)	Aggressiveness (Active)	Support (Active)	1) Shows Solidarity (Active)	Major change in the *Integrative* Dimension. Attitude: Cathexis in forms of Diffuse need dispositions. Relation to object: Particularistic
11) Shows Tension (Passive) 10) Disagrees (Passive)	Withdrawal (Passive)	Permissiveness (Passive)	2) Shows Release Tension (Passive) 3) Agrees (Passive)	Major change in the *Expressive* Dimension. Attitude: Certain affective tendencies held Neutral (Inhibition). Relation to object: In terms of given Quality-features of system.
9) Asks for suggestion (Passive)	Compulsive Performance (Active)	Denial of Reciprocity (Passive)	4) Gives Suggestion (Active)	Major change in the *Instrumental* Dimension. Attitude: Certain affective tendency allowed to issue into action. Relation to object: In terms of expected performance
8) Asks for Opinion (Passive) 7) Asks for Orientation (Passive)	Compulsive Acceptance (Passive)	Manipulation of Situation (Active)	5) Gives Opinion (Active) 6) Gives Orientation (Active)	Major change in the *Adaptive* Dimension. Attitude: Cathexis in terms of specific interests. Relation to object: Universalistic

Pattern-Responsibility Aspect (below double line)

The first important insight in this connection was that "over-conformity" should be defined as deviance. Alienation, the disposition to break away from the pattern of conforming behavior—i.e. of stabilized interaction, could then be paired with "compulsive conformity", the disposition to maintain it in the face of strain, which however would make *full* conformity impossible. This paradigm was thus formulated in terms of a theory of motivation, the foci of which were the conceptions of internalization of pattern, and of the ambivalent nature of psychological reactions to strain.

There was then introduced the conception that, whether the deviance was on the side of alienation or of over- or compulsive conformity, the direction of deviance could be either active or passive. What this meant was that *relative to stabilized expectations* i.e. to the institutionalized pattern, ego could deviate either by actively "taking the situation in hand", doing more in attempting to control it than the expectations called for, or he could deviate in the passive direction, falling short of asserting the degree of active control which the role-expectation called for.

These two axes of differentiation yielded the fourfold-classification which is presented under the heading of deviance in Fig. 3. At this point as pointed out it became evident that there had been a convergence with Merton's well-known paradigm of the relations between social structure and anomie.[15] It was also shown that a further significant sub-division of types of deviance could be worked out by using the additional distinction as to whether the focus of strain was on relations to the social object (to alter as a person) or on the pattern with which conformity was expected. This brought the whole classification very close indeed to that of the mechanisms of adjustment of the personality.[16]

The second section of Parsons' motivational paradigm was that concerned with the process of social control. As noted this was worked out in the first instance in connection with an attempt to state certain of the conditions of successful psychotherapy.[17] It borrowed directly from the psychiatric literature and particularly from insight gained in the course of training in psychoanalysis. Four essential conditions were distinguished (which must of course

[15] Merton, op cit.

[16] cf. *Values, Motives and Systems of Action.* Chapter II pp. 125ff and table p. 255. and *Social System,* Chapter VII, p. 259.

[17] cf. *The Social System,* Chapters VII and X, also "Illness and the Role of the Physician", *Am. Jour. of Orthopsychiatry,* July 1951.

be combined in the proper ways). These were, as noted, first the "support" of the patient in the sense of acceptance of him as a person, the existence of a "helpful", "understanding", non-punishing attitude on the part of the therapist. The second, permissiveness, meant that the therapist must be ready to permit, within limits, expression of sentiments and at least verbal behavior which would ordinarily be inhibited in the patient's other socially interactive relationships. Negative sanctions are to this extent suspended, and thus the patient is permitted openly to express his deviant wishes, attitudes and beliefs. Third, the therapist must not merely be negatively permissive but he must also refrain from reciprocating certain of the patient's overtures, that is those based on expectations that the therapist will undertake certain overt performances, which may be gratifying or frustrating from the patient's point of view. He must, as psychiatrists often say, not allow himself to be "seduced" into such reciprocation. When he does allow this, it is "countertransference". Finally, the therapist must carefully manipulate the rewards available to him, particularly those involved in his own attitudes of approval-disapproval toward the patient's behavior, since generalization along this axis is known to be so fundamental to interaction. In general an "interpretation" should be regarded as a deliberate intervention in the situation which is meant in part not only to aid in clarifying insight but to reward the patient for the insight gained through his successful "work" or to deny such reward when it has been expected by the patient.

It has further been shown[18] that this paradigm could be generalized and regarded as formulating essential features of the processes of social control, and of socialization in so far as the latter concretely involves reactions to strains. For example in funeral ceremonies there is support in the form of symbolic declaration of the solidarity of the bereaved with the collectivities to which they belong; there is permissiveness in the form of allowing or even prescribing "grief reactions" beyond the normal level of emotional demonstrativeness; there is denial of reciprocity for unduly extreme sentiments of grief, despair and sometimes hostility, and finally the reward system is definitely structured so as to put a premium on "getting back" onto the track of resumption of "normal" social functioning. Or, to take another example, the youth culture in our society may be analyzed from the same point of view. The solidarity of the peer group gives the individual a support which is not too closely bound up with the adult society rela-

[18] *Social System*, Chap. VII, final section.

tive to which he feels strain. Yet the adult society is distinctly permissive within certain limits relative to the "vagaries" of the young. At the same time there are very important denials of reciprocity both within the youth culture group itself, and vis-a-vis adults, and finally the reward system is by and large structured in favor of successfully "growing up".

Now it appears that the paradigms of deviance and social control can be put directly together in the manner indicated by Fig. 3. Each directional type of deviant act may in these terms be regarded as a way in which disturbances can be introduced in an equilibrated system of interaction. Then the corresponding category in the paradigm of social control may be regarded as a way in which a counteracting tendency to re-equilibration may take place. Thus an aggressive act from the present point of view is a disturbance of equilibrium in the sense that it weakens the solidarity of the parties to the interactive relationship. If solidarity is weak or deteriorating a supportive act may be a way of strengthening it. Secondly, withdrawal from fulfillment of normal expectations in any way is another form of disturbance; some adjustment must be made in the system to "take the place" of the expected performances. Permissiveness, on the other hand is a form of "equilibrating withdrawal" in that by the suspension of negative sanctions it permits release of tension without driving the actors concerned into antagonism or otherwise deviant performance. Third, compulsive performance is still another way of disturbing equilibrium in that, though ostensibly in line with the expectations of the role, it "overdoes" the part, and creates difficulties of adjustment for the other parties. Thus in a competitive situation, too great extra effort on the part of one competitor may force the others to extra exertions. The equilibration of a system that is, depends on the "gearing in" of the performance levels of the various participants so that too much performance by one is, if not adjusted to by the others, disturbing. Correspondingly, denial of reciprocity for a deviant performance, or conversely the introduction of a needed performance where there has been withdrawal, constitutes a step toward re-equilibration. Finally, compulsive acquiescence may be regarded as allowing behavior to be illegitimately rewarded; it is approving what in fact falls short of the requisite standards. The obverse of this is in turn the setting of rewards into an appropriate relation with performance again, refraining from rewarding below standard performance, and positively rewarding that which meets the standard.

The point of view from which this paradigm was originally formulated has introduced a "bias" in the sense that the processes of deviance and social control constitute a very important *special class* of the more general processes of disturbance and re-equilibration in social interaction. In the more general sense "disturbance" need not be deviance—thus every process of group task solution necessarily involves disturbances, which do not constitute contravention of any recognized norm, as for instance through the introduction of new information into the system. Bales' categories, as can be seen, formulate this more general case of the minor disturbing "movements" in the relatively stable process.

It should be very carefully kept in mind that in the actual process of interaction the succession of disturbing and re-equilibrating acts does not follow this specific pattern of sequence. The problem of the laws governing sequence is a distinct problem which we cannot follow out in this paper. For present purposes all we mean to say is that for every disturbance there is a corresponding mode of re-equilibrating process and vice versa. The interaction process is a process of action and reaction and the directions of disturbance and of re-equilibration correspond directly with each other.

One fruit of the placing of the paradigms of deviance and social control in this more general context of equilibrium of the interaction process is to throw new light on the significance of the distinction between activity and passivity and hence the inclusion of these categories in the paradigm. Social equilibrium, or more generally that of action as such, is an ongoing process which presupposes certain expected and continuing levels of performance at appropriate times. From the point of view of the equilibrium of the system as we are now analyzing it, the "active" phase of the process then may be regarded as *acceleration of the rate* of action process, while the "passive" phase is a *deceleration*, a slowing down, of that rate. In either case a disturbance of equilibrium results which in turn necessitates a process of readjustment throughout the system. Further this disturbance may or may not "fit" with a stable pattern of development. We shall see that it is of great importance that a conception of change in rate has entered into the general conceptual scheme with one of its original components, though it had not been clear just what the significance of this was when the deviance-social control paradigms were first formulated.

We must now take up the problems presented by the dimensions of the action frame of reference as these concepts have been reached from the two different sources of Bales' functional problems of a social system[19] and Parsons' and Shils' pattern variables. Perhaps the convergence of these two lines of thought presents the most important single aspect of the synthesis we are describing; it underlies the categorization of the interactive process which we have just reviewed.

The part of Bales' scheme which is most directly relevant here is the classification of the four functional problems of the social system which were made in turn the basis of the classification of types of acts for observational purposes. These, it will be remembered, were the "adaptive", the "instrumental", the "expressive" and the "integrative". Bales pointed out that the first three of these could be considered phases of the adaptation of the social system respectively to its situation, to the expectations of group performance, and to the motivational needs of its members as personalities. The fourth, on the other hand, must be considered to be a problem arising out of the complexity of the interactive system itself as an internally differentiated system. It was explicitly pointed out that "progress" with respect to any one or combination of the other three system problems might entail increasing strain on the integration of the system, and therefore call for action specifically oriented to restoring that integration.

In the light of the present developments it is a curiously ironic fact that Bales reserved the term *dimension* for a related but different set of concepts which refer essentially to modes of foci of differentiation of social systems in a structural sense, with reference to access to resources, to control of action, to prestige and to identification of an individual with the group. These were, that is to say, the main axes of role-differentiation in the system, but not, as we can now see, the dimensions of the process of action as such.

As noted above, Parsons' and Shils' pattern variable concepts were developed, not in connection with the analysis of the interaction process as such, but in the first instance in the analysis of social structure. After considerable use of the concepts on that level, it finally became apparent that they were more widely applicable and that as a system they were directly grounded in the frame of reference of action itself.[20] On that level and in that reference they have

[19] cf. *Interaction Process Analysis*, Chapter II, pp. 49ff. and Chapter V.
[20] cf. *Values, Motives and Systems of Action*, Chapter I.

been, as we have noted, extensively used for structural analysis both of social systems and of personalities, and of the structural articulations between them.

For a considerable period it has become increasingly clear that there was some fundamental connecting link[21] between the polarities of the pattern-variable system as these had been worked out, namely the motivational or attitudinal pole which was analyzed in terms of the categories of affectivity-neutrality and of specificity-diffuseness, and the situational or object-categorization pole which involved the categories of universalism-particularism and ascription-achievement, or as seems a more appropriate terminology for present purposes, quality-performance. Only the careful analysis of the relations of the pattern variables to symbolic generalization and patterning, however, has revealed just what this cross-system link is, and that it in fact formulates in another way exactly the same thing as did Bales' system-problem classification, including exact correspondence in the *number* of categories. It is necessary, therefore, to review briefly the main relevant considerations in the theory of symbolism, though these are more fully set forth in another paper.[22]

The importance of these concern the field of expressive symbolism, which has unfortunately been a seriously neglected field in the theory of action. The most important starting points are those noted above, that every symbol has *both* expressive and cognitive meaning-references, and that every overt act or performance of an actor is in one aspect an expressive symbol, whatever its other or "intrinsic" significances may be.

Symbols, however, seldom occur singly; they come to be organized in *systems,* by virtue of which the actor can be *oriented* in and to his situation. Such symbol systems must be organized both in the cognitive reference context as ways of ordering the object world in its significance for the actor's orientations or "interests", and in the expressive reference context as ways of ordering his attitudes, that is his cathexes, toward objects. Furthermore, and most important, both aspects must be articulated, they must be organized to form a *single system* of the actor's orientation. This

[21] That there is more than one such link will be shown in Chapter V below.

[22] A first attempt to push analysis in this field farther was made in *The Social System,* Chapter IX. The present remarks take their departure from that treatment. Further development will be found in the paper of Parsons, *The Theory of Symbolism in Relation to Action* which forms Chapter II of this publication.

system must be organized about axes which include *both* the cognitive and the cathectic references.

Organization of symbolic significances in systems is essentially what psychologists have come to call generalization. The organization in question takes place relative to *patterns* of generalization according to which, in the cognitive reference, objects are on the one hand discriminated and on the other *classed* together, and in the expressive reference, motivational components are discriminated or segregated and are *organized* together.

In the cognitive reference there are two cross-cutting ways of discriminating and organizing symbol-references. The one is defined by the universalism-particularism variable, the other by that of quality-performance. Universalistic organization is the most familiar pattern type of cognitive organization; it is the classing of objects together, and conversely discriminating them, by virtue of properties they have in common which are significant independently of any specific relation of the object to ego, for example, in terms of common shapes, colors or types of behavior. The particularistic mode of organization, on the other hand, is that in terms of the common belongingness of objects in a specific relational context relative to ego; for example by virtue of all being "ego's possessions". Any concrete object or event may be treated in terms either of universalistic or of particularistic significance to ego.

The other way of discriminating types of cognitive organization of symbols is according to whether or not the object, i.e. an event or some other object associated with an event, is or is not considered to be a *performance* of a social object, or significant as the consequence of a performance and hence as an expression of the *intentions* of the actor concerned.

Performances as objects or object-properties of the situation of action constitute the fundamental link between the situational and the motivational aspects of the action system. if the intentions which are "manifested" in a performance are *generalized* into a pattern of performance-intentions, we impute to the actor, not a series of discrete intentions, but an *attitude*, which, in the present terms, is understandable only as a case of the *symbolic generalization of cathexis*, which is the expressive counterpart of cognitive generalization.

The generalization of cathexis in turn is organized about two cross-cutting pairs of alternative modes. On the one hand there is the organization of particular cathexes and the symbols associated with them about the *total concrete object* as an entity, in the most important case a social object. It is this which is involved when we speak of an attitude of love or esteem, hatred or contempt for a *person* as such. On the other hand the same fundamental cathectic components, object-cathexes and their associated symbols, can be organized about particular *types of motivational interest*, cross-cutting the particularity of the concrete object, so that *any* object which meets the specifications of the interest type can be cathected, independently of its attributes in other respects.

The second pair of alternative modes of organization of cathectic generalization concern whether or not *any* cathectic interest, whether in a diffusely cathected concrete object or in a type of gratification significance, should be permitted to be released into overt action (performance) in the given specific situation, or is to be inhibited in the interest of the integration of the action system. The affective case constitutes the permission to "go ahead" the "green light" for positive overt action, while the "neutral" case is the "red light", the signal to hold up and wait. The assumption is that the object in question is definitely cathected. Therefore "neutrality" in the present case does not mean "indifference" but precisely the existence of "tension" because there exists an impulse to discharge into action, but at the same time an inhibiting force of some sort. This is a set of facts the significance of which was not directly appreciated until the most recent phase of the development of the present conceptual scheme.

Thus, making all due allowances for peculiarities of terminology which reflect the special paths by which the conceptions have developed, we may say that affectivity is directly linked with performance in that, *as distinguished from neutrality*, on the motivational side of the conceptual scheme it signifies the *release* of an impulse into actual overt behavior. Performance on the other hand is the corresponding behavior seen from an observer's point of view; that is to say, it is *the same thing as affectivity* with the "actor" seen as an *object* rather than as an agent of action.[23] This relation between affectivity and performance provides the prototype for treating all of the pattern variable components in terms of their relationships *across* the motivational-situational axis of the system rather than as confined to one or the other side of it.

If, in this manner, affectivity is paired with a counterpart from the cognitive-situational side of the system, namely performance, it is logical that its "partner" affective neutrality should also be paired

[23] The actor in question may be either ego or alter. As performer ego is an object to himself, as well as to alter.

with the corresponding component on the other side, namely "quality" or in the older terminology "ascription". The significance of this second pairing appears to lie in the relation between dynamic process, on the one hand, and its potentiality and consequences on the other hand. Looking at the motivational or "phenomenological" side, affectivity represents motivation *in action,* neutrality, motivation *ready to go into action.* Performance on the other hand, in terms of the actor as object, represents the actor *in the process of acting,* while qualities represent his attributes so far as either the action has been completed and the relevent qualities therefore constitute *consequences* of the process of action, or on the other hand they represent those features or attributes of the actor as object which are not at the moment engaged in performance, which include those which can potentially be changed through performance. Again, therefore, we are able to say that pairing a pattern variable element from the motivational side of the system with the corresponding one from the situational side enables us to gain the perspective that we are looking at essentially the same phenomena from two different vantage points.

We may sum up this aspect of the system by saying that a system of action is involved in what may be called developmental phases. The system or any given unit of it is, from the perspective of what may happen or be about to happen, in a "state of tension". This means that if certain conditions of motivation are given and not changed the system may, in the relevant ways, undergo a process of change which is directionally defined, that is, other things being equal, it can change *only* in the direction of "reduction of tension". Secondly, there is the phase of actual process of change which, according to the point of view, is formulated as affectivity or as performance. Finally, there is the stage of completion of the change which, from the point of view of what has happened in the system, of the new state, is a set of qualities of the objects which compose it; from the point of view of what *may* happen in the next phase of process, on the other hand, it is a neutrality aspect of the motivation system, it is tension not yet released into action.[24]

These two linkages across the system represent what is in the most immediate sense the "dynamic" aspect of the process. This process starts with tension, which is released into overt action, producing consequences, which in turn are the points of reference

[24] This conception of the phase process will be further elaborated in Chapter V below.

for the states of tension which in turn motivate the next series of performances. But this paradigm fails to formulate two other essential features of system-process, namely the relation of that process to the "intrinsic" features of the situation in which it takes place, and its relation to the state of integration or lack of it of the relevant system of action itself.

The former of these two additional points of reference may be formulated in terms of the relation between specific motivational interests and those features of situational objects which are intrinsically appropriate for or threatening to their gratification, namely in terms of the pattern-variable components of specificity and universalism. This connection may be interpreted to mean that the generalization of cathectic interests, that is their building up into attitudinal *systems* must be "oriented" to the *intrinsic* characteristics of the available object world. This, we may surmise, is the fundamental conception involved in the "reinforcement" theories of learning, namely that a *patterning* of orientation to objects which is not "rewarded", that is one which does not establish a gratifying relation to objects, must introduce a strain into the system of action. But this, in a different perspective, is *the same thing* as the symbolic organization of the cognition of objects in terms of those of their intrinsic features or properties which are independent of any particular relation to ego, above all of his "wishes". This aspect of the organization of action as a system concerns above all the relevance of the *givens* of the situation to its shaping. In a sense it is the obverse of the qualities which are the consequences of past performances. It is the qualities of a situation, *however produced,* which must affect or "condition" the *motivational consequences* of an act, and hence also affect the state of tension which is the motivational starting point of subsequent action. This is another way of saying that the success or lack of it of adaptation to situational exigencies of a system of action, is interdependent with the states of tension which motivate future performance.

Finally, the system of action itself may have greater or lesser degrees of integration which change as a function of all three of these other aspects of action process, tension build-up and reduction, adaptation, and actual instrumental performance. In a system of social interaction the focus of the integration problem is the solidarity of the members of the group with each other, which may be increased or decreased. The opposite of solidarity is antagonism or aggression displayed toward alter, where the relation to the task process calls for mutual support rather than mutual interference.

The concept of diffuseness formulates the organization of an actor's motivational or cathectic system relative to a particular object as a concrete entity, whether it be alter as a person or the collectivity of which both are members. In either case on the side of the structure of the object system it is the inclusion of alter or the collectivity in ego's particularistic relational system, and the adjustment of his motivation to the solidarity of that system, which constitutes the integration of the action system *both* in terms of his own motivations as such, and in terms of the relations of the relevant objects to him and to each other.[25]

It should now be evident that the four combinations of cross-system pattern-variable components which we have just reviewed are identical with the four system-problems of Bales' analysis which lay at the basis of his classification of categories of action. This convergence is not only found to hold on the basis of the foregoing abstract analysis, but it also serves to unify both the category system of Bales and the categories of the motivational paradigm of Parsons, both internally in each case, and in their relation to each other. This suggests that they formulate something of fundamental significance to the theory of action. Our next question is, what are these four system-categories?

III

The suggestion was first made by Bush[26] that what we have here are *the dimensions of a four-dimensional* space in the mathematical sense of that term. We would like to assume from here on that this interpretation is correct and attempt to develop the implications of this assumption for the nature of the variables involved and of the theoretical system in which they belong.

We will further assume that the space thus defined is "Euclidean" in the sense that, though it has four rather than three dimensions, it is "rectilinear," that there is continuous linear variation along each of the dimensions, and that time enters into the analysis of process in essentially the same way that it does in classical mechanics. Rather than attempting to justify these assumptions on general grounds, let us try them out to see whether they "work" in the sense that, when applied to the content of the theory of social in-

[25] It will be evident to the reader that the considerations just reviewed essentially recapitulate the Appendix to Chapter II above.

[26] Dr. Robert R. Bush in personal discussion with the authors.

teraction, they serve to organize and generalize our knowledge in this field.

On these assumptions one fundamental aspect of process in a system of action must be "movement" of units or "particles" in the space, that is change of location as defined and described in terms of the four coordinates of the space. In order to describe such a process determinately we must be in a position to locate the unit in the space relative to a point of origin, and thus to other units in a system, and to describe the change of location which has occurred in the course of such a process. We must, that is, be able to describe the location at an initial time t1 and a difference of location at a subsequent time, t2. Each location must be described in terms of *four logically independent statements of fact,* one for each of the four coordinates of the space, hence change of location must be definable as change relative to each of the four coordinates. Concretely, of course, it is entirely admissible that in a particular case of change there should be no change relative to one, two or even three of the coordinates. This would be described geometrically by saying that the movement was parallel to one or more of the coordinates. In mathematical terms this possibility is one test of the "orthogonal" character of a space.

For each dimension we will describe change of location in each of two sets of terms. On the one hand, looking at the process in the perspective of a "phenomenological" description of the motivational system of the actor, we will describe it as in some way involving a change in the gratification-deprivation balance of the actor. It involves, that is, an increment or decrement of gratification or satisfaction in the relevant sense. On the other hand the *same* process will also be described from the "behavioral" point of view, as a change in the organization of the *relations* between actor and situational object-system. Bales' "system-problem" terms do not discriminate between these two perspectives. The pattern variable terms of Parsons, on the other hand, are paired precisely with respect to this axis, one item from each pair describes the phenomenological aspect of the process, the other the behavioral aspect.

In order to clarify the meaning of this procedure we must both define the term "unit" and characterize what we mean by it in its relations to action systems. We may first distinguish three meanings of the term as follows: (1) A unit of measurement such as an inch or a degree of temperature by the Centigrade Scale. (2) A unit of *concretely observable* process or change relative to a system, which may or may not be measurable in terms of a single unit of measurement as stated under (1). Thus a change of position of a body of one inch in a given direction or a rise of temperature of a liquid of one degree centigrade may be an observable unit of process; (3) The particle or *unit part* of a system. In this case the processes observed under (2) are interpreted to be "manifestations" of processes in the system involving one or more units in the third sense. Thus the length of a streak on a photographic plate may be interpreted to measure the path of a planet relative to the rotation of the earth —the streak of light *is not* the planet but is interpreted as an observable manifestation of the change of location of the planet.

In the present discussion we are not concerned with the first meaning of the term unit, but with the third, and with the relation between it and the second. We may assume that what we actually observe in connection with action systems is "overt acts" or "performances". We divide the objects of these observations into units— these may be the behavioral unit acts of Bales' observation procedure or a system of such unit acts of any degree of complexity. In this connection it is essential to note that what is observed is not only the "performance event" itself but the actor whose performance it is and the "target" actor, individual or collective, to whom the act is directed. In addition the observation procedure places this event in a context—it is placed in a sequence of such acts so that it is related to antecedent events in the system and, through the concept of "expectations" to an estimate of probabilities of future events.

This unit may be referred to as the *minimum behavioral role*. This is the unit of observation in the interaction process but it is *not* the unit or particle of the *system* of action in the theoretical sense, and pari passu these observed events are not the locations or movements of the system unit in action-space but are *manifestations* of these locations or movements. We must *infer* from these manifestations what changes have occurred in the *intervening variables* of the action system. The unit which is the particle of the system then is a "hypothetical" entity,[27] not to be confused with the units of observation. It is *this* to which location and change of location in action space must be attributed, as well as the other properties to which we will refer later, namely rate of change of location, change in rate of change, and "motivational force", or *relative importance in the system*. This we will call the *system unit* as distinguished from the behavioral unit.

[27] It is at least close to the concept of unit act developed in Parsons' Structure of Social Action, esp. Chap. II.

Where the system under consideration is a system of social interaction the system unit is *always a role*,[28] whereas if it is a personality system, it is a *need-disposition*. A single action-movement which is conceived as part of a system of social interaction, is a minimum role in this system-sense rather than the behavioral sense. Correspondingly a single overt act, considered in its context in a personality as a system may be considered to be the behavioral unit which is a manifestation of a movement of one or more need-disposition units of the personality system. Finally, it should be entirely clear that *both* of these system-units involve the integration of "drive" organic energy with *cultural patterning*. The significance of this will be further discussed below.

Some of the methodological problems involved in this way of looking at action process will be further discussed later. Under these assumptions, however, we may now attempt to formulate as precisely as possible what change of location of a system unit with respect to each of the four dimensions means, as follows: The terms designating the first two dimensions have been changed slightly, and we hope improved, in Chapter V below.

1. *The Instrumental goal-achievement dimension,* G, characterizing the degree of involvement of motivation as affectively in process of overt performance.

   Location B of the system unit, a subsequent location, differs from location A, an antecedent one, in that, phenomenologically stated, there has occurred or "been produced" for the actor in question an increment or decrement of gratification relative to the consummation of a given particular goal-orientation, that is, the system unit is, according to the relevant indices, taken to be closer to, or farther away from a location defined as the state of consummatory gratification relative to the goal of a particular need-disposition. This is the case for an individual actor; for a collective actor the corresponding goal-state is an optimal *organization* of the gratification levels of the need-dispositions of the component individual actors. Stated in behavioral terms, B differs from A in that it is closer to or farther away from a location defined as "goal-attainment". The relation of ego to his situation or if a collectivity is the actor, of that collectivity in its relevant collective-role, has changed in the direction of the goal-state relation or away from it.

[28] For elucidation of both these concepts see *Toward a General Theory of Action*, Part I, Chapter I, the *General Statement*, and Part II.

2. *The Expressive dimension,* E, characterizing the component of neutrality-quality orientation, i.e. the degree of tension of motivation as neutralized by inhibition.

Location B of the system unit differs from location A phenomenologically in that "tension" has either been reduced or "built up". By this is meant that a system of motivational impulses, which by the neutrality of the orientation to objects of potential consummatory gratification other than the specific goal-state referred to under 1. above, is inhibited from discharge in performance, is increased or decreased in "strength", that is in "pressure to discharge in action". Stated in behavioral terms this has been an increment or decrement of "accomplishment". This means that "qualities" have become established in the relation of the actor to the object world which are *consequences* of the performance process, but which, having become established, are no longer aspects of performance itself, but have become independent of performance. This implies a close connection between the consequences of prior process and subsequent tension states.

3. *The Adaptive dimension,* A, characterizing the degree of cognitive learning of interest—specific relevance of properties of situational objects.

Location B differs from location A in that there has been produced an increment of reward-gratification or deprivation with reference to a specific motivational interest or type of them. The implication is that this increment is independent of goal-consummation gratification and should not be confused with it.[29] Behaviorally stated the change is one in the *organization* of the actor's (individual or collective) *relation* to the situation. He has "learned" by experience and become better adapted to the situation. This is saying that learned adaptation and secondary reward *are the same thing* seen from different points of view.

4. *The Integrative dimension,* I, characterizing the level of diffuse-particularistic integration of the system unit act in the system.

Location B differs from A in that there has been produced an increment or decrement of the "optimization of gratification"[30] for the system (if a personality) or of "adjustment" of the units

---

[29] It seems probable that it is legitimate to consider this increment as equivalent to secondary reinforcement, while that of goal-attainment is equivalent to primary reinforcement.

[30] *Values, Motives and Systems of Action,* Chap. II, p. 121.

in the system, if a social system. In either case it is a matter of the total consequent balance of the action-*system* in which the particular unit is integrated. Behaviorally stated the meaning is that there has been an increment or decrement of *value achievement of the system as a system,* that is in that position the unit has made a *contribution* to this achievement. System-integration is thus here regarded as a *dimension* in the theory of action, not merely as a "phenomenon".

These four directions of the movement or change of location of action are, we believe, the dimensions of a space. To complete the description and analysis of events in such a framework, we must specify certain additional facts about the units conceived as located and moving in such a space, and about the systems which are composed of a plurality of such units which together constitute a system.

The first, and a particularly strategic question is what is meant by the rate of change of location of such a unit in the space; closely related is that of what is meant by a change in the rate of change of such location. With respect to both of these we assume that the foregoing has adequately defined what is meant by the "direction" of a process. The direction of a change is understood to be the "resultant" of the motions with reference to the four co-ordinates of the space.

There are two levels on which we can attack the first problem, an "absolute" and a "relative" level. We may suggest that the problem as to what the rate of change may be in any absolute sense is a "pseudo-problem". This assertion implies that any system, as we have several times suggested, tends to have an established level or trend of process, that this process tends to go on unchanged unless interfered with. In action terms we have said that such a process tends to have its established levels of "performance."

If this tendency to constancy or "inertia" be assumed, then the problem may be stated in a relativistic way. The important problem is thus that of locating the points of reference relative to which variations in this rate of process are to be measured. This in turn seems to be inseparable from the question of the definition of the points of origin relative to which location in action space can be determined.

In three-dimensional Euclidean space, the choice of a point of origin is in principle completely arbitrary, and correspondingly the point of reference for the measurement of velocity and of change in velocity is also arbitrary. It seems at least doubtful whether this is true of the space of action as we have defined it, and of the conception of rate of process in such a system.

The problem seems to be connected with the fact that in some sense there are "boundaries" to the space of the theory of action, to which there are no close analogies in the space of classical mechanics. Three of these boundary-features should be called to attention. The first of these is involved in the conception of the goal-attainment of a system unit-act. The dimension of closeness or its reverse to attainment of such a goal seems to imply that that there is a state, with reference to the posited particular goal, of having attained it, which is contradictory to the conception of indefinite extension of the process in this direction. If the goal in question is to be relativized, there must be some sort of change in the point of reference. This of course in no sense excludes the possibility of a "nesting" relationship between goals, a problem which certainly needs special investigation.

The second "boundary-condition" concerns the dimension of tension. Whatever may be true of the upper limits of tension there is surely a conception of tension declining to a zero point. Conversely it also seems that the conception of negative tension does not make sense. In the light of the above discussion we can perhaps say that these two boundaries complement each other. They seem to mean that in some sense a system of action is not a "self-subsistent" system. There is an "input" of energy or "force" into the system which we may presume comes from the organism in a biological sense. This appears in the system as the state of "tension" relative to both the system and the unit act. Tension in this sense, however, runs on a declining gradient in the direction of goal-attainment. If there were only one goal in the system of action, goal attainment and the zero point of tension would be identical. But a system of action is a system composed of many such units, i.e. roles or need-dispositions, each with its goal. The tension state of any particular unit therefore expresses some kind of an "economic" or allocative balance as between the energy which is allowed to be involved in performance relative to the particular goal of the particular unit act, and other goals or "interests" of the system. It would seem that it is fundamentally for this reason that tension reduction and build-up must be treated as independently variable relative to goal-attainment.

The third boundary-feature of the system is concerned with the integrative dimension. This dimension evidently derives its importance from the fact that in the theory of action we are dealing with what has been called boundary-maintaining systems whereas the systems of classical mechanics are not boundary-maintaining systems. A system in mechanics cannot—given the laws of the conservation of matter and of energy—"cease to exist", it can only "change". But a boundary-maintaining system may cease to exist in that it becomes assimilated to its environment, that is the distinction between the phenomena within the boundary and those outside, disappears. Disintegration of a boundary-maintaining system is precisely this *disappearance of the difference* between "internal" states and the environment. This is what is meant by death in the biological sense.

The differential of internal and external states can be maintained only by a continual process of interchange across the boundary. This interchange includes the "consumption" by the action system of energy-input from extra-system sources, that is from the organism. It also includes the adaptive processes whereby the "functional needs" of the action system are met by the "utilization" of the resources of the situation, by the "facilities" available in the situation. The adaptive process, or "learning" as referred to above, may be conceived essentially as the process by which facilities come to be utilizable, and utilized in action. When matters are seen in this light, there is obviously a fundamental relationship between the integrative aspects of such a boundary-maintaining system and the adaptive aspects. Movement along these two dimensions must in the nature of the case be related but equally cannot be identical. Increase in integration of the system without reference to adaptive considerations is presumably impossible except within very narrow limits; it would be like an organism continuing to utilize energy without any food-intake. Adaptation, on the other hand, without the integrative processes would constitute simply the dissolution of the system, its assimilation to the environment.

The question of boundary-process may be clarified somewhat further. We must evidently assume *two* fundamental sources of influence on a system of action from outside. The first of these is the energy-flow into the system from the organism or organisms involved. This factor is not conceptualized in any of the four dimensions of process within the system itself, which amounts to saying it can affect only the *rate*, not the direction of these processes; it is not, we may say, a factor of "orientation".

The second fundamental source of influence from outside the system is through the *adaptive* processes which are conceptualized in connection with the movement of units, and of the system, along the third dimension discussed above. Here occurs the *cognitive* "input" across the boundary into the system, i.e. the input of "information". This input again must be classified in terms of two fundamentally different sources, though not channels. The first of these concerns the actor's own "perception" of non-social and non-symbolic objects.

An action system interacting only with a non-action environment is limited to perception-cognition in this sense as its source of "information". Correspondingly the instrumental dimension for-mulates the boundary-process of such a system in the opposite di-rection, namely that of what the system "produces", its "output" which, in terms of the system itself, is its own value-accomplish-ment, as distinguished from the adaptive relation to the environ-ment; this is *control* as distinguished from adaptation.

If, however, a system of action be conceived as interacting with other systems of action, there are further and to us fundamental complications of the boundary interchange processes. We may for-mulate one by saying that in this case input through adaptive proc-esses involves information received through "communication", that is information from other systems of action through *symbolic* media; certain of the objects of the situation, then are interpreted as symbols which have intended meanings given them by some actor. Conversely, of course, a fundamental part of the output of the system will consist in communications to other action systems, to personalities, collectivities or subsystems of them.

Both the input and the output of communication may have es-sentially the same significance to the system as does the perception of situational objects in a purely adaptive way, and as also does the control of them in the interest of instrumental goals. But in any given instance this need not be the case and for the interrela-tions of total systems of action it *cannot* be the case. This is es-sentially because, as we have pointed out, a performance in the processes of interaction *necessarily* acquires meaning as an expres-sive symbol. There is, therefore, not merely communication of "in-formation" in the purely cognitive sense, but of the intentions of the actor, that is of his attitudes. The stabilization of the mutuality of attitudes is, however, subject to the condition which, in social systems, we call "solidarity". This is essentially what we mean by the *integration* of a system of action, the organization of the cathexes of the sub-systems to constitute themselves into a system, so that there is no longer merely expressive communication *between* systems, but what were formerly discrete systems of action have now to a degree become one system, which has established boundaries vis-a-vis what is outside, what is to it the external situation. Within any such system then there are adaptive processes and instrumental performance processes of the role or need-disposition units vis-a-vis each other and vis-a-vis the system of which they are parts. But there is also expressive communication, and variation of integration as a function of the expressive factor.

It is in the light of all these considerations that the problem of what is meant by the rate of an action process must be approached. A constant rate will concern the utilization in the action system of the energy-input from the organism or organisms involved. This will be "converted" from "neutral" potentiality into affectivity-performance, to goal-attainment, finally to consequences. A constant rate will constitute a stabilized flow of such energy through the system producing a stabilized performance rate for the units in question and for the system as a system. We do not yet have technical measures of this flow, but the above considerations give us a definition of what is meant which is of sufficient precision so that the problem of devising measures should not present any insuperable difficulty.

The second question, that of what is *change* in the rate of action process has in essentials already been answered. What we have termed "activity" is, namely, to be understood as the acceleration of this rate relative to a given stabilized flow of the process, while "passivity" is the deceleration, the slowing down of the process, relative to stabilized expectations.

There is a final problem concerning the units of action systems and their relations to each other which must receive at least a tentative answer at this point. This is the question of what is meant by the "motivational force" or the potential of a system unit. We may take our departure from the consideration noted above that it is necessary to distinguish the dimension of goal-attainment from that of tension reduction, because the motivational energy of the system must be allocated between a plurality of units. It is a condition of order, that is of equilibrium, in a system of action that this allocation should be determinate, but it need not be equal. Essentially what this is, is the relative *importance* of the various units of the system in terms of their influence on processes in the system. In social system terms this seems to come close to what we mean by the *power* of an actor in a role, whether it be an individual or a collective actor. In personality terms there is need for a corresponding conception of the relative action-potential of the different need-dispositions in the system. Prestige, in the social system, on the other hand, is not this potential, but is one aspect of the set of consequences of past processes in the system by which the units have each become differentially adapted to their situations and thus fitted into the integration of the system. This is the ordering of the reward system in differential terms which must, in the nature of the case be relatively well integrated with the power system, but is not the same thing.

From essentially the same considerations we derive a tentative solution to the problem of the point of origin for analysis of processes in action-space. We may say tentatively that because of the boundary features of the space, which we have just reviewed, the point of origin cannot be arbitrary. The essential feature of these boundaries is that there must be distribution of energy within a system, and this system must be organized relative to that distribution and the components which are involved in it. Both the tension or expressive dimension and the integrative dimension formulate this reference, for each particular process, to features of the system as a whole. Hence the point of origin must be relative to the *particular system* which is being analyzed. We suggest tentatively that there can be *only one* point of origin for a given system. Changing the point of origin then would mean shifting to another system point of reference. We further suggest that this fact is of fundamental significance to the theory of action and its history. Keeping system points of reference, that is points of origin, straight has proved one of the most prolific sources of difficulty in the field. Because they have very often *not* been kept straight different treatments of the same problem, and of different problems have tended to be incommensurable. This has certainly played a major part in the conspicuous failure of social science to progress cumulatively.

If the point of origin must be relative to the particular system being analyzed, this has an important implication. For in the definitions both of the units of the system and of the system itself we have specifically included a set of patterns of culture which are internalized and institutionalized. It follows that the most elementary analysis of equilibrating processes in systems of action must assume constancy of these culture patterns. The problems of change in culture itself which of course are of overwhelming empirical significance, must involve additional considerations which we have not attempted to enter into here.

There is a further important problem about the point of origin.

This concerns its relation to the position of the observer. It is essential to the theory of action on its symbolic levels[31] that the observer must *communicate* through symbolic channels, directly or indirectly with his subjects of observation. The point of origin for an observer's analysis of a system of action process, then must be such as to *include himself in the system being analyzed*. This means, in social system terms, that the *role* of the observer must be explicitly analyzed and treated as part of the system.

This view confirms a previously common opinion that the interdependence of the material being observed with the observer was an essential feature of the sciences of action in a way which is not true for the physical sciences, at least in the case of classical mechanics. We cannot, however, agree with some, such as Wiener,[32] that this is a fundamental barrier to progress in our field. We feel that the theory of the social system possesses the resources, through its analysis of roles, to deal adequately with the problems. This consideration does, however, clearly explain some of the difficulties which have developed in the field of personality psychology through failure to take account of the role of the observer. This is indeed one of the most dramatic demonstrations of the fact that the theory of action is a *single* conceptual scheme, and that the study of personality is, beyond certain limits, severely handicapped without explicit use of the theory of social systems, even where the interaction of the personality in question with others is not being studied in any other respect than that implied by the fact that he is being observed.

The considerations which have just been reviewed may be summarized from one point of view by saying that the theoretical system with which we are here concerned is characterized by a fundamental asymmetry. It is a dramatic confirmation on a theoretical level of the soundness of our deductions, that the asymmetry in question turns out to be precisely an aspect of the "symmetrical asymmetry" of the pattern variable scheme which was first worked out in *Values, Motives and Systems of Action* and further developed and utilized in the *Social System*.

The essential starting point is the fact that at each "end" of the action system, (the attitude-organization end and the object-organization end) as formulated in pattern variable terms, there is a fourfold table of the fundamental possibilities of combination of

[31] *Social System*, Chap. XII, *Interaction Process Analysis*, Chap. II.

[32] In public lectures at Harvard University and elsewhere.

the components. These have been stated as the major classifications of personal and of social values respectively, or as those of
attitudes and of status-categorizations. (See *Values, Motives and
Systems of Action,* figures 3 and 4.)

If, as the original classificatory tables of pattern-variable combinations assumed, "random" combinations were possible across
the system, there would be sixteen possible "dimensions" rather
than four. The limitation of such combinations to the four we have
considered, involving as it does the exclusion of three fourths of the
logical possibilities, clearly implies certain fundamental assumptions or postulates.

The first assumption underlying the exclusion of certain of these
logical possibilities derives from the fact that the pattern variable
components themselves have from the first been treated as paired, so
that each pair states a single dilemma of choice. Then, secondly,
with respect to the "sides" of the system, each pair comes to be
associated with a pair from the other side; there is no crossing *as
between* these complementary pairs. This means that affectivity-
neutrality is paired only with performance-quality and specificity-
diffuseness only with universalism-particularism. Each of these
pairings and the exclusion of the other possibility implies one postulate. These turn out to be precisely the postulates which we have
derived above from considerations of the boundedness of the action space.

The first of these postulates is that a system of action is considered to involve a *one-way process.* As we have put it, "energy"
is continually "fed into" the system and "expended". There is no
spontaneous reversal of this process from sources within the system
itself. Energy is converted into goal-attainment and consequences,
but the latter cannot be directly converted into energy. Another
way of putting this point is to say that of the sixteen "regions" of
the space which lie between coordinates above and below a point
of origin, a certain negative region is excluded by this postulate.
Decrements on the instrumental dimension and the expressive dimension must, that is, stop at the zero point. Where tension is zero
there is no action and there can be no motivation to performance.
There can only be *distribution* of tension in the system, not an absolute deficit in it. Furthermore when all goals are attained action
must stop.

The second postulate concerns the relation between movement
on the adaptive and the integrative dimensions. It also says that
a negative region of the space is excluded as the location of a

unit act. This again is essentially to say that integration *cannot be negative*. The reason for this is, on the above assumptions, nearly obvious. It is that at the zero point on the integrative dimension the system as a system ceases to exist, the boundaries of the system, that is, disappear and it is assimilated to the environment. In action terms the distinction between actor and situation disappears; the system is *only situation to some other actor or actors*.

The limitations on pattern variable combinations across the system thus constitute essentially ways of formulating the two crucial facts about the system which we have stressed above. The first is that it is a system which "consumes" energy or motivational force, a law of conservation of energy thus does not apply to an action system as such. The second is that it is a system which requires *organization* relative to a situation or environment, organization which inhibits completely "free" interchange between internal and external systems. If either the energy input ceases or the organization is completely disintegrated the system as a distinctive, boundary-maintaining system ceases to exist.

It should be clear that action systems must be considered to be boundary-maintaining systems not *only* vis-a-vis non-action systems, i.e. physico-chemical systems or biological systems, but also vis-a-vis *other* action systems. The death of an individual constitutes in this sense the termination of his personality as an empirical action system concomitantly with the dissolution of the organism as a boundary-maintaining biological system. This seems to be the only way in which a personality as a system of action can radically "die".

But a social system may cease to exist by the disappearance of its boundaries both vis-a-vis the member personalities and vis-a-vis other social systems. Every collectivity is a social system in this sense. The significance of the fifth pattern variable, that of self-vs collectivity-orientation, for the present context emerges here. It states the fundamental fact that a social system can be dissolved and still leave the boundary-maintaining properties of the constituent personalities and of other collectivities in which they are involved, intact. This pattern variable constitutes the conceptualization of the fundamental fact that there is a special level of integration *within* and not merely *of* systems of action, namely that the interacting individual actors not only constitute *a* social system, but a system of social systems, of collectivities each of which can arise and be dissolved as a consequence of processes within the interaction system. Personalities as we know them could not be developed without involvement in collectivities in the sense in which we are now speaking of them. But this does not mean that the survival of the personality as a boundary-maintaining system is bound to the survival of any single *particular* collectivity. This may, along with the one-way process and the need for organization on the more general level, be regarded as a third *fundamental* property of systems of interaction.

We have self-consciously focussed our discussion on the interaction of a plurality of individual actors. We have, however, from time to time noted that there was a more general case of action in abstraction from interaction in this sense. This is the level in general treated in "behavior psychology". However, we feel that the property of collectivity-integration which emerges with social interaction, fundamentally underlies the properties of human personalities as systems of action as well as of social systems. More specifically the role of symbolic processes as distinguished from the more elementary sign processes seems to be inherently bound up with interaction and the integration of the individual in collectivities. From this point of view personality psychology as distinguished from behavior psychology must in the nature of the case be *social* psychology. It cannot abstract from the involvement of the individual not only in social interaction, but in collectivities which have the property of solidarity. This is perhaps another way of saying that the human personality must have a "superego".

IV

If we have succeeded so far in defining a space, the units which must be located in that space, the nature of change of location in the space and finally of the systems of units which are conceived as moving interdependently with respect to location, direction and rate of change of location as systems, the question next arises as to whether we are in a position to state any general conditions governing the equilibrium of such systems. This is essentially what is meant by the statement of the "laws" of a system, namely certain fundamental generalizations about the nature of the equilibrating processes such that it is possible, by applying them, to deduce the nature and directions of the changes which will take place in a system following what we have called above a disturbance of its equilibrium assuming that the system does, indeed, regain its equilibrium.

We would like to suggest that certain such generalizations have already been implicit throughout our discussion and that it is necessary only to make them explicit.

The first of these is the statement that a process of action including interaction between a plurality of actors, will tend to proceed unchanged unless impeded or deflected, that is unless what we have defined as a disturbance is introduced into the system. This generalization was explicitly stated by Parsons[33] and made by him the fundamental point of reference for the treatment of motivational process in the social system. It is obviously closely similar to the law of inertia in classical mechanics. It is another way of stating one aspect of the fundamental postulate that we are dealing with equilibrating systems.

The second generalization or law has been clearly implicit in our treatment of the interaction process as such. It is that, once a disturbance has been introduced into an equilibrated system there will tend to be a reaction to this disturbance which tends to restore the system to equilibrium. Qualitatively we have assumed throughout that the reaction will tend to be opposite in direction to the original disturbance; this is the essential meaning of the whole polarity of the scheme for the analysis of interaction which we have presented here. One way of putting it is to say that deviance must be counteracted by mechanisms of social control. We may suggest hypothetically that not only is the reaction opposite in direction to the disturbance, but that it is in some sense quantitatively equal in motivational force. This would make the generalization directly parallel to the law of action and reaction in mechanics. It is difficult to see how equilibrium could be maintained without this quantitative equality. So far as we know this generalization has not been explicitly stated before for all systems of action, but Bales has recently explicitly made it a fundamental assumption in the attempt to construct a mathematical model for certain empirical characteristics of the interaction process.[34]

The third generalization concerns changes in rates of action process. That such changes are dependent on something which is often called "effort" is very close to common sense. The factor of effort was given a prominent place in Parsons' *Structure of Social Action,* and may now be identified with that of activity-

[33] *Social System,* Chapter VI.

[34] One version of this model is briefly outlined in Chapter IV below.

passivity as discussed in the present paper. This latter statement should be held to supersede the earlier one because it is couched explicitly in terms of the relation of the effort factor to the equilibrium of the action system. It is held that either an increase or a decrease of effort will, relative to the established rate of action process, constitute a disturbance of equilibrium, a possibility which has been directly built into the paradigm of interaction set forth in Fig. 3 above. What is so far lacking is a quantitative statement and here again we would like to state in hypothetical form that the change in the rate of action process is directly proportional to the *magnitude* of the motivational force added to or withdrawn from the unit in question. In its qualitative form it may be maintained that we know pretty well what the generalization means empirically. Implementation and testing of the quantitative statement must await the development of satisfactory measures of the rate of action process, and hence of changes in that rate. There is no reason, however, if we know just what we want to measure, to believe that this will prove an insuperable task. Again, the resemblance of this generalization to the law of acceleration of classical mechanics is obvious.

Finally, there has also been implicit in our discussion a generalization about the integrative aspects of systems of action, namely to the effect that there must be a minimum of structural compatibility of the patterns of organization of the different parts of the system. We may put this in dynamic terms by saying that the survival of a pattern element within a system of action will be a function in part of its *contribution* to the integration of the system. This in turn will mean that once such a pattern of organization has appeared it will tend to be maintained in the system, or eliminated from it, as a function of this contribution, of its compatibility with others to form an integrated system. This may be called the law of system-integration. Unfortunately we do not now see our way clear to give it a quantitative formulation at this time, but this should be possible in due course.

In its phenomenological aspect as applied to personality systems this generalization would appear to be the "law of effect" in the version formulated by Olds in Chapter II of *Values, Motives and Systems of Action*.[35] This says that the confirmation of a learned pattern in a personality system or its elimination (ex-

[35] pp. 123-4. In this collaborative monograph authorship of specific points was not distinguished, but it should be acknowledged here that this insight was contributed by Olds.

tinction) is a function of the fact that the system is a system i.e. a boundary-maintaining system or as we say here that it has to maintain a level of integration as a system. In the behavioral version this is what, especially for social systems, has continually been said about the "functional prerequisites" of systems having to be met if the system is to survive. Hence it is by no means new.

We would like to raise the question without being able to answer it here, as to whether there is not some important general significance in the fact that with a system using a four-dimensional space, we have found four fundamental generalizations which are essential to defining the conditions of equilibrium of a system described in terms of that space. The reason this seems probable is that classical mechanics had three fundamental laws of motion, and operated in terms of a three-dimensional space. Moreover, the first three of our generalizations are clearly analogous to the three Newtonian laws, while the fourth equally clearly has to do with the fourth dimension of action space, the one which has no analogy in the space of classical mechanics. Furthermore it also seems evident that the necessity for both the fourth dimension and the fourth law derives from the fact that we are here dealing with boundary-maintaining systems.

If all this, which frankly involves a speculative element at present, is correct, then it would seem likely that there is a very important analogy between the scheme we have developed in this paper and the classical mechanics. If this supposition stands up to critical testing of a variety of sorts, it is evident that it should turn out to have far reaching implications in that it should open up possibilities of quantitative as well as qualitative systematization which are far beyond those which the sciences of action have yet attained.

For convenience we present succinct statements of the four generalized conditions of equilibrium or laws just reviewed as follows:

1. *The Principle of Inertia*: A given process of action will continue unchanged in rate and direction unless impeded or deflected by opposing motivational forces.
2. *The Principle of Action and Reaction*: If, in a system of action, there is a change in the *direction* of a process, it will tend to be balanced by a *complementary change which is equal in motivational force and opposite in direction*.
3. *The Principle of Effort*: Any change in the rate of an action

process is directly proportional to the *magnitude* of the motivational force applied or withdrawn.

4. *The Principle of System-Integration*: Any *pattern* element (*mode of organization* of components) within a *system* of action will tend to be confirmed in its place within the system or to be eliminated from the system (extinguished) as a function of its contribution to the integrative balance of the system.

V

If the theoretical scheme we have here been expounding possesses the degree of generality and of logical integration which we feel it does, it will certainly in time be possible through its use to derive a whole series of hypotheses for the treatment of empirical problems. To attempt to do this in the present paper would lead too far afield. Symbolic process is, however, as we have seen, of such fundamental importance for the whole enterprise in which we have been engaged, that we feel we must attempt briefly to relate the general scheme to this field.

In the first place the treatment of action as change of location in a four-dimensional space gives us a new way of defining what we mean by various kinds of "symbolic acts", while in the second place we can derive hypotheses as to the conditions which will favor the acquisition of the different kinds of symbolic significance by a situational object. Let us take the definition of symbolic acts first.

Symbolization is the attribution in both cognitive and cathectic contexts of a "secondary" significance to a situational object, secondary that is, relative to what may be called a "principal" object of cathexis or to a goal.[36] Put in terms of overt action, that is of behavior, such a principal act is what we have called a "performance" it is change of location on the instrumental goal-attainment dimension. A symbolic act must also involve some movement on that dimension, it must be an observable performance. But the act will be symbolic in so far as the movement on this dimension is *small* relative to that on one or more of the others.

Moreover, our dimensional scheme gives us a basis for discriminating three different kinds of symbolic acts according to which of the other three dimensions besides the instrumental is

[36] Whether the principal object itself should not also be considered as symbolized is a question which will be taken up in Chapter V below.

the one of greatest movement. Thus we may say that such an act is primarily an "expressive symbol" if the principal movement is on the expressive or tension-reduction dimension, if, that is to say, while the increment of instrumental goal-attainment is small, that of expression or tension reduction is large.

Similarly, the act is primarily a "cognitive symbol" if the principal dimension of movement is not the expressive but that of adaptation. Then the act will be primarily significant for the increment of adaptation or cognitive "learning" which it has produced while again the increment of instrumental goal-attainment is small. Action oriented primarily along the adaptive dimension then may be called "investigative" action.

Finally, what has been called "evaluative symbolism"[37] may, so far as it consists of overt acts, that is of performances, be interpreted as the case where the principal dimension of movement is the integrative dimension, and as compared with a small increment of instrumental achievement, there is a large increment (or decrement) of system-integration. Readers familiar with Durkheim's work will see immediately that, on the social system level just such a relatively large increment of integration is what he held happened to a social system through certain types of religious ritual. On the personality level correspondingly we may think of this as the case for certain "rituals" which serve the function of reducing anxiety. Anxiety may probably be interpreted to be an index of the danger of system-disintegration.

It should furthermore be clear that if this is a proper approach to the subject, only in certain cases should symbolic action be regarded as a process of "substitute gratification". This would be true only in the cases where the system itself was imperfectly integrated in such a way that the "normal" movement along one or more of the dimensions was "blocked". Interpretation of these statements of course involves complex problems which will have to be reserved for later consideration.

The obverse of the above classification of types of symbolic acts is the analysis of the bases on which situational objects acquire symbolic significance. Such significance, we may say, is acquired through the process we have called the "generalization of cathexis". When a principal object, i.e. a goal object or one cathected but not directly treated as a goal object, has become emotionally important, other objects in the situation, means objects, or merely those otherwise associated with it, also become cathected

[37] *Social System,* Chapter IX.

in such a way that there is a "symbolic complex" built up around the "principal" object.

Put a little differently, an object cannot acquire this secondary cathexis without being associated with a significant experience of the actor, that is the cathexis of a principal object and increments or decrements of gratification in relation to it. Then the kind of symbolic significance it acquires, and the standards of its selection as a significant symbol, or rejection as such, will depend on the kind of "significant experience" with which the object has become associated.

If the significant experience is instrumental goal-attainment, that is if the greatest action-movement is on this dimension, then associated objects will be primarily cathected in terms of their instrumental means-significance, that is if they are not themselves intrinsically significant as means-objects, as cognitive-adaptive symbols. They are *signs* pointing to the instrumentally significant features of the situational world.

If, secondly, the primarily significant experience is on the dimension of change in the expressive tension-level, objects will tend to be cathected primarily as expressive symbols—remembering always that the concrete symbol is both expressive and cognitive at the same time. It is important to note that the movement may be either in the positive or the negative direction. Hence either cognitive or expressive symbols may serve as "warnings" of feared deprivations as well as in the role of "promises" of expected gratification. By the same generalization of cathexis, then, the symbolic object itself evokes the same feeling that the principal object does, though not necessarily with the same intensity. Hence an expressive symbol may be directly enjoyed, or it may be directly feared itself. This is most important; it is not *only* a question of the "referent" to which the symbol points.

Finally, if the primary context of significant experience is that of system-integration, that is in social system terms the experience of enhanced or diminished solidarity with others in the collectivity, or in personality terms, that of reduction or increase of conflict, then the secondarily cathected object will tend to be an "evaluative" symbol. Thus we may speak of an experience of "religious conversion" as one of a feeling of resolution of conflicts, and of the religious symbolism associated with the experience as evaluative symbolism for the convert.

The general formula for the establishment of symbolic significance for an object, then, is that the object should be experienced as part of the situation in which there has occurred a significant action-movement, with a large increment of gratification or deprivation in at least one direction. The primary *type* of symbolic significance acquired by the object then will depend on which of the dimensions has been that of greatest movement. Finally, the movement may be positive or negative in direction; hence the significance of symbols will be differentiated relative to this polarity. A symbol may be positively cathected and signify possibilities or hopes of gratification; it may on the other hand be negatively cathected and signify possibilities and fear of deprivation. What is sometimes called "basic anxiety" is from this point of view, we may surmise, a pattern of generalization of negative symbolism which is, above all, deeply involved with the integration of the personality as a system.

VI

This paper has already become so long that only a few things can be said in conclusion. Clearly the ultimate test of the importance of the synthesis of previously distinct theoretical elements which we have presented here, will be found in the extension of the codification of existing empirical knowledge, and the further development of generalized knowledge through research. Both authors expect to devote much attention to these questions but even present tentative suggestions in this direction cannot be presented here. We must confine ourselves rather to the statement of a few general considerations which we would like to the reader to keep in mind in evaluating this paper.

The first, and in certain respects the most important of these concerns the range of applicability of the fundamental conceptual scheme which emerges. We feel that the new level of theoretical generalization presented in this paper strongly confirms the view we have previously held that the theory of action is a conceptual scheme which is not tied to any particular "level" of the study of action process from the microscopic to the macroscopic.

We suggest that the scheme advanced here is in its fundamentals applicable all the way from the phenomena of "behavior psychology" on pre-symbolic animal and infantile levels, to the analysis of the largest scale social systems. The main key to this scope of applicability lies in the fact that it is possible to treat what, on one level is a system, on the next "higher" level as a point of reference, that is as a "particle" or system-unit in a larger system. Thus what we have called the need-disposition is, from the point of view of elementary behavior psychology, a complex system of motivational and cultural components; but from the point of view of the analysis of a more complex sub-system of a personality, or of the whole personality as a system, it may be treated as a particle, as a system-unit in the above sense. That a need-disposition is *itself* a boundary-maintaining system is an essential condition of this treatment. Similarly, the minimal role unit of a system of social interaction may from one point of view be regarded as a complex system, composed of the requisite need-disposition components of the personalities of either ego or alter, and of certain situational components. But from the point of view of the analysis of a system of interaction it also becomes a system unit which can be treated as a unit in its involvement in the rest of the system. Again, the same can be true of more and more complex role-constellations. Finally a collectivity may itself be treated as an actor. This is essentially to say that, though obviously from another point of view it is a complex system, as a unit in an interaction process, a collectivity may also be treated as a system unit which may be located in action space and analyzed in interdependence with other units in the same system.

This is perhaps the most fundamental feature of the generality of the conceptual scheme we have presented. This generality has been evident in certain respects for a long time, and has been documented in our previous publications, but we are now able to state it, and its methodological basis, with much greater precision than before.

Such generality of application from the microscopic to the macroscopic levels must not be interpreted empirically without due allowance for phenomena which are emergent at different levels of organization of systems of action. We have repeatedly noted that perhaps the most fundamental of these is the development of true symbolization and thus of the possibility of culture. Closely related to this is the fundamental difference of system reference when the system is a personality or sub-system of it, from that involved when it is a society or sub-system of it. All such considerations must be kept clearly in mind in the use of the scheme. It is particularly important to realize that, as we have pointed out, this is not a scheme directly for the analysis of culture change, though it will surely be found that it is an essential part of the scheme necessary for such analysis. The phenomena of culture, its development and change, certainly involve factors not directly formulated in the present scheme. We have concentrated our attention on the processes of equilibration in carefully defined, indeed in a strict sense in hypothetical, systems of action.

In concentrating our attention in this way we have been very careful not to imply that there is any inherent presumption that empirical systems must remain in equilibrium, or return to any given state when the equilibrium has been disturbed. We merely use the concept of the equilibrating system as a theoretical model. Quite clearly the process of cultural change is, on certain levels at least, an example where a given initial equilibrium has broken down and been replaced by a new state of the system. The analysis of such processes requires further steps beyond those presented here. But we feel that they will be most successfully analyzed by extension of the scheme we have developed, rather than by replacing it with a totally different kind of scheme. However, we wish to make clear that we have carried our analysis only up to a certain point, and that before certain kinds of use of the scheme can become possible, it must be carried farther.

Pending this, however, we may note two extremely important fields of urgent work in other directions. We have long felt that the principal barriers to the cumulative development of the sciences of action did not lie *primarily* either in the difficulty of finding out the necessary facts, or in any inherent methodological limitations on the scientific study of human behavior, but rather in defining variables of sufficiently generalized significance which it was most important to measure, and then devising techniques of measuring precisely *these* variables. We feel that the most important direct contribution of the present paper lies in the progress it documents toward this goal. We have presented a scheme in which it seems to be implied that for a given system process in the action field a relatively *small* number of measures should be needed in order to achieve a highly generalized analysis from which definite deductions could be drawn. We must, that is, define a system, and define the number and character of the units in that system. We must be able to locate each unit in the space of action relative to a point of origin and thus to other units, and measure changes in that location for each unit over time. We should, finally, be able to measure rates of action process and changes in those rates.

We have pointed out that the behavioral units, which have to be the units of empirical observation, in all probability cannot be the system units. This is essentially to say that it is unlikely that the theory of action will be able to do without the use of intervening variables. But much progress has already been made in developing measures of certain behavioral units and in relating them to the concept of the theoretical system relative to which they are interpreted to have significance.

We feel that the scheme put forward here is sufficiently integrated to justify intensive effort on various levels to develop these measures of behavioral units which in the present terms can be shown to have specific theoretical significance.

The second main direction of effort which we suggest can produce very fruitful results, is work on the logical interconnections of the variables of such a system. We feel again, that our theoretical work has now progressed to a point where much more fruitful results can be expected from this type of work than in the past, in particular the path of the construction of mathematical models for various parts of the theoretical scheme seems promising.

Neither of these tasks should be conceived as important to the exclusion of codification of existing knowledge, or of extension of the theoretical scheme into the realms of analysis of change in the fundamental character of systems, that is especially change involving alteration in the cultural components. But we do feel that effort addressed to the measurement and mathematical tasks is likely to yield important scientific advances in the relatively short run.

CHAPTER 4

THE EQUILIBRIUM PROBLEM
IN SMALL GROUPS[1]

BY ROBERT F. BALES

THE PURPOSE OF THIS PAPER IS TO PRESENT CERTAIN EMPIRICAL FIND-
ings from the program of observation of small groups at the
Harvard Laboratory of Social Relations and to discuss their relevance to the theory of equilibrium developed elsewhere in this
collection of working papers.

Method

Some of these findings have been published previously, and
the reader is referred to these earlier articles for details omitted
here.[2] It will also be assumed that the reader is familiar with the
method of observation, recording, and analysis used in the direct
study of the interaction process as it takes place in our small

[1] The research reported in this paper was facilitated by the Laboratory of
Social Relations, Harvard University. The funds for the observation project
now in progress are provided by the RAND Corporation, Santa Monica, Cali-
fornia. I am indebted to Philip E. Slater, Research Assistant in the Laboratory
of Social Relations, especially for work on the latter parts of this paper on
problems of role specialization, and more generally for the many stimulating
discussions we have had on the research as a whole. Similarly, I owe much to
Christoph Heinicke, Social Science Research Council Fellow, for initial insights on the nature of the status struggle as it appears through the series of
meetings of our groups. This phenomenon will be described in later papers.

[2] Bales, Robert F., "A Set of Categories for the Analysis of Small Group
Interaction", *American Sociological Review*, Vol. XV, No. 2, April, 1950, pp.
257-263.

Bales, Robert F., and Strodtbeck, Fred L., "Phases in Group Problem
Solving", *Journal of Abnormal and Social Psychology*, Vol. 46, No. 4, October, 1951, pp. 485-495.

112   *Working Papers in the Theory of Action*

laboratory groups.[3] The observation categories are shown in Chart I. Certain aspects of their theoretical grounding in the general theory of action have been discussed earlier in this collection of papers.

Chart I
Set of Categories Used for Direct Observation of the Interaction Process

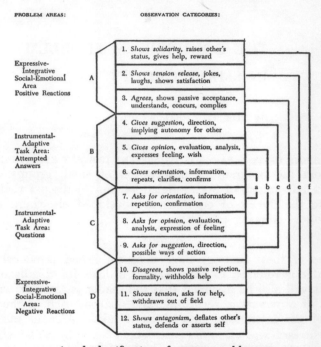

PROBLEM AREAS: OBSERVATION CATEGORIES:

A sub-classification of system problems to which each pair of categories is most relevant:

a. Problems of orientation
b. Problems of evaluation
c. Problems of control
d. Problems of decision
e. Problems of tension-management
f. Problems of integration

Bales, Robert F., Strodtbeck, Fred L., Mills, Theodore M., and Roseborough, Mary, "Channels of Communication in Small Groups", *American Sociological Review*, Vol. 16, No. 4 August 1951, pp. 461-468.

Bales, Robert F., "Some Statistical Problems of Small Group Research", *Journal of the American Statistical Association*, Vol 46, No. 255, September 1951, pp. 311-322.

[3] Bales, Robert F., *Interaction Process Analysis, A Method for the Study of Small Groups*, Cambridge, Massachusetts, Addison-Wesley Press, 1950.

Conditions of Observation

A number of different types of groups have been observed, in natural as well as laboratory settings, and some of the generalizations to be discussed were obtained before the present observational series was begun. For purposes of exposition, however, it will be simpler to confine the description of the conditions under which the generalizations hold best to the series of groups now under observation since these groups were specifically set up to epitomize the appropriate conditions.

Groups of sizes two through ten are under observation in the present series. Data for sizes three through six have been gathered. The groups are experimental discussion groups, each group meeting for four meetings. The subjects are all males, Harvard undergraduates, who are obtained through the Harvard employment service and typically do not know each other prior to the first meeting. In each of its four meetings, the group examines and discusses a "human relations case". A different case is used for each of the four meetings. Each case is a summary of facts, five pages in length, about a person in an administrative setting who is having some kind of difficulty with the men under him, and has some superior putting pressure on him to get some technically important job done. The summaries for a given case discussion are distributed separately to the subjects. After each member has read his summary the actual typed copy of the case is collected from each by the experimenter. The manner of presentation is such that the subjects are made specifically uncertain as to whether or not they possess exactly the same facts, but are assured that each does possess an accurate, though perhaps incomplete, factual summary.

The subjects are asked to consider themselves as members of the administrative staff of the central person in the case. He has asked them to meet and consider the case. He wishes an answer to two questions: (1) why are the persons in the case behaving as they do, and (2) what should he do about it. The members of the discussion group are asked to come to their decision in forty minutes. No leader is appointed. The host experimenter leaves the room. The discussion is observed through a one-way mirror and sound recorded. The interaction is observed and recorded in the categories shown on Chart I. After the meeting the members fill out a questionnaire asking certain questions about their reactions, their satisfaction, their relations to each other, and their opinions about their discussion group.

This particular concrete task has certain abstract characteristics which are important in eliciting a range of diversified behavior. The problems of *orientation, evaluation,* and *control* are each to a major degree unsolved at the beginning of observation. More specifically:

(a) With regard to *orientation,* members of the group have some degree of ignorance and uncertainty about the relevant facts, but individually possess facts relevant to decision. Their problem of arriving at a common cognitive orientation or definition of the situation must be solved, if at all, through interaction.

(b) With regard to problems of *evaluation,* the members of the group ordinarily possess somewhat different values or interests and the task is such that it involves several different values and interests as criteria by which the facts of the situation and the proposed course of action are to be judged. The problem of arriving at common value judgments necessary to a concrete plan must be solved, again, if at all, through interaction.

(c) With regard to problems of *control,* (that is, attempts of the members to influence directly the action of each other and arrive at a concrete plan) the acceptance of the task sets up in most instances a moderately strong pressure for group decision, with the expectation that the excellence of the decision can and will be evaluated by each of them as well as by the experimenter, so that the decision will affect their status. There are a number of possible alternative decisions or solutions, with uncertain degrees of potential frustration or satisfaction associated with various choices.

These abstract conditions, with emphasis varying according to circumstances, are met in very much this form and emphasis in a great many group conferences, work groups, committees, and the like. When group problems or tasks lack or greatly minimize any of the three abstract characteristics described above (a, b, c,) we speak of them as being "truncated". When these three characteristics are all present and marked, we speak of the problem as "full-fledged". We have felt that full-fledged problems give us a better opportunity to explore the range and interconnections of various sorts of social behavior, and so have begun to develop empirical norms and a body of theory around this particular set of conditions as a standard diagnostic task. Once this baseline has been established, other sets of conditions expected to have different results can be described as modifications or accentuations or reversals of the laboratory conditions. The more we learn about the typical effects of the particular diagnostic *task* we employ, the more we are able to use discrepancies from our typical baseline patterns of observed interaction as diagnostic indicators of the *personalities, culture,* and *role organization* of the participants, since these are all sets of conditions which influence the way interaction actually goes.

Under each mode of analysis discussed below some of the main uniformities of behavior we have found will be compactly stated. Space does not permit the presentation of the evidence in detail. In general, the patterns described and illustrated can be understood to refer to approximate or average uniformities in aggregates of large numbers of group meetings under randomly varying external conditions, and in addition, they can be understood to hold more uniformly and in particular under the full-fledged conditions of the standard diagnostic task described above.

The Profile of Activity and the Equilibrium Problem

One of the interesting characteristics of interaction is the distribution of total number of acts among the twelve categories, according to quality. A distribution of this kind in percentage rates based on the total is called a profile. An illustrative comparison of group profiles of two five-man groups working on the standard diagnostic task is shown in Table I.

TABLE I—*Profile of a "Satisfied" and a "Dissatisfied" Group on Case Discussion Task*

	Meeting profiles in percentage rates			
TYPE OF ACT:	Satis-fied*	Dissatis-fied**	Ave. of the two	Ave. rates by Sections
1. Shows Solidarity	.7	.8	.7	
2. Shows Tension Release	7.9	6.8	7.3	25.0
3. Agrees	24.9	9.6	17.0	
4. Gives Suggestion	8.2	3.6	5.9	
5. Gives Opinion	26.7	30.5	28.7	56.7
6. Gives Orientation	22.4	21.9	22.1	
7. Asks for Orientation	1.7	5.7	3.8	
8. Asks for Opinion	1.7	2.2	2.0	6.9
9. Asks for Suggestion	.5	1.6	1.1	
10. Disagrees	4.0	12.4	8.3	
11. Shows Tension	1.0	2.6	1.8	11.4
12. Shows Antagonism	.3	2.2	1.3	
PERCENTAGE TOTAL	100.0	100.0	100.0	100.0
RAW SCORE TOTAL	719	767	1486	

* The highest of sixteen groups. The members rated their own satisfaction with their solution after the meeting at an average of 10.4 on a scale running from 0 to a highest possible rating of 12.

** The lowest of sixteen groups. Comparable satisfaction rating in this group was 2.6.

In the present illustration the "satisfied" group attained a higher rate of suggestions, more often followed by positive reactions and less often by negative reactions and questions than did the "dissatisfied" group.

The profiles produced by groups, however, are not completely and radically different from each other. The profile produced by the average of these two illustrative groups is more or less typical of averages of larger aggregates under laboratory standard conditions. Attempted Answers, that is, giving orientation, opinion, and suggestion, are always more numerous than their cognate Questions, that is, asking for orientation, opinion, or suggestion. Similarly, Positive Reactions, that is agreement, showing tension release, and solidarity, are usually more numerous than Negative Reactions, i.e., showing disagreement, tension, and antagonism. Intuitively one would feel that the process would surely be self-defeating and self-limiting if there were more questions than answers and more negative reactions than positive.

On the average, for groups we have examined, the relations of amounts by Sections are about as they are in the illustration. The relations between the amounts can be viewed as the final result of a repetitive series of cycles, each of which consists of: (1) an initial disturbance of the system (precipitated by the introduction of a new idea, or opinion, or suggestion into the group) followed by (2) a "dwindling series of feedbacks" and corrections as the disturbance is terminated, equilibrated, or assimilated by other parts or members of the system. Attempted Answers, or as one might call them for the moment, "Initial Acts", account for a little over half (or 57 percent) of the total activity, with Positive and Negative Reactions and Questions accounting for the other half, roughly.

Looking at the *Reaction* side alone, and assuming it to be 50 percent of the total, about half the reactions (or 25 percent of the total) are Positive and presumably terminate the disturbance introduced by the initial action. The other half of the time the Reaction fails to terminate the disturbance. Of this non-terminating portion again, about half (or 12 percent of the total) are Negative Reactions, which typically precipitate another Attempted Answer, thus beginning a repetition of the cycle. Of the remaining hypothetical 13 percent or so, about half (or 7 percent) are Questions, which also typically precipitate another Attempted Answer. If about 7 percent of Attempted Answers are in direct response to Questions, these might well be called "Reactions", thus leaving the relation of "Initial Acts" to "Reactions" about 50-50, as assumed above. One might say that quantitatively (as well as qualitatively, by definition) interaction is a process consisting of action followed by reaction. The balance of action with reaction is one of the equilibrium problems of the system.

Act to Act Tendencies and the Equilibrium Problem

A more detailed understanding of the equilibrating tendencies by which the characteristic profile arises may be obtained by examining the frequencies with which each type of activity tends to be followed by each other type. Two input-output matrices showing these act-to-act tendencies are presented in Tables II and III. These particular matrices were obtained by tabulation from the interaction tapes of the total sixteen sessions of the four five-man groups of the present observation series. The total number of output acts occurring after each input type of act is considered as 100 percent, and the probabilities for each type of output act are derived by a percentage breakdown.

TABLE II
MATRIX OF PROACTIVE TENDENCIES
OUTPUT PROBABILITIES FOR A GIVEN INPUT.
16 MEETINGS OF 5-MAN GROUPS

Category of Prior Act (Input Type)	Category of following Act (Output)												Total percent
	1	2	3	4	5	6	7	8	9	10	11	12	
1 SHOWS SOLIDARITY, raises other's status, gives help, reward:	—	6.8	9.1	22.7	29.5	18.2	—	4.5	2.2	—	—	6.8	99.8
2 SHOWS TENSION RELEASE, jokes, laughs, shows satisfaction:	1.6	37.5	1.6	6.3	21.9	9.4	.8	1.6	2.3	3.1	3.9	10.2	100.2
3 AGREES, shows passive acceptance, understands, concurs, complies:	3.0	4.6	6.6	9.7	41.6	22.1	2.8	2.1	.7	5.1	.8	.8	99.9
4 GIVES SUGGESTION, direction, implying autonomy for other:	2.6	4.8	1.6	55.6	19.3	9.6	1.0	2.6	.6	1.0	1.0	.3	100
5 GIVES OPINION, evaluation, analysis, expresses feeling, wish:	2.3	4.4	1.6	5.0	60.1	17.0	1.8	4.4	.7	.9	1.4	.3	99.9
6 GIVES ORIENTATION, information, repeats, clarifies, confirms:	.2	2.1	.2	3.4	22.6	61.4	4.7	2.8	1.3	.4	.8	.2	100.1
7 ASKS FOR ORIENTATION, information, repetition, confirmation:	1.1	1.1	1.1	6.5	19.4	38.7	21.5	7.5	1.1	1.1	1.1	—	100.2
8 ASKS FOR OPINION, evaluation, analysis, expression of feeling:	—	3.2	—	9.7	31.2	26.9	4.3	19.4	2.2	2.2	1.1	—	100.2
9 ASKS FOR SUGGESTION, direction, possible ways of action:	3.2	6.5	—	16.1	22.6	19.4	3.2	—	19.4	6.5	—	3.2	100.1
10 DISAGREES, shows passive rejection, formality, withholds help:	1.2	2.5	1.6	6.6	51.4	21.8	4.1	2.5	.8	1.6	5.3	.4	99.8
11 SHOWS TENSION, asks for help, withdraws "Out of Field":	—	4.2	2.1	8.3	45.8	35.4	—	2.1	—	—	2.1	—	100.0
12 SHOWS ANTAGONISM, deflates other's status, defends or asserts self:	5.9	27.5	—	5.9	19.6	7.8	5.9	2.0	—	—	3.9	21.6	100.1

Category of Prior Act (Input Type)	1	2	3	4	5	6	7	8	9	10	11	12	Total percent
1 SHOWS SOLIDARITY, raises other's status, gives help, reward:	28.4	11.9	3.0	13.4	14.9	11.9	4.5	4.5	—	3.0	1.5	3.0	100.0
2 SHOWS TENSION RELEASE, jokes, laughs, shows satisfaction:	.7	68.2	3.2	3.1	10.2	6.7	2.2	1.5	.3	1.7	.6	1.5	99.9
3 AGREES, shows passive acceptance, understands, concurs, complies:	.6	2.7	15.9	8.5	40.8	21.4	2.3	3.0	.9	2.7	1.0	.2	100.0
4 GIVES SUGGESTION, direction, implying autonomy for other:	1.3	6.7	46.0	8.6	9.2	8.8	2.3	1.5	1.5	12.4	1.3	.4	100.0
5 GIVES OPINION, evaluation, analysis, expresses feeling, wish:	.6	4.3	48.9	2.2	19.2	6.3	2.3	2.8	.3	11.8	.6	.6	99.9
6 GIVES ORIENTATION, information, repeats, clarifies, confirms:	.6	5.8	35.0	3.6	15.2	24.0	5.6	1.3	.4	5.7	1.1	1.7	100.0
7 ASKS FOR ORIENTATION, information, repetition, confirmation:	—	1.0	5.6	.7	10.0	73.7	5.6	1.0	.3	1.6	—	.7	100.2
8 ASKS FOR OPINION, evaluation, analysis, expression of feeling:	1.5	5.4	9.2	2.4	45.9	13.2	10.7	3.0	.5	4.4	2.0	2.0	100.2
9 ASKS FOR SUGGESTION, direction, possible ways of action:	—	13.2	—	35.8	28.3	9.4	1.9	1.9	—	3.8	3.8	1.9	100.0
10 DISAGREES, shows passive rejection, formality, withholds help:	.3	6.6	12.4	5.2	25.0	13.5	3.6	2.0	.3	24.2	3.9	3.0	100.0
11 SHOWS TENSION, asks for help, withdraws "Out of Field":	4.1	7.2	5.2	2.1	39.2	22.7	2.1	4.1	—	4.1	9.3	—	100.1
12 SHOWS ANTAGONISM, deflates other's status, defends or asserts self:	1.0	18.1	4.8	3.8	12.4	11.4	1.0	3.8	—	5.7	1.9	36.2	100.1

Category of following Act (Output)

TABLE III
MATRIX OF REACTIVE TENDENCIES
OUTPUT PROBABILITIES FOR A GIVEN INPUT.
16 MEETINGS OF 5-MAN GROUPS

It will be noted that two matrices are presented, one called a Matrix of Proactive Tendencies, and the other a Matrix of Reactive Tendencies. A single matrix could be produced, of course, by omitting this distinction, but such a matrix would ignore the fact that the action "changes hands" at certain points, from one member to another. And this fact is crucial, since the equilibrium problem of social systems is not simply one of a certain "balance" in the relation of qualitatively different types of acts to each other, as shown by the profile. It is at the same time, and just as intrinsically, a problem of a certain balance in the way in which these activities are distributed between separate members. The distinction between "proaction" and "reaction", for the matrices presented, hinges on the member-to-member oscillation of activity. Very simply, an act which is a direct continuation by the *same* member who has produced the last act is called "proactive". An act which follows immediately the last act of *another* member is called "reactive".

The distinction is based on a suggestion by Murray:

"I . . . suggest . . . that the term *proaction*, in contrast to *reaction*, be used to designate an action that is not initiated by the confronting external situation but spontaneously from within. An action of this sort is likely to be part of a serial program, one that is guided by some directional force (aim) which is subsidiary to a more distally oriented aim. As a rule, a proaction is not merely homeostatic, in the sense that it serves to restore the organism to a previously enjoyed equilibrium or state of well-being. If successful, it results in the addition or production of something—another bit of physical construction, let us say, or more money in the bank, or greater social cohesion, or another chapter of a novel, or the statement of a new theory. The integrates of serials, of plans, strategies, and intended proactions directed toward distal goals constitute a large portion of the ego system, the *establishment* of personality which inhibits impulses and renounces courses of action that interfere with progress along the elected paths of life."[4]

The operational definition of the distinction for purposes of tabulating from interaction records does not correspond perfectly to

[4] Murray, Henry A., "Toward a Classification of Interactions," in *Toward a General Theory of Action*, Parsons and Shils, Editors, Harvard University Press, Cambridge, 1951, pp. 439-440.

Murray's theoretical distinction, but the basic idea is the same. In face to face interaction it is true by and large that the first act of a person following the last act of some other is "provoked" by the last act of the other as the "stimulus" and thus has a "reactive" quality. Conversely, it is sufficiently true that as a person continues talking his activity tends to change to a "proactive" quality, directed adaptively and instrumentally to the achievement of more distant aims. The activity is now *directed toward* the external confronting situation, including the situation external to the group as a whole, rather than immediately *initiated by* it, as in the "reactive case". It might be noted in passing that the term "initiation of action" is ambiguous, in that it is often defined empirically as the total of *all* types of activity "given out" by a specific individual, but usually carries the theoretical *connotation* of "proaction".

The Matrix of Proactive tendencies shows very clearly that when the same person continues talking, after having given an act of orientation, opinion, or suggestion, the probability is very high that he will continue with the same type of activity (probabilities of about .61, .60, and .55) presumably in a connected "serial program", to use Murray's term. When he does not continue with the same precise category of activity, the probability is still relatively high that he will carry on in one of the three types called Attempted Answers. If his preceding act was a Question of some type, and he continues himself instead of yielding the floor to some other, the highest probabilities are that he will either repeat or go directly ahead with an Attempted Answer. Indeed, the tendencies to continue proactively in the Attempted Answer area are very strong, even when the member has begun his participation with a Reaction to the other. As we all know, an act of agreement is often a way of "getting one's foot in the door" in order to go ahead and present one's own ideas. And similarly, when one has given a disagreement, he is very likely to go ahead and "tell why". In both of these cases, the tendency to present the argument in terms of "opinion" rather than "facts" is notable.

If the preceding Reaction was far over on the affective side, however, there are appreciable tendencies for the member to continue in the affective area. If one's former act was a display of antagonism, the present act is likely to be another, unless it passes over into tension release, either of which is more probable than a direct return to the task area. Similarly, when the last act was one of tension release, the next act is likely to be *another* act of tension release, and the tendency to continue with an act of antagonism (possibly a joking one) is still appreciable. Once such a cycle of antagonism and tension release is set in motion, it appears to have a tendency to continue until presumably the major potential of implicit tension is "bled off" to a substantially lower level. Similar cycles also appear between showing solidarity and showing tension release, although they do not appear on this matrix because of our scoring convention (now changed) of scoring "jokes" in category two, as well as laughs. We now score the jokes themselves in either category one, or category twelve, according to whether the butt of the joke is outside the immediate group, or a member of it. This convention appears to us now to more satisfactorily represent affective dynamics of the process, but as a result of the change we obtain considerably more scores in category one than previously, and a few more in category twelve. The implication of the scoring change is simply that we now assume, on the basis of experience and intuition, that one of the reasons the number of acts in these two categories was formerly so low (of the order of one or two percent) is that in our particular type of groups, the management of positive and negative affect is typically accomplished in a "joking" rather than in a "serious" manner. Whether joking or serious, however, these cycles of affective activity, once started, have a tendency to "carry on", just as do the "serials" of instrumental-adaptive activity.

As we think of the matter, the instrumental-adaptive activity of the preceding participant tends to build up tensions in the present participant to some point where he enters the process and changes to activity of an expressive-integrative relevance, which tends to "bleed off" the tension to some point at which he changes the focus himself and continues again with instrumental-adaptive activity. The problem of equilibrium is essentially the problem of establishing arrangements (or an "orbit of activity") whereby the system goes through a repetitive cycle, within which all of the disturbances created in one phase are reduced in some other. The dilemma of all action systems is that no one disturbance can be reduced without creating another.

The individual personality is such an action system, and some of its cyclical tendencies can be seen in the Proactive Matrix. The combination of two or more personalities in interaction, however, is also an action system. Indeed, this is the level on which the systematic properties can be seen most fully articulated in overt observable behavior. The "switch-over" from reactive to proactive behavior can be seen in the individual person as he continues his participation, but the switch-over from proactive to reactive is most notable at those junctures in the process when the action changes hands. What happens to the quality of action when the action changes hands may be seen in the Matrix of Reactive Tendencies.

When the prior act of another member has been an Attempted Answer, the highest probabilities are that the present act will be a Positive Reaction, specifically an agreement, rather than a continuation in the task area, although there are appreciable tendencies for the reacting person to continue directly with further opinion or information. Probabilities of positive reactions (for these groups) far outweigh probabilities of negative reactions, and this is generally true, though occasionally we observe groups where it is not the case.

Theoretically, we tend to assume that a preponderance of positive reactions over negative is a *condition* of equilibrium or maintenance of the steady state of the system. The reasoning goes something like this: We assume that the instrumental-adaptive goals of the system involve the maintenance of a certain level of accomplishment output, and that this level *tends to fall* without the constant application of effort, energy, and activity applied successfully to the realities of the external situation. But the level of *accomplishment* can not be maintained for long without also maintaining the level of diffuse *satisfaction*, which depends upon the achievement of expressive-integrative goals. The full stable "orbit" will have to include tension release, gratification, and a feedback of positive sanctions to the person(s) performing the instrumental activities, in such a way as to "reinforce" them (in the learning theory sense), either in keeping them doing what they are doing, or in keeping them generalizing appropriately from their former accomplishments. Negative reactions tend to inhibit the behavior which preceded, but do not provide the basis for establishing a stable, positively defined orbit. Nor does generalization from negative reactions help appreciably in finding a positively defined orbit. It simply tends to cancel out or inhibit possible untried orbits, while the unstable "seeking" or "trial and error" fluctuation of the system continues.

Furthermore, each failure, and each negative reaction, tends to result *in its own right* in disturbance, and thus reduces the satisfaction levels directly. Assuming a quantitative equivalence of units of action observed (a shaky, but not inconceivable assumption), one might conclude that at least one positive reaction would be required for each negative reaction, simply to counteract the disturbances introduced by the negative reactions. On these assumptions, if positive reactions are only equal to negative reactions, the system barely manages to counteract the disturbances introduced by the "friction" of its own controlling apparatus, and the accomplishment and satisfaction levels will tend to sink because of lack of effort and instrumental activity applied constructively and successfully to the situation of the system. One concludes that the accomplishment and satisfaction levels can only be maintained in a steady state if an orbit is found in which positive reactions preponderate over negative. The degree to which they must do so in order to maintain steady levels will then depend upon such factors as levels of expectation or aspiration, the stringency of situational demands, and the abilities or resources of the actors in relation to aspirations and situational demands.

One obvious inference from this theoretical formulation is that the levels of satisfaction of members at the end of a problem-solving attempt will be a function of the degree to which positive reactions have outweighed negative reactions during the process. The two illustrative profiles given earlier demonstrate this relation. There are a considerable number of ways of constructing single indices from the balance of rates in the profiles which give reasonably good predictions of satisfaction. We do not yet know which of these is best in general. Several we have tried tend to yield correlations with average satisfaction at the end of meetings ranging from about .6 to .8.

Another possible inference is that the satisfaction ratings of individual members will tend to be a function of the preponderance of positive reactions received over negative reactions received by that member. We have not thoroughly explored this hypothesis as yet, but there are some indications that higher status members tend to receive higher relative proportions of positive reactions, and in general have higher satisfaction ratings. The degree of satisfaction, we believe, as a working hypothesis, tends to be highest with the members of highest status, and to grade down as status grades down. On the basis of the theory, however, one should definitely not expect perfect correlations, either between total group profiles and average post-meeting satisfactions, or between positive reactions received by individual members and their individual post-meeting satisfactions. The reason is that starting levels are typically not known, and that other factors such as stringency of situational demands, abilities or resources of the members, and the content and stringency of levels of expectation or aspiration are believed to be involved also. Much work remains to be done in this direction.

On the Matrix of Reactive Tendencies it will be noted that the tendency to reply to an Attempted Answer of the other with a Positive or Negative Reaction increases from a prior act of giving orientation to one of giving opinion, to one of giving a suggestion. One might say that the "urgency" of giving a Positive or Negative Reaction increases as the proaction becomes more "directive" or "constricting". An act of giving orientation has only a probability of about .06 of provoking a disagreement. An act of opinion, however, has a probability of about .12 and an act of suggestion has a little higher probability. But an act of suggestion is a little less likely than an act of opinion to provoke an agreement. If one makes an index by representing the probability of disagreement as a percentage of the probability of agreement the index rises from .16 in response to an act of orientation, to .24 in response to an act of opinion, to .26 in response to an act of suggestion. The difference between the last two is very small, but in the expected direction. It should be pointed out that on the Proactive Matrix the probability that a member will follow a disagreement with an act of opinion is very high, .51. Consequently, the replies to opinion on the Reactive Matrix are often replies to an opinion which was in support of a still prior disagreement. If one took the trouble to segregate those cases where the acts of orientation, opinion, and suggestion are given without prior disagreement, it is likely that the differences between them would be greater.

The notions that proaction is likely to provoke reaction, that the probability of reaction increases as the process passes from problems of orientation, to evaluation, to control, and that the reaction will tend to swing to the negative side as the implications of the acts become more "directive" and "constrictive" are fundamental to the theory of equilibrium problems in small groups. The problem appears in many guises, and solutions are worked out in many directions, as will appear later in the discussion of the way in which participation tends to get distributed between members, the way in which quality of activity tends to move through a series of phases constituting a closed cycle in time, the way in which number of members affects the process, the way in which differentiated roles tend to appear, and the way in which the structure of roles tends to shift though a series of meetings.

On the Matrix of Reactive Tendencies the probabilities that

a Question from the other will provoke a complementary or cognate Attempted Answer are seen to be very high. There is perhaps . nothing very remarkable about this, but it does provide evidence of a kind of "reasonable continuity" in the process—the persistence of the system in an instrumental-adaptive direction of movement, once started, in spite of the fact that the action changes hands from one member to another. Questions provide a means of turning the process into the instrumental-adaptive direction of movement, with a low probability of provoking an affective reaction, and are an extremely effective way of turning the initiative over to the other.

Our impression is, however, that in our groups the number of questions which arise out of a self-conscious anticipatory attempt to guide the process in this way is comparatively small. They probably appear more often after strains arise out of earlier failures, as a result of disagreement, argument, and "backtracking" from premature attempts to proceed more "directively". Questions provide a "neutral way out"—a "patch up" procedure of last recourse when negative reactions are anticipated if one goes ahead himself. At least this way of looking at the process gives a reasonable explanation as to why the rates of Questions are in general so low (about half that of Negative Reactions). Questions constitute the last of the "dwindling series of feedbacks" mentioned earlier, and tend to be called into play only after more direct and obvious feedback controls have failed to equilibrate the system. Since they tend to prevent the asker from going ahead to give his own ideas, they provide little opportunity to raise one's status, but rather hand this opportunity over to the other. Thus, one might suppose, where competition is high (as it is generally in our initially leaderless groups) there will be a tendency to avoid them except as a last resort. Those who have a fixed high status, and those who have essentially accepted a low status, can "afford" to ask Questions, but not those who are in the thick of competition.

The tendency for antagonism to provoke antagonism is even more marked when the action changes hands (in the Reactive Matrix) than when the same person continues (in the Proactive Matrix). Similarly, in the Reactive Matrix, showing solidarity tends to provoke a like Reaction. Either type of marked affect tends to lead to tension release, and this type of activity, when once tripped off, is more likely to continue than any other type. "Laughter is contagious" as the saying goes. In the present context it is another instance of the tendency of the system, once started, to continue in a given direction of movement until checked by other factors. It is interpreted as a mechanism by which massive changes in the tension level take place in a short length of time, and typically appears only periodically, with intervening periods of tension build-up, as will be pointed out later in the discussion of phase movement.

The interpretation of the rate of tension release for given groups is a vexed problem. According to our present thinking, a "moderate rate" (around 7 or 8 percent) is associated with successful equilibration after normal hazards. Very low rates lead us to expect high residual tension, and very high rates lead us to look for extraordinary sources of tension. Levels of satisfaction as measured by post-meeting questions would appear to give us some entree to this problem, but the complex determinants of satisfaction have already been pointed out.

These problems of interpretation are general, however, not specific to certain types of acts or results of acts. The whole implication of an equilibrium theory as an interpretive device is that the determinants of any part of the process, or any result of it, are complex, and should be sought in some kind of complicated balance of the system as a whole, rather than in a maximization or minimization of supposedly isolated factors. The understanding of a *repeated* phenomenon in this type of approach lies in showing how it fits into a system, or constellation of interlocking systems, as one link in a closed, repetitive cycle of activities or orbit which constitutes the moving steady state of the system as its equilibrium is persistently disturbed and reestablished.

The Who-to-Whom Matrix and the Equilibrium Problem

A further unfolding of the equilibrium problem may be seen by a closer examination of the way in which participation tends to be distributed among members. The total number of different possible combinations of who is speaking and to whom for a given time period is called a "who-to-whom matrix". The scoring system recognizes acts addressed to the "group as a whole" as well as to specific individuals.

An aggregate matrix of a collection of 18 sessions of six-man groups (all types of activity) is presented in Table IV as an illustration. The aggregate matrix is produced by rank ordering the members of each separate session according to the total amounts of participation given out, and then summing together all rank one men, all rank two men, all rank one men speaking to all rank two men, etc.

Table IV—Aggregate Who-to-whom Matrix for 18 Sessions of Six-Man Groups*, All Types of Activity

RANK ORDER OF PERSON ORIGINATING ACT	Speaking to Individuals of each Rank:						Total to Individuals	To Group As a Whole	Total Initiated
	1	2	3	4	5	6			
1		1238	961	545	445	317	3506	5661	9167
2	1748		443	310	175	102	2778	1211	3989
3	1371	415		305	125	69	2285	742	3027
4	952	310	282		83	49	1676	676	2352
5	662	224	144	83		28	1141	443	1584
6	470	126	114	65	44		819	373	1192
Total Received	5203	2313	1944	1308	872	565	12205	9106	21311

* These groups were observed before the standard laboratory task was evolved. The general features of the standard task groups are similar.

The pattern of distribution is different in detail under different conditions. For example, groups with no designated leader generally tend to have more equal participation than groups with designated leaders of higher status. However, in spite of these differences, the distribution of total amounts of participation of each member, as well as the pattern of who talks how much to whom, (and how, qualitatively) seems to be subject to system-influences, which tend to produce similarities from group to group, and some regular gradations by group size.

These generalizations may be illustrated in part by reference to Table IV. If the personnel are arrayed in rank order according to the total amount they speak ("basic initiating rank") we then find that they are spoken to in amounts proportionate to their rank order. Roughly speaking, each man receives back about half as much as he puts out in total. It will be remembered that something like half of all interaction is "reactive" and each man spends a certain portion of his time reacting to the initial acts of others. The amount of time spent reacting to specific other individuals rather than proacting to the group as a whole, however, differs according to the rank of the member. The profiles of participants tend to change systematically as we proceed downward in rank. High ranking men tend to have more proactive Attempted Answers in their profiles and to address more acts to the group as a whole than lower ranking men, while low ranking men have more "Reactions", both positive and negative, and address more of their acts to specific individuals. Quantitative differentiation in participation is accompanied by, or is symptomatic of, qualitative differentiation of roles of members. For example, the top man tends to give out more information and opinion to specific individuals than he receives, while, on the contrary, low men give out more agreement, disagreement, and requests for information than they receive.

If this is true one might expect quantity of participation to be related to the status hierarchy of the members. We typically find that the order produced by ranking individuals according to their "basic initiating rank" on total amounts of participation is fairly highly correlated with the order produced by their own ratings of each other as to "productivity", i.e., who has the best ideas, and who does the most to guide the discussion effectively. Similar findings are reported by Norfleet[5] and Bass[6] with correlations of

5 Norfleet, Barbara, "Interpersonal Relations and Group Productivity", *Journal of Social Issues*, Vol. IV, No. 2, Spring 1948, pp. 66-69.

about .95 in each case. Strodtbeck[7] finds in addition a fairly dependable connection between amount of activity given out and probability of winning in contested decisions, which is a kind of measure of power or influence. The empirical correlation between status in some generalized sense and amounts of participation given out and received seems to be pretty well established, but perfect correlation is definitely not to be expected in general.

Such approximate generalizations, once established, can typically be used to produce further valuable diagnostic information, as will be shown later. Any specific group, or some particular types of groups, may present exceptions, in one or more particulars, depending on the conditions operating. Exceptions to the empirical rule give the investigator the cue to look for exceptional conditions. For example, we have often found particular exceptions to the expected correlation between amount given out and amount received in cases where one of the members disagrees with the others persistently, and so tends to attract or receive a disproportionate amount of communication. Festinger and Thibaut[8] have produced this effect experimentally. We have found similar exceptions to the generalization when two highly interactive and agreeing members form a sub-group or coalition vis-a-vis a third neglected or rejected member.

Size of group is obviously an important condition affecting the distribution of activities. From present indications it appears that the top man in groups larger than five or so tends to speak considerably more to the group as a whole than to specific individuals in the group, as in Table IV. All other members tend to speak more to specific individuals (and particularly to the top man) than to the group as a whole. Each man tends to speak to each other man in an amount which is a probability function of both his own rank on outwardly directed remarks, and the rank of the other on the receiving of communication.[9] As groups increase in

[6] Bass, Bernard H., "An Analysis of Leaderless Group Discussion", *Journal of Applied Psychology*, 33 (1949), pp. 527-533.

[7] Strodtbeck, Fred L., "Husband-Wife Interaction over Revealed Differences", *American Sociological Review*, Vol. 16, No. 4, August, 1951, pp. 468-473.

[8] Festinger, Leon, and Thibaut, John, "Interpersonal Communication in Small Groups", in *Theory and Experiment in Social Communication* by Festinger et. al., Research Center for Group Dynamics Institute for Social Research, University of Michigan, Ann Arbor, 1950, pp. 37-49.

[9] See Keller, Joseph B., "Comment on 'Channels of Communication in Small Groups", *American Sociological Review*, Vol. 16, No. 6, December 1951.

size, a larger and larger proportion of the activity tends to be addressed to the top man, and a smaller and smaller proportion to other members. In turn, as size increases, the top man tends to address more and more of his remarks to the group as a whole, and to exceed by larger amounts his proportionate share. The communication pattern tends to "centralize", in other words, around a leader through whom most of the communication flows.

But if the situation is one in which *inter*action is expected by the participators, there would seem to be a top ceiling for the top man somewhere around 50 percent, apparently connected with the general tendency for interaction under such expectations to come to a system-closure, such that each "action" of one member, as it were, tends to be countered with a "reaction" from some other. Even if the top man is initiating most of the action, he still has to expect that he will receive a "feedback of reactions", both of a positive and negative sort, that will tend to equal the amount of action he initiates. It may very well be that the expectation of "equality" which is so often present in groups of our culture, refers rather to this over-all balance of action and reaction than to an equality of amounts of output of all members, which in practice, is never found.

Thus it can be seen that the differentiation between members as to specialized roles and status, is intimately related to the equilibrium problem. The tendency for the system, once started, to continue moving in the same direction until checked by opposing forces, is reflected in the tendency of given members to continue proacting until checked by other members. Negative Reactions appear to act as such a check, presumably through learning mechanisms. Their regular appearance should be viewed as a check on the widening of status differences, as well as a result of "objective mistakes" and task attempts which fail to appeal on other grounds. But if, as we have hypothesized, the system cannot maintain a steady state without a preponderance of positive reactions over negative, then in the equilibrated system more task attempts will be rewarded than punished, and they will be attempts by specific persons.

Here enters the crucial importance of "generalization" in the learning theory sense. Insofar as a given person "gets on the right track" and receives Positive Reactions from other members, he will be reinforced in his direction of movement, and will tend to keep on talking. He will "generalize" from the premises, logical and emotional, which underlay his original successful attempt.

This is the "growing point" of the system of common symbols or group culture, as well as of role differentiation. And reciprocally, the other members will "generalize" from his earlier attempts, gratifying in some sense to them, to an expectation of further effective behavior on his part. The member begins to build a "specialized role". Insofar as the activity he performs is felt to be important in terms of the functional problems of the group, its goals and value norms, the "status" of the member will begin to rise. There will be a "generalization" from the specific *performance* of the person to a *qualitative ascribed* "position" in the group which bears a rank relation to other positions similarly developed. It is apparently in some such terms that one may understand the tendencies toward gross differentiation of amounts of participation given and received, the qualitative differences by rank, and above all, the emergence of a "top man" in larger groups, with an amount and quality of activity radically discontinuous with the more or less equal rank intervals between the other men. A system can not achieve a steady state without generalization, but the operation of generalization produces a differentiation of roles which introduces new strains. The price of accomplishment is differentiated status.

It should not be assumed, however, that once generalization in its various aspects has resulted in an ascribed status and role for a man, that his position is now stable. There are apparently a number of ways in which it may be undermined and subject to later shifts, two of which may be mentioned as likely. The first is that the effects of his role-specialized behavior, even if it does not change, put other members under ambivalent strains of some sort which gradually lead them to shift their perception of, attitudes toward, or behavior addressed to him. The second is that the psychological effects of holding a given position may result in gradual *changes* in his behavior (either by "overconfidence", "dissatisfaction" or in some other way) which finally "break through" stereotyped perceptions of his previously established role and become obvious to the other members, with a resulting shift in their attitudes toward him. In other words, the problem of equilibrium is relevant on the more macroscopic levels of role structure and in longer changes over time, as well as on the more microscopic levels we have so far discussed. The unfolding of the equilibrium problem on these levels will be discussed later in this paper. First, however, it may be useful to present, in a very tentative way, a sample of the type of statistical models we have been "playing with", which ignore these more macroscopic equilibrium problems of larger scale "social structure change".

A Statistical Model for Exploring the Matrix Equilibrium Problem

Some characteristics of the hypothetical learning process just described can be formalized slightly in terms of a statistical model. The model presented below is the fifth of a series of models which have been informally explored and discarded as their deficiencies forced to clearer awareness the sorts of assumptions which appear to be necessary to "reproduce" the characteristics of the average process as we have found it empirically. The present model has been barely explored as yet, and is by no means expected to be the last of the series. It is presented simply as another step in what is hoped to be the right direction. This model which we call T_5 (T for "temporary") takes the act-to-act tendencies represented by the Proactive and Reactive Matrices as given, makes certain additional assumptions about the effects of learning mechanisms and generalization as discussed above, and attempts to determine whether, if these givens and assumptions are true, the who-to-whom matrix we find for groups of each size will turn out to be the equilibrium state of the system.

No formal mathematics have been employed. The model is set up for easy "Monte Carlo" calculation. The results to be obtained are thus exceedingly "approximate". They have been quite adequate however, to show that previous models could not possibly be satisfactory, and this is all that is required for progress. To lighten the boredom we have typically employed an actual group of people, each of whom is given an identical set of Proactive and Reactive Matrices (thus erasing all "personality differences") and a table of random numbers. The process proceeds by a series of probability choices according to a set of "Rules of Order" administered by the experimenter. Still another person takes down the scores as they are determined by the probability choices, and these scores are later tabulated and analyzed just as we analyze actual scores. To forestall any misunderstanding it may be repeated: the group of people is in no sense necessary—the whole operation is defined by rules and probability choices and can be performed by a single statistical clerk. However, to do the calculation as a game gives an excellent setting for spotting specific deficiencies and artificialities of the model.

For use in the model, the probabilities in the Proactive and Reactive Matrices given earlier are translated into spans of random numbers, so that one can make a probability choice by drawing from a table of random numbers. For example, take the probabilities for what happens next following an act in Category 1 in the Proactive Matrix. The probabilities add to 1.000. Random numbers 001 to '000 are taken to represent this range. The probability that the output act will be in Category 1 is zero on the table, so no random number span is assigned. The probability that the output will be in Category 2 is .068, so the span of random numbers from 001 to 068 is taken to represent this probaaility. The probability of an output in Category 3 is .091, so the span of random numbers from 069 to 159 is taken to represent this probability, and so on.

Model T₅

The first two elements of the model are the two act-to-act matrices, represented in terms of random numbers, as explained:

The Matrix of Proactive Tendencies
(See Table II)

The Matrix of Reactive Tendencies
(See Table III)

The next two elements of the model are two tables which represent, not the *tendencies,* as above, but the *opportunities* arising out of the status order, and modified by a "learning" process, as explained in the Rules of Order.

The Table of Proactive Opportunities

This table contains a set of probabilities, one for each man, adding to 1. Initially each man's probability is $\frac{1}{N}$, where N=number of members in the group. However, Man 1 is designated for purposes of this model as "Leader", and he is given special treatment as indicated later. In the event a man's probability is to be increased, as under Step 8 in the Rules of Order, a suitable operator is applied which increases the probability of the given man and decreases the probability of each of the others, with the probabilities still adding to 1 after the operation.

Practically, the change will be accomplished in this Model T₅ by the following crude method. A set of numbered tags will be used, the numbers indicating the identification numbers of the members. Initially an equal number of tags (say 10) will be put in a hat for each man. When a probability choice is to be made, a tag will be drawn, and then returned. When a man's probability is to be increased, a single tag bearing his number will be added to those already in the hat.

Mathematically, this is a very awkward operator. However,

with the present mechanical method the operation is very easily performed.

The Table of Reactive Opportunities

This table contains a set of probabilities, one for each man, adding to 1. Each man's probability will be set at $\frac{1}{N}$, where N=number of members in the group. These probabilities are not changed.

Practically, the probabilities will be represented by the assignment of an appropriate span of random numbers to each man, and the choices will be made from a random number table.

Following is the Table to be used for a six man group:

Random Numbers:		Man Designated:
001–167	=	1
168–333	=	2
334–500	=	3
501–667	=	4
668–833	=	5
834–1000	=	6

Rules of Order for T_s
Proaction:

1. A man is chosen from the table of *Proactive* Opportunities (it may be any man) and the Process goes to Step 2.

2. The quality of the man's proaction is chosen by probabilities from his Matrix of Proactive Tendencies, from the row of the preceding input act* and the Process goes to Step 3.

   (*Note: If there was no preceding act—that is, if the present act is the first of the run—the present act is arbitrarily chosen as an act in Category 6).

3. The proaction is delivered to a given target as follows:

   a. If the man *just received a Positive Reaction* (or if his present act is the first of a run) the present act is delivered to the *group as a whole*, and the Process goes to Step 4.

   b. If the man has *just given a Positive Reaction*, and he is now continuing, the present act is now delivered to the *group as a whole*, and the Process goes to Step 4.

   c. If the man has *just given an Attempted Answer, a Question, or a Negative Reaction to a specific individual or to the group as a whole*, the present act is now delivered to the same target, and the Process goes to Step 4.

Choice of Proaction or Reaction:

4. The number of a man is drawn by probabilities from the Table of *Proactive* Opportunities, and a decision is made as follows:

   a. If the number of the man is that of the man who *just spoke*,* he is allowed to *continue Proaction* and the Process returns to Step 2.

   b. However, if the number is *different* from that of the man who just spoke, he is now required to *stop speaking* and another man is chosen to *continue with a Reaction*, as the Process goes on to Step 5.

   (*Note: If the group as a whole delivered the last act (as in Category 2) any man drawn may be considered as having just spoken.)

Reaction:

5. The man who just spoke is *excluded* from the *Table of Reactive Opportunities* and a *different* man is chosen from this Table by probabilities. The Process then goes to Step 6.

6. The quality of the man's Reaction is chosen from his Matrix of Reactive Tendencies, from the row of the preceding input act, and the Process goes to Step 7.

7. The reaction is delivered to a given target as follows:

   a. The act is delivered *to the man who just spoke*, and (unless the exception under "b" applies) the Process goes to Step 8.

   b. If the act under "a" is an act in Category 2 (Tension Release) .each other man in the group is allowed to deliver an act in Category 2 to the same man, (but the receiver of these laughs does not deliver such an act to himself). The Process then goes on to Step 8.

Reward and Punishment

8. Depending upon the quality of the act, and who receives it, the Table of Proactive Opportunities may be changed, as follows:

   a. If the *"Leader"* receives the act, *regardless of its quality*, he is "rewarded" by an increase in his probability of speaking again in the Table of Proactive Opportunities, and the Process goes to Step 4.

   b. If any other member receives the act, a change may be made or not, as follows:

      1. If he receives a *Positive Reaction*, he is rewarded, as above, and the Process goes to Step 4.

2. If he receives a *Negative Reaction,* he is punished by a decrease in his probability of speaking again in the Table of Proactive Opportunities, and the Process goes to Step 4.

3. If he receives a *Question or an Attempted Answer,* no change is made, and the Process goes to Step 4.

This particular model has not been in existence long enough at the point of this writing to provide data which might be presented. However, it includes one feature which previous models did not contain—the fact that one person is designated in the very beginning as "Leader". It also assumes that there will be no change in leadership, and indeed, that the equilibrium problems of role organization, once roles get specialized, are much simpler than we know them in fact to be. Some of these problems will be discussed later.

The "Leader" is rewarded by an increase in probability of speaking *each* time he speaks, regardless of the response. All other men are rewarded when they receive a positive response, and punished by a decrease in probability when they receive a negative response. All men are started equal, but with say 10 tokens each, so that one punishment does not extinguish the probability of speaking again.

The "rationalization" of the model, so far as it goes, is this: Any model generally similar to this one, so far as I can see, will only produce the aforementioned radical discontinuity between the top man and the others if the top man is somehow singled out for distinctive treatment. Otherwise he can not get so far ahead as he actually does. Of course the probabilities of speaking could be set on an empirical basis, but this would defeat the purpose of the model, except as a device for obtaining sampling distributions. It is hoped that there is some set of assumptions which will regulate the process in such a way that the empirical gradients will appear as an equilibrium state of the system. The problem is to discover some such set of assumptions.

One possible procedure is to employ further matrices which members use in speaking to the top man. This would involve constructing such matrices so that the probability of the top man receiving agreement (rather than disagreement) is enhanced, or even set to the point where disagreement is not received. However, empirically we know that the top man *does* receive disagreement—in fact he receives, absolutely, more than any other member, just as he receives absolutely more agreement. His ratio of agreement to disagreement may, however, be somewhat higher than other members.

This will come about automatically, however, I think, for the rest of the members on the gradient, if not the leader, by the working of the model. That is, a man obtains the opportunity to go ahead by receiving agreement. Those who go ahead will have higher totals of amounts given out—or vice versa, those who are found with higher amounts given out will also be found to have received more agreement, since that is the mechanism by which they got ahead. All will be held down by disagreement however, to some extent, with the exception of the top man. He will receive the full probability of agreement in the model, whereas the others will all have been held down.

The reward of the top man each time he speaks can be given some rationalization in various ways. One can assume that the leader is the man who is speaking as the expression of a self-consistent set of norms, and is internally rewarded by the "knowledge that he is right", no matter what response comes from others. For the same reason, he can receive disagreement and antagonism without abandoning his self-initiating and self-rewarding tendencies. If his status is the highest in the group, and he is the source of authority, it is as if he "can do no wrong" and disagreements from other members are taken simply as signals that they are confused, in error, or deviant. It is then the leader's job to "remain steadfast", and to correct the deviance by his own consistent attitude and administration of rewards and punishments. So long as his status is the highest in the group, his positive and negative responses function as rewards and punishments to the other members, but not vice-versa.

The original sources of such a position might be assumed to be various. They might proceed from some initial positive affective reactions of the members to the leader. The leader in this case is the major target of positive affect in the group—the "sociometric star". They might proceed from the identification of the leader with a set of norms or a coherent symbol system, where both the leader and the members identify with the symbol system and the leader is identified by the members as the "true spokesman and interpreter" of the symbol system. Both of these sources would involve a kind of "generalization" of response. In the first case affective responses of liking are organized by generalization so that the leader is persistently "liked" in spite of variability or his behavior. In the second case affective responses of evaluation and of agreement with verbal or symbolic propositions are generalized in such a way that new propositions appropriately linked with (or "deduced from") the existing symbol set are also felt to compel agreement.

There is a third case, perhaps, where one might say that whatever will tend to "insulate" a given man from the ordinary influences men have on each other by reward and punishment will tend to produce an "Archimedean Point" for change and readjustment of the system around the unyielding and stable element. The psychotic or semi-psychotic personality, or the rigidly neurotic one can thus be seen to answer the formal requirements perhaps as well as the former cases. By extension one might say that if one wishes to move a system as a leader, he must be able to "take it"—i.e. take disagreement and antagonism, without reacting in the usual way. The refusal of the therapist to assume a full reciprocity of relation with the patient is a case that is formally similar, in this "immovable" quality. The therapist often differs from other leaders and influencers of behavior, however, in that he takes a "passive" immovable role rather than an "active" one, as in the case of the charismatic leader.

The preliminary character of this speculation is obvious. In fact, it clearly overlooks the complications introduced by the fact that the role of "Leader" in the sense of the man with "the best ideas" or who "does most to guide the discussion" tends *not* to be the sociometric star, as will appear later in this paper. This model, T_5, is simply not complicated enough to handle this problem. Perhaps it will suggest, however, the way in which an effort toward more formal models can play a part clarifying the assumptions involved in the type of equilibrium theory toward which we are aiming, and give some inkling as to how they may be handled formally as they get too complicated for intuitive grasp.

Phase Movement and the Problem of Equilibrium

Changes in quality of activity as groups move through time in attempting to solve their problems may be called phase patterns. The pattern of phases differs in detail under different conditions. However, these changes in quality seem to be subject to system-influences which produce similarities from group to group. An increase of task-oriented activities in the early parts of a meeting, that is, Questions and Attempted Answers, seems to constitute a disturbance of a system equilibrium which is later redressed by an increase in social-emotional activities, that is, both Positive and

Negative Reactions.

Part of our observations prior to the development of the standard diagnostic task were kept by time sequence. Each available meeting was divided into three equal parts, and the amount of each type of activity in each part of each meeting was determined. The meetings were divided into two kinds: those which were dealing with full-fledged problems (essentially problems of analysis and planning with the goal of group decision as described for the standard diagnostic task), and those dealing with more truncated or specialized types of problems. Those groups dealing with full-fledged problems tended to show a typical phase movement through the meeting: the process tended to move qualitatively from a *relative* emphasis on attempts to solve problems of *orientation* ("what is it") to attempts to solve problems of *evaluation* ("how do we feel about it") and subsequently to attempts to solve problems of *control* ("what shall we do about it"). Concurrent with these transitions, the relative frequencies of both *negative reactions* (disagreement, tension, and antagonism), and *positive reactions* (agreement, tension release, and showing solidarity), tends to increase. Chart II presents the summary data for all group sessions examined in the phase study.

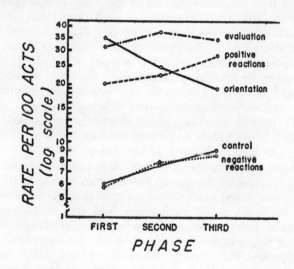

The underlying theory as to why the phase movement just described is characteristic of full-fledged conditions is again a system-equilibrium rationale. An individual may be cognitively oriented to a situation and speak of it to others in cognitive terms without committing himself, or the other when he agrees, either to evaluation of it, or an attempt to control it. But in speaking to the other in evaluative terms he attempts to commit both himself and the other to some assumed previous orientation, and further, if he suggests a way to control the situation by joint cooperative action, he assumes both previous orientation and evaluation. When the problems of arriving at a common orientation and evaluation of the situation have not been substantially solved by the group members, attempts at control will meet with resistance on the part of the others and frustration on the part of the person attempting to exercise the control. Probably generally, unless there are contrary cultural, personality, or group organizational factors, the interacting persons tend to avoid or retreat from this frustration-producing type of interaction by "back-tracking" toward orientation and evaluative analysis until the prior problems are solved.

In addition to their task problems, the members of any cooperating group have problems of their social and emotional relationships to each other to solve and keep solved. Efforts to solve problems of orientation, evaluation, and control as involved in the task tend to lead to differentiation of the roles of the participants, both as to the functions they perform and their gross amounts of participation. Some major features of this differentiation have already been described in the presentation of findings about the matrix. Both qualitative and quantitative types of differentiation tend to carry status implications which may threaten or disturb the existing order or balance of status relations among members. Disagreement and an attempt to change existing ideas and values instrumentally may be necessary in the effort to solve the task problem but may lead, nevertheless, to personalized anxieties or antagonisms and impair the basic solidarity of the group.

This impairment, or the threat of it, we may assume, tends to grow more marked as the group passes from emphasis on the less demanding and more easily resolved problems of cognitive orientation on to problems of evaluation, and still more acute as it passes on to its heaviest emphasis on problems of control. It will be recalled that this notion appeared earlier in the examination of act-to-act tendencies. This assumption seems to be a more generalized way of stating the findings of certain other studies. For example,

Lippitt[10] found negative reactions to autocratic control or leadership in boys' clubs under certain conditions, while Rogers[11] and his associates tend to find a minimization of negative reactions on the part of clients when the counselor confines himself to nondirective (or, in our categories, orienting rather than evaluating or controlling) types of activity. The present assumption may be regarded as a generalization of this connection between degree of control and negative reactions, so that it is viewed as applying to different points in the process of the same group, not simply to differences between groups. Thus, a series of changes in the social-emotional relationships of the members tend to be set in motion by pressures arising initially from the demands of the external task or outer situation. These social-emotional problems tend to be expressed in overt interaction as they grow more acute—hence the increasing rate of negative reactions.

However, at the extreme end of the final period, assuming that the members' attempts at control over the outer situation and over each other are successful and a final decision is reached, the rates in Categories 1, 2, and 3 also to rise to their peak. In other words, one might expect the successfully recovering group to confirm its agreement and to release the tensions built up in its prior task-efforts, repairing the damage done to its state of consensus and social integration. We note joking and laughter so frequently at the end of meetings that they might almost be taken as a signal that the group has completed what it considers to be a task effort, and is ready for disbandment or a new problem. This last-minute activity completes a cycle of operations involving a successful solution both of the task problems and social-emotional problems confronting the group. The apparent incongruity of predicting a peak for both negative and positive reactions in the third phase is thus explained. Negative reactions tend to give way to positive reactions in the final part of the crudely defined third phase.

Changes in role structure and the equilibrium problem

We now consider a series of role changes which take place on "the next rung up" the ladder of microscopic-to-macroscopic contexts in which the general theory of action systems can be applied.

[10] Lippitt, R., "An Experimental Study of Authoritarian and Democratic Group Atmospheres". *Stud. Topolog. Vector Psychol.*, No. 1, Univ. Ia. Stud. Child Welf. 1950, 16.

[11] Rogers, C. R., *Counselling and Psychotherapy: New Concepts in Practice* Boston, Houghton Mifflin, 1942.

Changes in quality of act from one act to the next are on a very microscopic level as to time span involved. Changes in rates of acts of various types through the course of a single meeting are on a more macroscopic level. As we have seen, very much the same sort of general system theory can be applied to both, with proper allowance for changes in conditions which will surely be characteristic of any shift up or down on the microscopic-macroscopic ladder. We now proceed up another rung of the ladder to consider changes that take place from meeting to meeting in a time span of four meetings. And for the present analysis, we shift from a primary emphasis on consideration of interaction rates to a consideration of more "generalized" or partially "structured" roles as reflected in post-meeting ratings and choices of members by each other. Much more detailed treatment of changes within the four meeting time span, using interaction rates as well as post-meeting measures will be given in later publications.

The essential rationale for the ratings and choices we ask members to make at the end of meetings is rooted back in the four types of system problems discussed in the other papers of this collection as the "dimensions" along which system change takes place—the instrumental, adaptive, integrative, and expressive. For present purposes we link the instrumental and adaptive dimensions together to obtain one "pole" of specialization: the instrumental-adaptive pole. On the other side we link the integrative and expressive dimensions together to obtain the integrative-expressive pole.

Toward the instrumental-adaptive pole we distinguish two types of roles: The first is a role emphasizing specifically task-oriented achievement addressed to the problems of the external situation confronting the group. In terms of the type of task we give our groups, this role appears to be fairly well defined operationally by answers to the question: "Who contributed the best ideas for solving the problem? Please rank the members in order. . . . Include yourself." The second type of instrumental-adaptive role we distinguish is one which emphasizes regulation or management of the group process in the service of task oriented achievement—a role approximating that of "chairman" or perhaps in a more general sense that of "executive", (as contrasted with that of "technical specialist" which is the first type of role above). We attempt to get at the second type of role by the question: "Who did the most to guide the discussion and keep it moving effectively? Please rank the members in order. . . . Include yourself."

Toward the integrative-expressive pole we also distinguish two sub-types of roles, but this time according to a "positive-negative" distinction rather than according to an "external-internal" distinction as above. The questions we ask here are fairly orthodox sociometric choice questions—essentially "Who do you like in rank order" and "Who do you dislike in rank order", although we ask them in a somewhat more complicated way that would take unnecessarily long to describe here. Detailed description of scoring methods will also be omitted—by inverting ranks it is possible to obtain high scores for top ranking men and low scores for low ranking men. This is done for greater intuitive ease in grasping the meaning of the data. I shall refer to high ranking men as "receiving the most votes", sacrificing accuracy a bit to convenience.

Now, according to the line of thought embodied in the sample statistical model for reproducing the matrix, and its "rationalization", one might make the following sorts of inferences: Since a man may receive agreement for advancing ideas which appeal to other members, or for making neutral suggestions with procedural content rather than task content, or simply because people like him emotionally, and since agreement tends to encourage a man to go ahead and talk more, we might suppose that such men would tend to have high rates of participation. Conversely, since disagreement tends to discourage a man from talking, and since disagreement is often a manifestation of dislike, we might suppose that dislikes would tend to center around men with low rates of participation. And since the model makes no assumptions about the incompatibilities of these various roles (excepting the incompatibility of Liking and Disliking) we might suppose that the same man—"The Leader" —might receive the most votes on all three roles—Best Ideas, Guidance, and Best Liked, and that another man—"The Scapegoat"— at the bottom of the heap might receive the fewest votes on all three of these virtuous roles, but the most on Dislikes. The simplest assumption is that the votes on each of these roles will grade according to Basic Initiating Rank—the rank on total amounts of participation given out. Such a group we might call a "simply organized group", meaning that no matter what criterion of status were chosen, it would place the men in the same rank order of relative status. Now those who are acutely aware of the lack of such perfect integration of various criteria of status in larger social systems will be likely to suspect that small groups will not be so "simply organized" either. Nevertheless, we had evidence of some appreciable degree of positive correlation of these various status criteria with Basic Initiating Rank, and the hypothesis of the "simply or-

ganized group" was adopted as a working hypothesis for the first
ordering and examination of the data.

Our first major insight with regard to what we now regard as
a basic problem of role structure was obtained from a tabulation
of data from twelve meetings of five-man groups (twelve instead
of sixteen because of absences in four meetings). No distinction
was made as to which meetings in the series of four were represented. The identity of men was not preserved from meeting to
meeting. We simply took each meeting, listed the men in rank order
of total amounts of participation given out, and recorded "the number of votes received" on each role. Then the data for all rank one
men on total acts initiated were pooled, and so for all rank two
men, and so on for the five. The fact that Joe Smith might have
been rank one man in the first meeting, rank two man in the sec-

CHART III

"Total Number of Votes Received" on each of four roles, pooled for men
of each basic initiating rank as of each meeting. (Data from
twelve assorted meetings of four five-man groups).

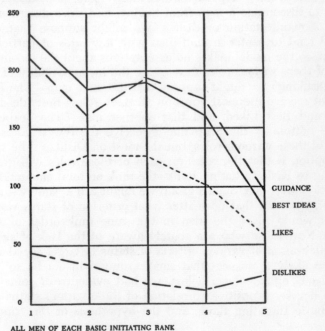

ALL MEN OF EACH BASIC INITIATING RANK

ond, and so on, was ignored. The data are represented in Chart III.

First it may be noted that there is a general gradation of votes on Best Ideas and Guidance by Basic Initiating Rank as expected by the working hypothesis. Second, note that these two curves are very close together and move in the same way, indicating the relative lack of segregation of these roles from each other. But there is a departure from the prediction of the working hypothesis: on both curves the second man is unaccountably low.

But a more serious departure from the prediction is in terms of the curve on Likes. There the top man is unaccountably low, and the second man is highest in the group—by an insignificant margin, but still enough to give birth to the idea: can there be any connection between the fact that the second man, who is unaccountably low on Best Ideas and Guidance, is also Best Liked? Can it be that he is avoiding too heavy participation in the instrumental-adaptive area? Can it be that the man who is participating most heavily and is receiving the most votes on Best Ideas and Guidance is provoking dislikes and losing likes? Here we note the Dislike curve. Contrary to the prediction of the working hypothesis the top man receives *most* Dislikes, and they grade down by rank —until we come to the bottom man, and here the curve shows an upturn. The upturn is consistent with the scapegoat hypothesis.[12] Looking again at the Like curve, we note that although the second man is receiving more likes than the top man, actually both are depressed in terms of an expectation of an evenly graded curve. The new hypothesis is strengthened: there must be something about high participation and specialization in the technical and executive directions which tends to provoke hostility.

Here I think it can be seen that we are dealing with the same equilibrium problem encountered before in attempting to understand the uniformities of the profile, the matrix, and the phase movement. Movement in the instrumental-adaptive direction tends to upset the equilibrium of the system, and recovery mechanisms must be worked out if the system is to turn full cycle and regain equilibrium. The more "directive" and "constricting" the quality of activity, the more likely it is to arouse negative reactions. If a man begins to specialize noticeably in this direction, the negative reactions tend to be centered on him. The displacement of hostilities on a scapegoat at the bottom of the status structure is one mechanism, apparently, by which the ambivalent attitudes toward

[12] Similar curves are found in 3 and 4-man groups. The 6-man groups introduce a special complication at a level of subtlety which is inappropriate to these preliminary generalizations.

the instrumental-adaptive specialist—the "top man"—can be diverted and drained off. The centering of positive affect on a secondary man is another mechanism by which the solidarity of the group—its integration as a collectivity of persons—can be re-established. Such a man can be warm, receptive, responsive, and rewarding, can "conciliate" and "bind up the wounds", without diverting the movement of the system too far from the kind of movement in the instrumental-adaptive direction which is also felt to be necessary. He can do this because he does not assume the "responsibility" for the movement of the system in these directions, but leaves this to the technical or executive specialist.

But suppose the best liked man is not willing to do this? Suppose that his perceptions of the likes of others "goes to his head" and encourages him to begin to "take over" from the technical or executive specialist? He is in a position to command considerable support, and the "top man" is in a vulnerable position because of the latent or overt hostility centered on him. Or suppose, on the other hand, that the top man is emotionally unable to stand the hostility, or is unable to tolerate the fact that not he, but another, is best liked? The top man is under strains, we might suppose, to try to "undercut" his nearest rival. Here are the seeds of a fundamental status struggle, exceedingly damaging, in potentiality, both for the instrumental-adaptive achievement of the group, and for its affective integration. This, as I see it now, is the core of the status struggle we see our groups go through in the course of their four meetings. The first meeting is typically rather cautious and tentative, and such "simply organized groups" as we do find, tend to be found at the end of this meeting. With the second meeting, the role structure which has crystallized, if at all, in the first meeting, is challenged in a status struggle which may result in either confirmation of the first structure, or an exchange of status positions between the top two or three men. If the original structure "holds up", the group may begin to "level out", and the status struggle slacks off. If a new man comes to the top, the *new* structure is challenged in the third meeting. Some groups apparently arrive at a fairly stable differentiated structure, others never do. Things go "from bad to worse", with a last meeting that breaks records for disagreement, antagonism, tension, perhaps tension release, and other signs of serious strains and an inability to achieve an equilibrated role structure.[13] However, the stable structure is never, in

---

[13] This discussion of structure changes by meetings is based upon findings which will appear in a separate paper.

our data, a "simply organized" one. It is rather one in which differentiated roles have appeared, in which one specialist "undoes" the disturbance to equilibrium created by another, and in turn is dependent upon another to remove the strains he himself creates—the total constellation of specialists being one which allows or aids the system to establish a full orbit in its dimensions of necessary movement.

Furthermore, there are probably "typical" solutions which tend to be found with considerable frequency, and may in older and more permanent types of groups, give rise to cultural arrangements and supporting symbol constellations including explicit ritual. Three constellations which are exceedingly ubiquitous, in a cross-cultural sense, come to mind as possibly significant in this connection. They are incest taboos, totem taboos and rituals, and scapegoat patterns. In the experimental small-group setting, of course, nothing concretely resembling these exceedingly complicated and elaborate cultural complexes appears, but certain functional equivalents may be possible.

There is some reason to believe that one possible arrangement by which the status struggle between the top instrumental-adaptive leader and the best liked man can be prevented or stabilized is the formation of a kind of "coalition" between them, such that the two tacitly agree, as it were, not to undercut each other, which is to say, not to be "seduced" into attempting to form a coalition with lower status members in order to displace each other. If such a coalition can be formed, it becomes quite difficult for lower status members to revolt, unseat the top men, or develop the norms of the group in any different direction.

Does this bear any resemblance, in functional terms, to the incest taboo as a cognate mechanism in the nuclear family? Is the incest taboo, at least in certain of its aspects, a kind of coalition between the father (in some family systems comparable to the senior technical and executive specialist) and the mother (similarly often the first major target of positive affect)? Such a coalition could be a powerful mechanism for forcing the socialization of the child, by putting him in a position where he must accept the authority and values of the father in order to obtain gratification, rather than allowing him to retain and overdevelop an affectively gratifying relation to the mother which would leave him insufficient incentive to acquire the skills, values, and other characteristics of the adult role. It may well be, I think, that the ubiquity of the incest taboo as it applies in the nuclear family, is simply another case of the much more general equilibrium problem.

Similarly with totem taboos and rituals. This is not the place for an adequate attempt to examine the problem, but the killing of the totem on certain ritual occasions is certainly suggestive of a ritual display of aggression against the principal authority figures, and the eating of the totem can be viewed as an "undoing"—a re-acceptance of the target of aggression after all. In some cases, as Frazier documents at length, the king himself is killed—the king becomes the scapegoat. In many other cases, as we know, some low status person or group is victimized. These facts are well known, and on one level, fairly well understood. The only new emphasis here, if any, is the suggestion that these patterns, culturally elaborated and various in form, can be viewed as particular cases of mechanisms relevant to the much more general problem of equilibrium, which has cognates on every level, from the most microscopic to the most macroscopic.

These are frankly and obviously speculations at this point. But perhaps they will indicate by example some of the ways in which small group study can form a bridge between the most abstract concepts and generalizations of action theory on the one hand, and the more concrete and elaborated problems of full-scale social systems on the other. To get back to the small group level (and to the point where hard numbers are still considerably behind the graceful soaring of speculations), I think it may be well to indicate briefly some of our earliest findings relating to the "insight" born of the slender evidence of Chart III.

The findings for our five-man groups prompted an investigation into our data on comparable groups of other sizes. In this investigation we made use of all the data available at that time, i.e., 61 group meetings. This represents 14 completed groups (four meetings each), and 2 uncompleted groups (two and three meetings respectively). Five of the completed groups were 6-man groups, four were 5-man, four were 4-man, and one was a 3-man group. Both of the uncompleted groups were 3-man groups.

Our analysis deals with five roles, hypothesized as having leadership potentialities, and capable of being simply derived from our data. These are:

(1) The Top Initiator, i.e., the man who initiates the most interaction, as determined by the "who-to-whom matrix". This role will be designated hereinafter as "TI".

(2) The man who *receives* the most interaction (designated RM), as determined by the who-to-whom matrix.

(3) The man who "has the best ideas" (designated BI), as determined by the rankings made by the members in the post-meeting questionnaires.

(4) The man who "does the most to guide the discussion" (designated G), as determined by post-meeting questionnaire rankings.

(5) The man who is best liked (designated L), as determined by the sociometric ratings in the post-meeting questionnaires.[14]

The question now arises, which of these roles represents "The leader"? Our findings suggest, I think, that this question is in one sense meaningless, since all of these roles are "leadership" roles. To think in terms of "*a* leader" is, however, not only traditional, but useful, and a partial answer to the question can be found. A section is included in the questionnaire at the close of the last meeting of each group, asking the subjects to rank each other in terms of whom they considered to be the leader of the group, taking all four meetings into consideration. With these rankings as a base we should be able to get a rough notion as to which of the five roles are considered *by the subjects* to be most closely related to overall "leadership".

Unfortunately, the available data on this question are rather inadequate, since we have only ten separate groups who gave usable "leader" rankings. Table V, however, shows the results, which are at least suggestive. The figures represent the number of cases in which the chosen "leader" corresponded with the man who played the role in question most often during the four meetings. The decimals are created by ties in the role rankings, the incidence of which is, in our data, statistically small but methodologically provoking.

Table V suggests that the Best Ideas and Guidance roles are most closely associated in the subjects' minds with leadership, and that the Best-Liked role is *least* closely associated with leadership. Additional confirmation for this hypothesis may be found in the fact that in *no* case was the "leader" neither the Idea man nor the Guidance man. That the Best-Liked role was associated at all with leadership may therefore have been due to the fact that these two instances were also the *only* ones in which the Best-Liked role and either the Guidance or Idea roles were played by the same man.

[14] It should be emphasized that in all of the presentation which follows we are dealing only with "top" men on each of these criteria.

TABLE V

Subject's Concept of Leadership

	(10 Cases)
ROLE TYPES	Number of Groups in which person described as "Leader" played the role most consistently over the four meetings
TI (Top Initiator)	5.3
RM (Received Most)	5.5
BI (Best Ideas)	7.5
G (Guidance)	7.5
L (Liked)	2.0

The five-man group data indicated some specialization of role, in that the Best-Liked role was differentiated from the others by actor. Table VI shows the degree of role specialization among all of the five roles. The figures here represent the number of cases (in percentages) in which any pair of roles were played by the same man. Once again it is apparent that the Best-Liked role is the most specialized, in the sense that the man playing this role is least likely to play another role simultaneously. The two roles most closely associated, in the minds of the subjects, with "leadership"— Ideas and Guidance—are played by the Best Liked man only 30 percent and 27 percent of the time, respectively.

TABLE VI

Matrix of Role Correspondence

Percentage of Meetings in which each type of two-role combination was performed by the same man.

(61 Cases)

	TI	RM	BI	G	L
TI		62.3	60.3	44.6	25.4
RM	62.3		45.6	35.6	37.7
BI	60.3	45.6		54.9	30.0
G	44.6	35.6	54.9		27.0
L	25.4	37.7	30.0	27.0	
Totals	192.6	181.2	190.8	162.1	120.1

It is rather surprising that all of the figures are as low as they are, since presumably there is a tendency, in those roles determined by subjects' rankings (BI, G, and L), toward carryover from one ranking to another. For example, it seems likely that if subject A likes subject B best, and rates him most highly on Guidance, he will be somewhat inclined to rate him highly on Best Ideas. Be that as it may, the closest correspondence among these three roles is that between BI and G, which is only 54.9 percent, while the highest figure in the entire matrix is 62.3 percent (TI and RM).

The totals in Table VI provide a crude measure of the degree to which each role is likely to be associated with others, or conversely, the degree to which it is specialized. Once again the Best-Liked role shows the least correspondence with other roles.

The Best-Liked role is not only differentiated by actor from the other roles in the overall picture, but also shows *increasing* differentiation over time. This is especially true vis-a-vis the two "leadership" roles, the Idea and Guidance roles. Table VII shows the trend over time of correspondence between the Best-Liked and Idea roles and between the Best-Liked and Guidance roles. The percentages indicate the number of cases in which such correspondence occurred, by meetings, and Chart IV represents these trends graphically.

TABLE VII

Changes over time in the percentage of cases in which the "L" role coincides with the "B" and "G" roles.

(61 Cases)

MEETING NUMBER	I	II	III	IV
L with BI	64.4	18.8	23.3	10.7
L with G	40.6	35.6	12.0	17.9

CHART IV

Change over time in Percentage of cases in which Best Liked man played other roles (by meeting)

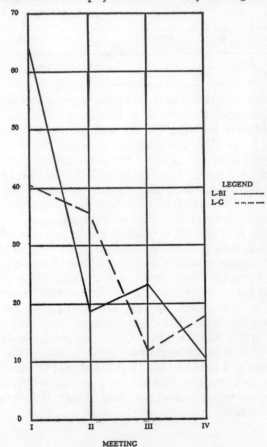

LEGEND
L-BI ———
L-G — — —

MEETING

CHART V

Change over time in Percentage of cases in which Best Liked man played "Leader" roles (BI and G), Average of two curves in Chart IV (by meeting)

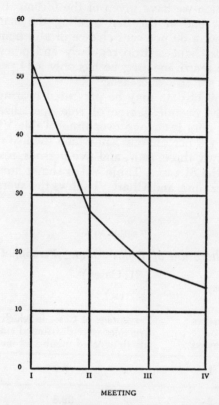

MEETING

Since the Idea and Guidance roles are equally "leader" roles, yet to a considerable degree differentiated by actor, it would perhaps be useful to average the two sets of figures. That is, the merely moderate degree of correspondence between Ideas and Guidance means that when Best-Liked is associated more with one, there will be a partial lessening of its association with the other. This is apparent in Chart IV, in which the two curves show a strong tendency to diverge at each point.

When the two sets of figures are averaged, the curve in Chart V is obtained. This curve might be said to represent the change in correspondence over time between the Best-Liked role and the "leader" role (as suggested by Table V). This is perhaps the most striking presentation we have given of the incompatibility of these two roles. At the end of the first meeting the man regarded as "Leader" has about a 50 per cent chance of also being Best Liked. From then on his chances drop regularly and precipitously, until at the end of the fourth meeting he has only a 14 per cent chance, and his chances are still decreasing.

One further bit of data may be presented bearing on the question: What is the *overall* degree of role specialization in these groups, and how does it change over time? Table VIIIa shows the number of cases (in percentages) in which the five roles were performed by one, two, three, four, and five persons, respectively, and the average for the 61 cases. Table VIIIb shows how this distribution changed over time, and Chart VI shows the average trend over time.

TABLE VIII

Allocation of Roles Among Personnel

(61 Cases)

(a)

NUMBER OF PERSONS	Percentage of Cases in which the five roles were distributed among the designated number of men
1	8.2
2	39.3
3	45.9
4	4.9
5	1.6
2.52	Average number of men playing five roles

(b)

Changes over time
(*by meeting*)

NUMBER OF PERSONS	I	II	III	IV
1	25.0	6.3	—	—
2	37.5	43.8	33.3	42.9
3	31.3	43.8	60.0	50.0
4	6.3	6.3	6.7	—
5	—	—	—	7.1
Average Number of Men	2.19	2.50	2.73	2.71

The average number of persons playing the five roles was 2.52, but this average tended to increase over time, showing an increase in role specialization. To be sure, the change illustrated in Chart VI is a small one, but interestingly enough, it is considerably greater than the change by size, which appears in Table IX.

We can conclude from these findings that some degree of role specialization is the rule in groups of this kind, and that such specialization tends to increase over time. The "simply organized group", in which one "leader" plays all five roles, is a comparatively rare occurrence in our data, and where it does appear, it tends to break down, in time, as Chart VII illustrates.

The implications of these preliminary findings are important in making distinctions between different types of leadership situations. We might tentatively advance the proposition that the traditional sociometric methods of determining "leaders" are appropriate only to situations where there is no specific and well-defined instrumental task. As soon as such a task is introduced there arises a demand for the performance of the new roles which the task creates. Initially the best liked man may perform these roles, but as time goes on, a dissociation takes place: either (1) someone else who can perform these new roles more successfully comes to the fore, or (2) the sociometric leader becomes a task leader and ceases to be best liked.

CHART VI

Index of Role Specialization (by meeting)

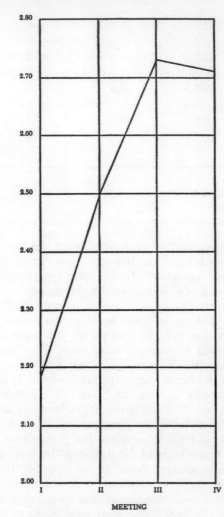

TABLE IX
Index of Role Specialization by Size
(61 Cases)

SIZE GROUP	Average Number of Men Playing the Five Roles
3-Man	2.50
4-Man	2.50
5-Man	2.50
6-Man	2.59

CHART VII

Changes over time in Percentage of cases in which
one man played all five roles. (by meeting)

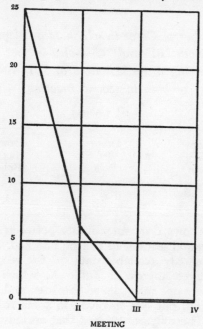

Essentially, it appears, we are dealing with the same problem of equilibrium that helps us understand the more microscopic levels of the profile, who-to-whom matrix, and phase movement. There we noted that as the quality of action moves from orientation to evaluation to control, negative reactions increase. Each transition, we may even say each instrumental *act*, disturbs to some degree the equilibrium which the system has achieved. The larger the disturbance, the more pronounced the negative reactions will become (thereby intensifying the need for reëquilibrating acts to occur). The Idea man is the one most prone to equilibrium-disturbing acts through his constant movement toward the instrumental goal, and hence he is most likely to arouse hostility. The value of the role he plays is so great for the group, however, that there are severe limitations on the amount of hostility which can be directed toward him, and as a result much of it may be displaced onto someone with low status. But at the same time this hostility places a strain on the friendly feelings of the group toward the Idea man, thereby lowering his sociometric position.

TABLE X

Number of Cases in which Man Playing
Both "BI" and "L" Roles in first
Meeting drops "L" Role or "BI" Role
or both in second meeting.

(10 Cases)

Drops "L" Role	Drops "BI" Role	Drops Both Roles
0	9	1

This tendency toward incompatibility between sociometric stardom and instrumental leadership can be handled, as we have said, in two ways. The only available data on the relative frequencies of these alternatives appear in Table X, which deals with ten cases in which the same man played the Idea and Best-Liked roles in the first meeting, but was involved in some role change in the second meeting. These figures suggest that an individual is unlikely to give up his high popularity position in order to become an instrumental leader. We might even guess (although this is a rather big jump) that some fundamental inability to "take" hostility was the origin of his striving for sociometric leadership in the first place. We appear to have arrived at a place where research on personality factors can be integrated most effectively with small group research.

We have begun to develop a systematic picture of the constellation of dynamically related roles that the group process tends to generate as a result of its equilibrating tendencies. We should now like to know more about the personality factors which cause particular individuals to seek to attain, or withdraw from given types of roles in this constellation.

CHAPTER 5

PHASE MOVEMENT IN
RELATION TO MOTIVATION,
SYMBOL FORMATION,
AND ROLE STRUCTURE

BY TALCOTT PARSONS,
ROBERT F. BALES
AND EDWARD A. SHILS

I. Introduction

In this paper, the last of the series of working papers in this collection,[1] we attempt to work through our major concepts again, tightening up their logical relations, removing inconsistencies where we have been able, drawing new deductions, and generally attempting to produce a more coherent and rigorous theoretical structure than we had earlier. It hardly need be said that we are not entirely satisfied with the results. There are many difficulties which prevent us from drawing sufficiently rigorous deductions, some of which we know about, and no doubt many others which we hope our colleagues will call to our attention. We regard this simply as another platform from which to work, and hope that the reader will regard it in a similar way. In particular we may mention that some changes in terminology have been made, to which we will call attention in appropriate places.

We will build on the analysis of Chapter 3 above, utilizing the fundamental concepts developed there and elsewhere in our work. The most important of these are, we may remind the reader, the

[1] It may be useful to state again that the papers in the collection are printed in the historical order in which they were written.

conception of four dimensions, which correspond to the four system-problems of Bales and which are defined in terms of the pattern variable concepts of Parsons and Shils; the conception of location and movement; the interaction categories of Bales, which are also articulated with the pattern-variable concepts; the paradigms for the analysis of deviance and social control of Parsons' earlier publications; and the analysis of symbolism and symbolic process developed in Chapter 2 above.

We make four major assumptions in our analysis of boundary-maintaining systems which are composed of a plurality of units, or "particles". We assume first, the *principle of inertia*, namely that a unit or "particle" always tends to move in the same direction at a constant rate unless deflected or impeded. Since the behavior of units in systems is concerned, this is empirically a limiting case. In no concrete case of system-process can this constancy of direction and rate be maintained for any span of time, since the interdependence of units is the very essence of the conception of system. Hence, the conception of *orbit* in mechanics is a relevant analogy here. The unit in a stable state of the system will tend to follow a sequential *pattern of changes* of direction as its relations to the other units in the system and to the external situation change over time. This sequence may be oscillatory or cyclical or it may have some other form, but it will always involve changes of direction (and of rate). These changes will, furthermore, not be entirely random, they will always follow a pattern, although there may be some random elements intermixed with the pattern. This conception of the orbit of the action-process is integral to that of phase movement which will figure prominently in our subsequent discussion. It is applicable both to the unit and to the system as a whole, the latter distinction being a matter of points of reference, not of the concrete structure of processes.

Second, we assume the principle that *action and reaction* tend to be equal in "force" and opposite in direction. We interpret this to be another version of, or a premise underlying, the conception of system-equilibrium. No more than the statement of the principle of inertia does the statement of this principle imply that actions and reactions *empirically* are always equal and opposite; it does imply that where they are not equal and opposite, a problem is presented. The conception of equilibrium implies that where they are not, the source of the discrepancy, the excess or deficit of "input" must lie *outside* the set of variables which constitute the stable state of the system. For example, in a process of small group interaction the source of discrepancy may be in situational change or in the personality system of one of the members.

Third, we assume a *principle of acceleration* which asserts that changes of rate of process must be accounted for by "forces" operating on (or in) the unit(s) in question. An increase of rate implies an "input" of energy from a source outside the unit in question, and a decrease of rate, a loss of energy, an "output" of some sort from the unit. This whole problem of input and output with respect to action systems will be taken up after we have had the opportunity to lay the proper groundwork for its consideration.

Fourth, we assume the principle of *system-integration*. We interpret this to mean that, *independently* of the operation of the other three principles, there is an imperative placed on systems of action which requires that pattern-elements in the organization of their components should be compatible with each other while maintaining the boundaries of the system vis-a-vis its external situation. Put a little differently, the consequence of the continued coexistence of incompatible or conflicting patterns will be, in the milder cases, tendencies toward change of state and low levels of integration, and at the extreme, dissolution of the system.[2] We therefore assume that the incorporation of a new pattern in conflict with some pattern already present in the system—including of course the development of emotional investments in both—will set up tendencies to resolution of the conflict. The most radical resolution would be the extrusion of one or the other pattern; but short of this, various types of accommodation and adjustment which amount to a change of system state may be found.

Major Problem Orientations

Central to our scheme of analysis is the conception of action as a *process* occurring in or constituting boundary-maintaining *systems* conceived within a given frame of reference. This frame of reference involves, above all, the four dimensions which in Chapter 3 we derived by bringing together the four system-problems of Bales and four of the five pattern-variables of Parsons and Shils.

[2] In Chapter 3 we pointed out that this principle of system-integration was a more general statement of what had been meant by the "law of effect" in psychology. We would like to suggest here that it is fundamentally the same as "natural selection" as that principle is used in modern biological theory; that its importance is a consequence of the existence of boundary-maintaining systems, a property shared by organisms and systems of action.

The two postulates which we discussed in Chapter 3 as underlying the pattern-variable antitheses mean that the dimensions constitute not just a list but *two pairs of opposites*. Hence their order is not arbitrary. These two postulates were, it will be remembered, first, that of the *one-way* character of the action process, from motivational input toward gratification, and second, that of the independence of adaptive and integrative exigencies, which we now interpret to be involved in, or to be another way of stating, the assumption that we are dealing with boundary-maintaining systems.

We have noted above that a given amount of motivational energy cannot, at the same time, be both expended on an instrumental process and "stored up" for later use: these are independent directions of its flow. Correspondingly, if such energy is to be activated it cannot in the same degree be both devoted to the manipulation of objects (including other units in the system) in an instrumental sense and to the expression of attitudes of solidarity or antagonism with them at the same time. Both components are present, but they cannot both be maximized at the same time, it is in this sense that they are antithetical. This is another manifestation of the general antitheses which were built into the original pattern-variable scheme, according to which an orientation cannot be both maximally universalistic and particulistic at the same time or both affective and neutral.

The dimensions are, we assume, essentially directional coordinates with reference to which the process of action is analyzed. Motivational energy entering the system from an organism cannot simultaneously operate in all the possible processes which go to make up the system. It must be specifically *located*, in the sense that it must be allocated to one or more units of the system. But at any given time this unit must be located at some definite point in the action space, and must be moving, i.e. changing its properties, in a definite manner. The dimensional scheme assumes that energy must either be "stored up" in the reservoir or it must be "expended" through transformation into gratification (satisfaction). There must be a balance between these since it is by definition (if the dimensions are independent) impossible for the same quantum of energy to go in both directions at once. Similarly there is a basic alternative as between orientation to adaptive and to integrative exigencies. The one involves primacy of the cognitive-instrumental components of the orientation system, the other of the expressive components and both cannot have primacy at the same time.

Within this dimensional framework, then, we conceive of process as occurring in a system which is treated as a point of reference. The system operates through the interaction of its member units. Every change of state of one unit, i.e. in its location in relation to any or all of the dimensions, in its energy charge, etc. will affect all the other units in the system and in turn the effects of these effects on the other units will "feed back" to the original unit. We conceive here of an unbroken "circular" process of interdependence which is analyzed in terms of the concept of equilibrium. Because of the dominant role of symbolism in action, of which we have spoken so often, we assign to the process of communication a particularly crucial part in the mechanisms of this interdependent equilibrating-disequilibrating process. Bales' twelve categories of interaction are primarily to be interpreted as types of communication, seen within this framework, and it is through them that the "feed back" processes occur.

From these fundamental premises of a four-dimensional scheme and a conception of a boundary-maintaining system of interdependent units, we derive next the conclusion that systems of action must be treated as *differentiated* systems. It then becomes clear that this differentiation will work out in two ways. Since we are dealing with processes which occur in a temporal order, therefore we must treat systems and the processes of their units as changing *over* time. The major uniformities of process occurring in a given time period as over against those uniformities which precede or follow it in time, we shall call the *phases* of action pattern, and a major part of our discussion below will be devoted to the discussion of these phases.[3]

The differentiation of action process over time is one of the two major modes of its differentiation. The other is the differentiation of patterns which are relatively constant *through* time. Essentially we may say such constancies are repetitive elements in phase or orbit patterns of the process. When we say that one unit is differentiated from others with respect to leadership in the task-fulfillment process, we do not mean to say that it—e.g. the member of a small group—displays no activity in the social-emotional sphere, but that overall he displays more of certain types of activity than do others in the group, and that these activities are concentrated at certain phases of the system-process. It is these uniformities of pattern which recur through a succession of phase-movements or cycles of them to which we refer as the *structural* patterns of a system of action. In the following, therefore,

[3] An empirical analysis of phases in small groups will be found in Chapter 4.

we will treat the phase patterns and the structural differentiation of systems as derived from the same common roots in the general character of action process, as analyses of *the same concrete phenomena* seen only in somewhat different perspectives.

In discussing phases, however, it is essential to keep in mind the difference between the phases of change of state of the system as a system on the one hand, and of each unit of the system on the other. Phases of system state are, we assume, to be regarded as resultants of phase changes in the units which are also systems. There is no one-to-one correspondence between the phase of a system and the phases of the constituent units at any point in time. On the contrary, it is inherent in the conception of differentiated system process that different units should, at any one time, be found at different phases of their process patterns. In order to keep this distinction clear we have taken the liberty of borrowing from mechanics the term "orbit" to designate the phase-pattern of a unit in the system, as distinguished from that of the system as a whole. An orbit then is a pattern of successively differentiated states of the unit of a system, analyzed with respect to the dimensional scheme: it is compared and articulated on the one hand with the phase-patterns of the orbits of other units, on the other with the phase pattern of the system as such.

The distinction between unit and system is, of course, relative. What is a unit in terms of one point of reference may always be treated as a system from another; this view of macroscopic-microscopic relations is fundamental to our whole treatment of action. But within this relativity it is always essential to be clear what is the system-reference; we should be clear whether we are referring to the system as such, the system within which it is functioning, or the systems of the units which constitute it.

The conceptions of action-process and the relations between units in systems constitute one major framework for our analysis. Intertwined with this but requiring somewhat separate analysis are two related sets of considerations. The first has to do with the basic duality of the action frame of reference, a duality which consists in the fact that every action phenomenon involves the relation of actor and situation or object. The second set of considerations has to do with the crucial position of symbolic processes in the action frame of reference.

We have insisted all along that action is a one-way process. This does not preclude the existence and fundamental importance of a duality of aspects of this process. The one-way character of the process we have deduced from the nature of motivational energy—the fact that it is "expended" in action. We assume throughout and will discuss in some detail below that there is, if not a law of conservation of motivational energy, a law of "equivalence" in the sense that this energy does not simply disappear, but "produces" some kind of consequences, that there is a balancing of input and output. We believe, though at this time we cannot prove, that this is a quantitative balance which will eventually prove to be reducible to terms of numerical equivalence. Indeed we feel that such a postulate is integral to the conception of equilibrium itself, which is obviously central to our whole analysis, and that the principle of the equivalence of action and reaction which we have stated in Chapter 3 is in fact a statement of this postulate.

Therefore we have endeavored in what is said below to approach the conceptualization of this balance in such a way as to be in conformity with our postulate of one-way process, by using the concepts of gratification and satisfaction to designate the outputs which in any action process balance motivational input. But this aspect of our conceptual scheme takes account only of one aspect of the duality of actor and object. There is, we suggest, a process not only of the creation of motivational states in the units of systems of action as a consequence of the investment of motivational energy in their action, but there must also be *process* with reference to the objects, and their relations to the action system must *change* through action, just as much as does the motivational state of the actors.

Our whole analysis of these problems is focused on processes of and in *systems* of action. Therefore we have found it necessary to distinguish two fundamentally different classes of consequences of action process so far as the object components are concerned. On the one hand we think of changes in the *relations* of the system or of motivated units in the system to objects including the system or one or more of its units as objects. This aspect, following the terminology of *The Social System*, we will deal with in terms of the category of "possessions", subdivided into facilities and rewards. The second class concerns the *properties* of the system and of their constituent units as *themselves objects*. Here we speak of the processes of learning in their broadest sense as the processes by which the properties of action systems become changed, and of the output of such processes as "accomplishment" as distinguished from "achievement" of valued relations to objects of possession. We have above given ground for the view that accomplishment consists in change in the symbolic pattern of the meaning components of an action system, which, when a stable state has been reached, we would speak of with reference to a personality system as "internalized" and with reference to a social system as "institutionalized".

As a process of output contrasted with the inputs of motivational energy, of perception of objects, of facilities and rewards as the two primary categories of possessions, we thus treat the learning process as "opposite" in directionality from the motivational input processes. This must not be interpreted as a denial of our postulate of the one-way character of the process of action. It refers to what happens to the components out of which action systems are built up, the production, out of objects and their prior system of relationships, of a new pattern of these relationships which itself produces new objects that had not previously existed.

The performance processes by which motivational energy is transformed into gratification and satisfaction, and the processes of acquisition of possessions and of learning by which new objects and new object-relations are produced, form the locus of the mechanisms of the process of action. Essentially what we are attempting to do in this analysis is to provide a framework for the development of more detailed analyses of the patterns of interdependence involved in the processes of action.

The distinction between performance and learning aspects of action process forms the basis for a further classification of types of process in systems, which has emerged from our work and will be treated in some detail below. In general we feel that the type of analysis which Bales has presented of the processes of interaction in small groups, in the most extensive form yet attained in Chapter 4 above, provides a model for the typical performance process where the primary concern is not with changes in the properties of the group and its constituent role-units, but with task-performance, that is. in the terminology we are adopting here, with attainment of a system-goal. The general type of analysis here developed can, we feel, be extended from the microscopic study of small groups under controlled conditions for short periods to large-scale social phenomena over longer periods and with appropriate modifications, to the analysis of personality as a system.

Bales' analysis, however, has not been extended yet to cases where vicious circles of deviance become firmly established, nor the processes by which these vicious circles can be reversed, in the processes of therapy and through other modes of social control. It was an entirely unexpected outcome of the work done in preparation for writing this chapter that the basic pattern of phases which Bales had developed in the study of small groups and which appears to be capable of generalization beyond that for a variety of types of performance processes, turned out to fit with remarkable exactitude the basic processes of social control and of socialization, if it were applied *in reverse*. That is to say, the patterns of behavior which are characteristic of the later phases of a performance process, namely tension release and the affirmation of solidarity, must come in the early phases of processes of social control and socialization; only when their consequences have been worked through is it then possible for the learning of specific content to take place. We might say that in the performance case, the processes of task-orientation create social-emotional strains which must be worked through before the group is ready for a new phase of goal-attainment. In the case of learning, on the other hand, a social-emotional foundation must be laid down before the more specific orientations can be assimilated. All of this will be analyzed in some detail in sections 2 and 3 below.

The more detailed treatment of the structure of systems of action has been reserved for the final section of this chapter. We have done this because we wish to emphasize as strongly as possible that structural analysis is not theoretically independent of the analysis of process. but makes use of the same fundamental components and relations. Above all we have noted that the phases of system-process are derived from the same roots as are the modes of structural differentiation of systems. We did not feel that this crucial proposition would be fully clear to the reader unless we had taken him through the whole analysis of process before we confronted him with our approach to the analysis of system-structure.

In concluding these introductory remarks, we feel it desirable to refer to the difficulties of presentation of the type of analysis we are here concerned with. Our concentration on systems and their properties means that there are inherent limitations on the adequacy of discursive exposition. We must adopt some tabular form which makes it possible for the reader to grasp the inter-relations of a variety of factors simultaneously. But in the absence of an adequate mathematical model, any feasible form chosen necessarily involves elements of arbitrariness which all too readily become distortions. We have chosen one such mode of presentation in the sections which follow, but in order to counteract any tendency to reify such a scheme, we have thought it best to say explicitly that it is arbitrary, that there are many possible types of models appropriate to the fundamental ideas, that we have experimented with several and are looking for others. We feel that in the present stage of development of this type of theory it is exceedingly important to be highly pragmatic about these matters and to try out a variety of devices. Only in such a way can we be protected against a premature rigidity of formulations which may be an artifact of a method of presentation rather than an inherent consequence of relations in the subject-matter itself.

This problem in particular touches the relations between Bales' categories of interaction and the other components of our conceptual scheme, namely the system-problems and pattern variables reinterpreted as dimensions, the input-output categories, the paradigms of deviance and social control, and the categorization of structure. We have long been aware that the interaction categories constituted more detailed "indices" of what we regard as the critical variables of the system. It seems to us now that these indices can be related to the fundamental variables, not just in one "right" way, but in more than one way. More work will need to be done before we feel that we can confidently limit ourselves to any one of the possibilities and ignore the others.

II. The System As a Point of Reference

We would like to enlarge a bit on this section on the importance of being aware of the variety of possible system-references. We conceive the conceptual scheme of the theory of action to be applicable over a range running all the way from the behavioral systems of elementary organisms to the most complex social and cultural systems, and on the human level, from the elementary learning processes of the infant to the processes of development of historical change in the most complex societies. At every point, the scheme deals with at least *two* adhacent "levels"—the level of unit and that of system. One must be clear whether the "point of reference" of his concepts is the *unit* or the *system of units*, otherwise he is plagued with subtle semantic ambiguities that are extremely difficult to resolve.

The microscopic-macroscopic range which is in the center of our attention in this paper is cross-cut by the complication involved in the relations between social systems and personalities as systems. Since in this paper we are directly concerned only with systems of social interaction we will not attempt to explore this aspect of the matter thoroughly here but will refer the reader to the treatment of it by Parsons and Shils in *Values, Motives and Systems of Action.* Here we need only to emphasize that we do *not* consider a personality to be a microcosm of a social system or conversely a society to be a "projection" of the personalities of its members. Though not only interdependent but interpenetrating, personalities and social systems are independent system references neither of which is reducible to terms of the other. This will be taken for granted in all the discussion which follows.

In considering microscopic-macroscopic relations, the point of reference we have tried to maintain all the way through this paper, and which should be adopted in the reading of the tables and in

Figure 1. *The System, Member Units, and Situation*

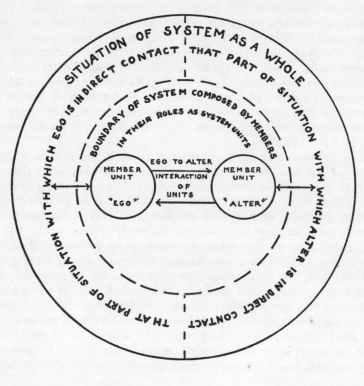

finding the appropriate referents of the concepts, is the *system*. Every system is conceived to be made up of two or more *units* or *members* which interact with each other. The system is conceived to be embedded in an environing *situation*. Each unit of the system typically has direct contact with some parts of the situation environmental to the system as a whole, but typically not with all. Similarly, each unit in the system has direct contact with some other units in the system, but not necessarily with all. The system as a whole may be said to change its relation to its situation *only through the interaction* of its units with each other and with entities outside the system. Similarly, the system is conceived to change its internal state only through the interaction of its units. Figure 1 illustrates the logical relation of these terms.

The position of the system with regard to its situation is described in terms of the four dimensions. Conversely, the four dimensions are dimensions within which *the system* moves. The units move the system but their own locations are specified only with regard to their effect on system movement. When we speak of "adaptation," we mean the adaptation *of the system* as a whole to its situation, which is achieved through the interaction of member units. When we speak of adaptive-instrumental activity, we mean the *inter*action of member units viewed in terms of its relevance to *system* adaptation. And so on for each of the other dimensions and types of activity. We intend never to speak of a unit without implying the existence of other units with which it is in interaction.

The important thing to note is that with the system as the center of the analysis, the member is treated as a *unit*, that is, the unit is treated as *undifferentiated*, as if it were not a system, but as if it were a *particle*, and is described only in its relation to other particles or a system of particles. This is an extremely difficult point of view to maintain, unless "common sense" habits of thinking are overcome, since another of our fundamental postulates is that whatever one may choose to treat as a unit for a given analysis, may, *by the appropriate shift in point of reference*, be treated as a system, itself made up of member units of some kind. It is upon this assumption that we maintain that the conceptual scheme can be applied up and down a wide range of microscopic and macroscopic systems. But when the scheme is applied to a more microscopic or macroscopic system, *the point of reference changes*, and hence the empirical referents of all the concepts and variables also change.[4] And from any vantage point, there will always be member units which from *that* vantage point are not analyzed as systems, but treated as units or particles, with certain given properties that are not treated as problematic. The maintenance of this perspective constitutes *one* of the principal differences between technical theoretical analysis as we are attempting it here, and the "common sense" treatment of the same empirical materials.

To illustrate briefly, the interaction of a small group of persons may be taken as a system, and their interaction classified with reference to the system they compose. This is what Bales does when he classifies the activities of the group he observes. The member units are persons in their capacities as actors in that group. The persons are treated as units, each is given an identification number, and particular acts are attributed to a particular person *as a unit*. To put it in the obverse, the act is *not* attributed to some *part* of a personality, such as the ego, or the unconscious, or a particular need or the like. This would be to treat the personality as a system on an inappropriate level of analysis. One obtains some description of the properties of a given person or unit *later,* by adding up his "profile"—all the acts he performed,—but one does not know, at this point in the analysis, to what degree the profile is a function of different parts or needs of the person in interplay with each other, and to what degree it is a function of the position of the person in the group. One can most appropriately say that he has a picture of the "orbit" that this person has travelled in reference to the group or system process as a whole, which is the point of reference.

If one wishes to account for the properties of something formerly treated as a unit, in terms other than its membership in a system, then one *changes the point of reference,* and now treats the former unit as a system. Thus, one might wish to change his point of reference and center his analysis on one of the individuals as a personality system rather than as the incumbent of a single role.[5] The personality will be treated as made up of member units of

[4] The reader will note that the theory of mechanics applies what is logically, exactly the same procedure.

[5] We emphasize that the "personality" as a *total* system of action reaction cycles is *not* a more microscopic system than the small group in a *single* action reaction cycle. The range from microscopic to macroscopic we think of as involving the time span required for some relevant action-reaction cycle of the system to take place, and the number of member units necessary to take into account.

some kind, possibly need-dispositions. One will now trace the relation of the system—the personality—to its situation, in terms of the interaction of the need-dispositions with each other, the kinds of internal conflicts involved, the compromises and coalitions between needs, and the resulting structure. One would never speak of a need-disposition without assuming other need-dispositions with which it is interacting.

On the other hand, one might wish to understand more about behavior in a group than he can understand by considering it as a system on that level, and so might shift to a more macroscopic level, taking as his point of reference the system which is some larger organization of which the group is a part. In this case, the larger organization is the system—the point of reference—and the particular group is now treated as an undifferentiated unit, in interaction with *other units* which make up a larger system. On this level one would never speak of this group without assuming that there are other groups (units) with which this one is in interaction. When we speak of an entity as a unit we thus abstract from its *internal* structure and processes and attribute all observations to the unit as such. But this does not imply that it does not, as a unit, have *several* properties.

In actual research, of course, one pursues the analysis on as many levels as he likes, or feels he needs to, but he should be aware of the various levels, and be quite clear as to what he is taking as the system point of reference when he attempts to apply these concepts to his empirical material. If the level is not kept clear, each concept will have multiple referents, the descriptions given of a single referent or piece of behavior will conflict with each other, and intolerable confusion will result. For example, a single concrete act of a given individual may be said to have a *goal-attainment* emphasis, as a piece of neurotic acting-out (when the personality of the individual is taken as the system point of reference) an *integrative* emphasis as an act of compromise (when the interaction process of a small group is taken as the system point of reference) and an *adaptive-instrumental* emphasis as an item in a factual report handed to a staff superior (when the larger organization is taken as the system point of reference). This is simply another way of saying that our only way of describing behavior in this conceptual scheme is in *relational* terms—that is, in relation to some system taken as the point of reference. If one wishes to take measurements from several points of reference, he should realize that the measurements are apt to differ.

Now a closely related, but not identical general point must be made, namely, that a certain *time span* is inevitably assumed when one speaks of a system. The system consists of the interaction of units, and this means that some process of action and reaction of units has to completed before one can give a description of any *state* of the system as a whole, or any change of state. This is important in understanding the figures and charts which follow. There is a time span assumed, and the cells describing different phases of the system have a temporal relation to each other as well as a point of reference which is a system made up of member units. If we assume that as a logical minimum for constructing our categories we will have to take into account at least two member units, then it seems to follow that our time span will have to involve *at least* four temporally distinct segments: 1) a segment during which the system is described as a latent structure, potentially ready to function in some way, 2) a segment during which one member unit acts, 3) a segment during which the other member unit reacts, and 4) a segment during which the system is described in terms of its resulting latent structure, possibly changed in some way from its former state. The numbers of stages of interaction between the two latent segments are in reality likely to be far more numerous than the minimum of two mentioned above. All that we wish to stress here is that the process in time comes full cycle and even though the content of the latent state is different at the end from what it was at the beginning, both are latent. It should be stressed that the second latent state is not at all necessarily the final state of the system or subsystem under consideration. The cycle between latency (1) and latency (4) is a microscopic oscillatory movement within a macroscopic movement which in its turn might also display this oscillatory tendency.

The exposition about a particular table starts with an "input" of some kind in the latent cell, the process is traced through the other three phases, involving actions and reactions of member units, and an "output" of some kind is traced back to some result in the latent cell again. In other words, time segments 1 and 4 as described above are both represented in the latent cell, and the other cells on the figures describe events in time segments 2 and 3. The reader should note especially that the four time segments described above can *not* be matched in a one-to-one relation with the four cells representing phases of system movement. The latent cell does "double duty" by representing both the "before" and "after" states that are inferred. It should be clear that any finite set of concepts constructed to be applicable to an infinite one way process of empirical events will have to ignore time differences at some point, and treat the end of some series of events as the beginning of a new cycle somehow comparable to the last.

Thus although in the first half of this section we discussed system-references as though they were relevant only to unit-system interrelations at a given moment in time, the concept of system-reference is applicable on the intertemporal scale as well. It is indeed a further complication of the more elementary system-reference problem. Just as there are system-reference problems arising from the simultaneous coexistence of units, their inclusive subsystems and their still more inclusive systems, so there are system-reference problems in which the units, subsystems, systems and so on are strung out along a time dimension, with the number and properties of units remaining relatively constant throughout. Many macroscopic problems are not problems of the large scale system with a larger and more differentiated structure; many of them are indeed primarily intertemporal system-reference problems. Microphasic movements of units or systems are embedded in macrophasic movements of varying orders of inclusiveness. A system such as a small group or a family has its characteristic sequence of phase movements over a single hour. It has its characteristic longer phase movements over a week, over a month, over a year, and over longer periods of time.[6] Each more inclusive or macroscopic phase is composed of a series of the microphasic movements, the orbits of the unit or system in the microphase having forms which are correlated to the macrophase. There is not however, a one-to-one correlation of particular phases on the more microscopic and macroscopic levels. Indeed, while a system is in a given macrophase, its temporal subsystems are likely to have been passing through a whole series of cycles of microphases.

We will sometimes couch our descriptions in terms of a small group as the system point of reference, sometimes in terms of larger organizations made up of groups as the member units, sometimes in terms of personalities, sometimes in terms of a larger temporal span, sometimes in terms of a very brief observational span. Some ideas are more easily understood on one level than another, and in general we will try to take the easiest way. We

[6] The kind of phenomena to which we refer have been treated by investigators of business cycles under the names of "long waves" and "short waves". Cf. J. Schumpeter. *Business Cycles.*

hope to keep the reader warned when we shift the system point of reference, but freely admit that we have ourselves had many confusions on this problem, and can hardly hope we have removed them all.

III. Phases as Related to the Pattern Variables

In Chapter 3 it was stated that there are certain inherent affinities between attitudinal (a) and object-oriented (o) pattern variable alternatives. They were the following:

1 Affectivity (a) — Performance (o)
2 Neutrality (a) — Quality (o)
3 Specificity (a) — Universalism (o)
4 Diffuseness (a) — Particularism (o)

These we defined as the dimensions of action space. There seems to be a second set of affinities among pattern variable alternatives when grouped across the attitude-object line. They are the following:

1 Specificity (a) — Performance (o)
2 Affectivity (a) — Particularism (o)
3 Diffuseness (a) — Quality (o)
4 Neutrality (a) — Universalism (o)

This second grouping has, in the work leading up to this paper, assumed a significance of which we were not aware when Chapter 3 was written. Two aspects of this significance may be mentioned here because they will figure prominently in the subsequent discussion. In the first place, in combining components from each of two dimensions they have a relation to the *order* of phase processes. For example, as shall see, the adaptive dimension (in pattern variable terms, specificity—universalism) is the focus of the adaptive phase. But the relation of specificity to performance points the direction of transition to the subsequent phase of goal attainment while that of universalism to neutrality points to the relation to the antecedent phase of latency. Secondly, these combinations are important in analyzing the directions of the processes of symbol formation and integration in the course of learning. Both aspects of their significance will be elaborated below.

There are other logical and empirical possibilities of grouping across the attitude-object line, but they do not seem to possess the inherent affinities which can be discerned in the above two sets of clusters and especially in the first set.

Each *attitudinal* variable, we find, by scanning the two arrangements, is linked with two different *object* categorizations. (For example, in the first arrangement, specificity is linked with universalism, and in the second, with performance.) Similarly, each *object* categorization is linked with two *attitudinal* variables. (For example, universalism is linked with both specificity and neutrality.) These four variables thus constitute a cluster, made up of two attitudinal descriptions and two object descriptions. By combining the two above arrangements in this fashion we arrive at four such clusters, as follows:

(1) Specificity (a) — Neutrality (a) — Universalism (o) — Performance (o).

(2) Affectivity (a) — Specificity (a) — Particularism (o) — Performance (o)

(3) Diffuseness (a) — Affectivity (a) — Particularism (o) — Quality (o).

(4) Neutrality (a) — Diffuseness (a) — Quality (o) — Universalism (o).

The clusters of pattern variables derived in this manner define the phases of the system which is our point of reference. To obtain Figure 2 we visualize the pattern variable clusters within each cell, give the cell an appropriate name, and move the pattern variable designation to the sides of the table. The pattern variable description of each cell is then read by reference to the row and column in which it falls. The four phases thus are defined in terms of the associated overt activity, type of orientation to objects, and type of attitude, as follows:

Phase A=Adaptive-Instrumental activity associated with the phase of maximal *Adaptation*. Orientation to objects marked by *Universalism* and *Performance*. Attitude marked by *Specificity* and *Neutrality*.

Phase G=Expressive-Instrumental activity associated with the phase of maximal system *Integration*.[7] Orientation to objects marked by *Performance* and *Particularism*. Attitude marked by *Affectivity* and *Specificity*.

Phase I=Integrative-Expressive activity associated with the phase of maximal system *Integration*.[7] Orientation to objects

[7] System integration is distinguished here from the "pattern" integration which is central to analysis on the *cultural* level. In this paper the term integration will, unless otherwise specified, refer to system integration.

marked by *Particularism* and *Quality*. Attitude marked by *Diffuseness* and *Affectivity*.

Phase L=Symbolic-Expressive activity associated with the phase of maximal *Latency*. Orientation to objects marked by *Quality* and *Universalism*. Attitude marked by *Neutrality* and *Diffuseness*.

The relations of these variables to each other are illustrated in Figure 2, with slightly more expanded descriptions of the nature of the process characteristic of each phase. It will be noted that each phase is defined by a given combination of four pattern variable alternatives, two of which refer to the way in which objects are categorized in activity appropriate to that phase, and two of which refer to the kind of attitude held toward the objects in that phase. It will be noted that the pattern variable pairs held to characterize each of the dimensions as treated in Chapter 3 appear in the same paired form here.

A "phase" may be regarded as the changing state of the system through some interval in time, when its movement in a given dimension is maximized relative to its movement in the other three dimensions. Phases are *technically* described by the specification of the direction and amount of movement taking place within the time interval on *each* of the four dimensions, but for purposes of convenience, are named in terms of the dimension of major movement. An act is conceived as exerting some kind of directing influence on the movement of the system, and may thus be described by the direction of movement of the system, which it signalizes.[8] A series of "pure types" may be visualized, which coincide with the maximum point of the phases. Bales' interaction categories are described in this way later. On the other hand, a given act may have appreciable components of more than one phase, and so tend to "pull the system" toward a new phase. This case is very important in the analysis of deviance and social control, as we shall see later.

The system problems as described in earlier papers may be thought of as problems of maximizing the movement of the system in *each* of the four dimensions. Since preponderance of all phases cannot be achieved at one point in time, the system goes through phases or time cycles in which first one direction of movement

[8] This seems to us to underly the (often loose) attribution of "functional significance" to an act. The looseness will usually turn out to be attributable to inadequate specifications of system references.

and then another is preponderant. The overt acts are thus "addressed to" or are "associated with" the solution of system problems,

Figure 2

Phases in the Relationship

of a System to its Situation

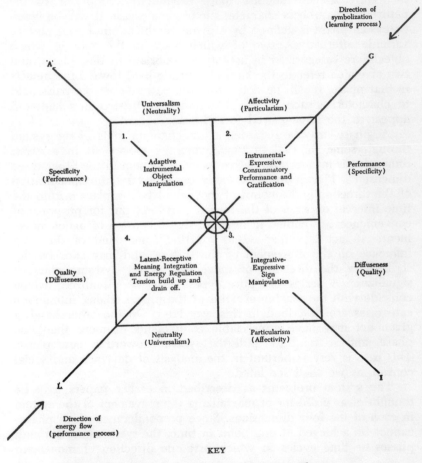

KEY

1. A—Adaptive Phase   3. I—Integrative Phase
2. G—Goal Gratification Phase   4. L—Latent Pattern Maintenance Phase

and by the frequency of their occurrence hold the system within given phases, and move the system from one phase to the next. These types of overt action or categories of interaction are marked by characteristic types of attitudes which can be described by the pattern variables. The pattern variables, as we have seen, also describe the dimensions. These classifications are thus extremely closely related to each other, and indeed, as we believe, describe simply different aspects of the same thing. We will now describe each phase a little more fully.

A. *Adaptation.* Successful adaptation involves (a) an accommodation of the system to inflexible "reality demands", and (b) an active transformation of the situation external to the system. In both instances there is a consequent emphasis on cognitive orientation. The eventual mastery of the external situation through instrumental activity necessitates "realistic" judgments in terms of generalized predictions concerning the behavior of objects. Hence, the relation of actors to objects needs to be *universalistic*, that is, cognizant of the characteristics of the object in relation to other objects or as a member of a class of objects with predictable characteristics. It is necessary, moreover, if the situation is to be "mastered" and not simply "accommodated to", for these universalistically defined properties to be perceived and dealt with in specific contexts of relevance to given goal-interests. Hence the character of the attitude tends to be marked by *specificity* of interest.

Instrumental activity involves some kind of manipulation of objects which changes their relation to each other, as distinguished from simply accommodative changes of the system as actor in relation to them. The relations of objects to each other will not change in the desired way unless they are indeed connected with each other in some more or less determinate relation of "cause and effect". In instrumental activity the actor manipulates objects and relations seen as "causes" in order to obtain certain "effects". Hence, for the actors, the emphasis in orientation to the object tends to be on an "operational definition" of the object, what effects it is producing or will produce when he manipulates it in a given way. These objects, of course, in social interaction, include persons seen in terms of what they are doing, how they are performing, what they can or will do, and include ego's performance as well as alter's. In our terminology this is an orientation to the object in terms of its *performance*. Finally, in this context, where the goal is not yet attained and where one must deal with objects in a "realistic" way, it is necessary to inhibit affective or emotional reactions to the objects in order to avoid being drawn off toward other goals, to avoid making inappropriate choices as to how the objects shall be treated, and to avoid premature relaxation of instrumental efforts. Hence the attitude tends to be marked by a certain inhibition or *neutrality*, with affect to some extent held neutral.

G. *Goal Gratification or Enjoyment of Goal-state.* In the phase of goal attainment two of these characteristics remain the same, and two change. The interest in the object is still segmental or *specific* and it is still viewed in terms of what it does toward the gratification of the need, that is in terms of *performance*. But the other two variables change.

Goal attainment involves intrinsically gratifying activity. It is the culminating phase of a sequence of preparatory activities. Any anterior instrumental-adaptive activities were associated with an inhibition on tendencies toward premature gratification, that is, were pursued with an attitude of neutrality. Then, when the culminating activities are about to be carried out, the inhibition on gratification is suspended and *affectivity* suffuses the goal consummative activity. Similarly, the relation to the object no longer tends to be universalistic, concerned with realistic prediction of later effects or relation to other objects. It gives way to a relation of *particularism* where the object is a goal object, to be possessed, consumed, enjoyed, or appreciated, and its particular relation to ego is the important thing.

I. *Integration.* The phase of integrative activity is linked to the goal gratification phase, (as that phase was to the adaptive) by the possession of two common characteristics, and a change of two. The attitude toward the object is *affectively* toned, and the relation to the object is *particularistic*. Successful integration involves a determinate set of relations among the member units of the system such that it retains and reinforces its boundary-maintaining character as a single entity. Expressive activity associated with the integrative problem involves a discrimination between social objects which are system members and those which are not members, or, with regard to non-social objects those which are and are not possessions. It involves a generalized and durable affective attachment to the system members in place of universalistic assessment of properties shared with non-members. Hence the relation to the object is marked by particularism and affectivity.

However, the specific interest in specific goals characteristic of the goal-attainment phase gives way in the integrative phase to a diffuse interest, and the object tends to be regarded in terms of its diffuse or global quality, rather than its specific performance as related to a specific goal. The particularistic attachment to the object, stressing its membership in the same system with ego rather than its specific role or status in the system involves a whole inter-related constellation of interests held in common. The elements of more specific interest in the attachment which must of course operate in any integrated system are evaluated as secondary. It is alter in his diffuse quality as a system-member rather than alter as an incumbent of a specific status or performer of a specific role to whom ego is attached. Hence the character of the attitude is marked by *diffuseness* and the important thing about the object is its *quality*.

L. Latency. During periods of suspension of interaction, there exists the imperative, if the system is to be renewed, for the motivational and cultural patterns to be maintained. During this period, they may be said to be in a state of latency in the sense that they are not positively and grossly visible as they are when the system is in active interaction. Nonetheless they are, as long as the group retains its life, in operation. They operate in their latent phase above all as limits on commitments to other systems of action which might otherwise hamper or prevent the reactivation of the system.

To put the matter somewhat differently, a system is confronted by the necessity, as a precondition for its continued existence, of maintaining and renewing the motivational and cultural patterns which are integral to its interaction as a system. This involves both their maintenance in a condition of latency and under certain conditions their expression. The latter involves moreover the expression of the motivations and cultural patterns which are integral to the system and those which are integral to the units. These unit motivations and cultural patterns may be in themselves in conflict with the motivations and patterns integral to the system but their expression periodically is usually a prerequisite of the system's continued or renewed functioning.

The maintenance of motivational and cultural patterns is necessary however, not only when the system is in a state of subsidence or suspension, but also when one particular action phase is preponderant. Thus, in the phase of integrative preponderance, the cognitive patterns appropriate to activity in Phase A (Adaptive-instrumental) will be in abeyance, i.e. subordinated, conversely, in the phase of adaptive-instrumental preponderance the cathectic patterns of object attachment will be in abeyance, in this special sense there is a latent phase in effect during any active interaction phase. The system-problem of pattern maintenance or renewal in this situation of active interaction bears a definite resemblance to the system-problem of maintenance during the suspension of interaction. Indeed it may be open to interpretation as to whether we should not regard this as the latency phase of a unit of the system regarded as a subsystem. Similarly the symbolic expression of a pattern in the latency phase of the system may be regarded as the goal-gratification phase of a unit in its subsystem process.

The latent phase is the phase of relative "before" and "after" quiescence by comparison with the intervening phases of the cycle. One might say that it is marked by "inactivity",[9] but this is only a relative matter. It is more accurate to say that this is a phase of no observable interaction between the units as members of the system which is the point of reference. The units of the system however, are themselves systems, and are internally active, with tension building up, draining off, patterns being maintained and consolidated and the like. Though interaction between member units is minimal, expressive acts may occur which may be read as indices of the subjective state or latent pattern of the member unit as a motivated entity and through this of the system. These expressive acts are the externalization of an internal motivational state of the unit in relation to some cathected object. The acts are not directed toward consequences for the system. So far as the unit is concerned its self—contained qualitive state is the important thing. Although, if directly observable, such acts entail physical movement, and sometimes even extremes of physical movement, they do not constitute movement of the system of member units which is the point of reference. Thus, unless interaction of members takes place, these acts do not move the system toward system adaptation, system goal-attainment, or system integration, but leave it in the same latent patterned state.

However, internal states of member units of this kind, latent patterns, have in their earlier process of formation, by learning, involved both overt activity with other member units and external objects. Hence the latent state is "object oriented". This is shown by the fact that expressive acts may be evoked in the presence of originally cathected external objects, or some sign or symbol of them as visualized internally by the actor. But the important thing about the object is not what it *can* do if properly manipulated,

9 As will be seen later, no overt interaction types are assigned to this phase.

but rather what it already *does* to the emotional state of the actor, through the associations it carries. In other words, the orientation to the object is primarily in terms of its *quality*. In this the L phase is like the I phase. It shares a second characteristic with the I phase which is the *diffuse* character of the many interests which may be involved, threatened, or pressing for goal-gratification.

Unlike the I phase, however, the internal activity of member units in the latent phase is marked by *neutrality* rather than freely released affect. Seen from the point of view of its significance for the system the primary feature of the latent phase is the latent reservoir of patterned but inhibitional motivational potential in which it consists. It constitutes a fund of rising or falling tension available for utilization in action. Hence a guarded neutrality or inhibition of attitude characterizes the latent phase, which can, however, pass over into affectivity by tension releasing activity as a "safety-valve". Even in these cases of affective breakover, however, the function of expressive acts often turns out to be the conservation and regulation of energy in conformity with a latent pattern, and not simply the "expenditure of energy" or release of tension. In the characteristic of guarded neutrality, the latent phase shares a common characteristic with the adaptive phase, to which the system may next pass. It also shares with this phase the characteristic of a *universalistic* orientation to objects, which is to say that the meaning of the object has been "internalized"—the signs and symbols standing for it have been connected with the signs and symbols standing for other objects, both cognitively and affectively, and the whole constellation of symbols and meanings constitutes an inter-related, generalized, symbol structure. The object is seen in relation to associated objects, and is manipulated both by logical rules and along gradients of cathectic generalization. The object, including the system and its units as objects, is one of a class of objects in one way or another equivalent to it— the mark of a universalistic orientation. This kind of "internalization" in fact, is a precondition of latency, as well as a characterization of it.

The phases which we have described are not merely descriptions of different possible states of systems. There are determinate dynamic relations among them, in consequence of the one way flow of motivational energy. There is a general tendency for systems to move towards the G (goal-attainment) phase through either the A (adaptive) phase or I (system-integrative) phase. The system-economy necessitates, after prolonged action in one phase, a shift to another phase to reestablish the balance of the system and to meet the system problems which had been disregarded while the system was in the former phase.

From empirical research such as that reported in Chapter 4, certain generalizations of phase sequence have been established. The sequence we use as an expositional model here seems to be roughly applicable on both microscopic and macroscopic levels in a variety of substantive contexts. This model of phase sequence does not however commit us to the contention that no other phase sequence is possible. On the contrary, they are in fact most certain, and in later sections on *therapy*, and *socialization*, we deal with certain reversals of this model. All that we would contend is that there are dynamic relations between the phases in the order that we have presented them. This *particular* dynamic relation seems to hinge on the fact that each of the phases possesses certain attitudinal or object orientation similarities or consequences in relation to its adjacent neighbors. These consequences, we think, tend to be one factor in the passage of the system from one particular phase to another. On the other hand, there is another obvious factor in that heavy concentration of activity in one phase, say the adaptive, tends to create particularly acute deficits in its "opposite"—in this case, the integrative. This tendency for opposite phases to alternate in rapid succession is seen in the act-to-act sequences as observed on the level tapped by Bales' interaction categories. Data are presented in Chapter 4 which show that opinion—(classified as associated with the adaptive problem—see later)—alternates rapidly with agreement and disagreement (classified as associated with the integrative problem, see later). The succession of phase emphasis through the meeting as described in Chapter 4 tends to be from *adaptation* (emphasis on orientation), to *goal-gratification* (emphasis on suggestion and tension release), with a last minute touch of *integration* (emphasis on solidarity). The empirical order of phases, we assume, is dependent upon the balance and fluctuation of inputs from outside the system as well as internal dynamic interdependences, and so regular phase movements are in a way a limiting case, dependent upon unusual stability of inputs, a relatively closed system, and a number of other factors. In all likelihood phase patterns will also tend to differ according to the place of the system on the microscopic-macroscopic time range, and according to a number of unknown factors, such as "ease of communication" between units in the system, number of units etc.

In spite of these reservations, we will continue for purposes of exposition to treat the phase movement A—>G—>I—>L, as a handy idealized" model.

The above schematic exposition suggests a solution for a problem of terminology which has plagued us over a considerable period and which, as is so often the case, has, we now find, covered over a substantive difficulty. This touches the use of the terms "instrumental" and "expressive". The term instrumental has shown a tendency to cover *both* what in the dimensional sense we have previously called adaptive and instrumental, leaving no appropriate term for the goal gratification state, whereas something similar has happened with respect to the term expressive and what in the dimensional sense we have previously called integrative and expressive.

In Chapter 3 above we used these terms to distinguish two of the four system problems which we also defined as the dimensions formulated by the combination of the pattern-variable components respectively of performance, affectivity and of quality-neutrality. At the same time we have used these two terms to designate broad trends of "directionality" on the orientation of action, namely, instrumental as concerned with interest in attainment of specific goals in relation to adaptive exigencies and correspondingly expressive as concerned with "direct" acting out of a need-disposition or internalized pattern without reference to a goal state requiring adaptive manipulation as a means to its attainment.

We propose in the following discussion to attempt to avoid confusion by reserving these two terms for the latter meanings. We will therefore speak of the four dimensions as those of adaptation, goal gratification, system-integration and latent pattern maintenance. These terms now take the place of what we formerly meant to designate by the "four system problems" as named by Bales. In tabular forms:

Adaptation—Bales' former "Adaptive Problem" (Universalism-Specificity)

Goal Gratification—Bales' former "Instrumental Problem" (Performance-Affectivity)

Integration—Bales' former "Integrative Problem" (Particularism-Diffuseness)

Latent Pattern Maintainance—Bales' former "Expressive Problem" (Quality-Neutrality)

The term goal gratification is nearly self-explanatory while that of latency stresses the variability with respect to which motivation and pattern is on the one hand held in the reservoir or on the other hand released into action. This is in accord with use of the term neutrality in the pattern-variable sense as one of its designations.

Goal-gratification and latency then designate antithetical, i.e. *independent directions* of the disposal of the inflow of motivational energy into the system. The instrumental *use* of this energy then represents the *transition* from latency to goal-gratification or investment *via* adaptive processes whereas the term expressive designates its discharge without reference to adaptive exigencies, but because of the phenomenon of expressive communication and its relation to the problem of order this is a process peculiarly bound up with integrative exigencies.

IV. *Phases as Related to the Interaction Categories*

In this section we consider the relationship of Bales' interaction categories to the more general concepts of phases and phase movement which we have introduced above. Perhaps it will be best to begin with the problem as to where, on the scale of micro-to-macroscopic treatment of systems, these categories are appropriate descriptions of the interaction of member units.

The categories are named in a way meant to be descriptive of overt acts of communication, largely but not exclusively verbal, in face to face discussion situations. The small group of persons, in direct communication through a limited time span of perhaps one to three hours is the most common system referent with which they have been used. Each behavioral act that occurs is categorized in terms of its type of relevance to *that* system of member units, and the goals which are known or assumed to be the focus of expected accomplishment during that time period.

It is obvious that such meetings of small numbers of persons in limited periods of interaction are typically "embedded" in larger system contexts, involving larger numbers of people working through longer time spans toward more general and distant goals. The members are often in "representative" roles, as the delegates or leaders of sub-groups which are the member-units of the larger system. This is true even in laboratory-formed groups. The subjects already have some kind of relationship to the experimenter(s) at the time they begin their technically observed interaction, whether they are his students, whether he has hired them, or whether he has simply persuaded them to come and participate in his experiment. In a time sense, they are first and last, persons in the role of "subjects" vis-a-vis the "experimenter", and second, or in between, they are members of a group which he asks them to form. Part of their behavior vis-a-vis each other is best understood by reference to this over-lying system context.

One of the basic strategic problems in small group research in the laboratory is how to handle this problem most effectively for research purposes. For example, one can attempt to make this relation to the overlying system as stable and unchanging as possible, by use of a single host-experimenter and standardization of procedures of recruiting, introduction of members, and instructions for the task. One can attempt to minimize further *inter*action between the small group as a unit and the rest of the team of experimenters and observers by use of one-way observation screens. One can include observation procedures specifically designed for content analysis of those aspects of behavior which appear to be most directly a function of the relations of the subject group to the experimenter, and take this into account in the interpretation of results. And so on. Practically, there is no such thing as a sterile, isolated group with no relation to larger system contexts.

Nevertheless, one should not fall into the trap of assuming that everything that happens in a small group is to be attributed to "outside influences". For the period when the members are in direct communicative contact they do influence each other, and do participate in a tangible "interaction system", which has the general properties, in greater or lesser degree, of all systems of social interaction, wherever they may fall on the microscopic to macroscopic range. The interaction categories as developed and used by Bales are verbally described for the use of an observer on a level of concreteness and specificity appropriate to a particular type of rather microscopic system, but they are based on a conception that there are general properties of action systems, and are assumed to have cognate forms on other levels of analysis. This was the conception from the first, and the present section is an attempt to work out more systematically, and show more clearly how they are related to other general categories which were worked out from starting points at other levels of system analysis, particularly the pattern variables of Parsons and Shils.

In many small groups one can say that in a certain sense, not much goes on except talking. The members are discussing verbally, and the concrete goal of the particular meeting is arriving at some sort of "decision", or a series of them. The members have other work and activities as part of a larger organization, and they meet together periodically to inform each other how things are going, to get things straightened out, iron out their differences, and to come to certain understandings or agreements as to how they will carry on when they separate. In the context of the larger organization as the system point of reference, the single meeting of members may have primarily an *"integrative"* significance. Their *"adaptive-instrumental"* work for the organization typically separates them physically and puts them under various sorts of pressures, frustrations, or leads them to make new inventions or developments, which, until they get together again for "reintegration", cannot be absorbed or taken into account by other units in the organization. They talk about these things when they get together. The activities significant for the larger organization, (including the non-verbal ones of course, as well as the verbal) are the *subject matter* of the talk in the meetings. These activities are *referred to* through the use of signs and symbols, but, for the most part they are not "what is going on now". "What is going on now" is talk or symbol manipulation which has a reintegrative goal by reference to the larger organization. One can say that the macroscopic system (the larger organization) is "represented by" the members present, and "referred to", in the present microscopic system (the group meeting) through the use of symbols.

One can probably say that the typical relation of symbol manipulation to the more extended interaction system it guides and in a sense controls (like a servo-mechanism) is a microscopic relation. The relation of such a microcosm to macrocosm is an extremely complex and subtle one. For example, we may note that the microcosm is not simply a reflection or map of the macrocosm, but is a *constitutive part* of it, as well. Figure 3 may give a crude illustration.

Figure 3. Microcosm to Macrocosm Relation

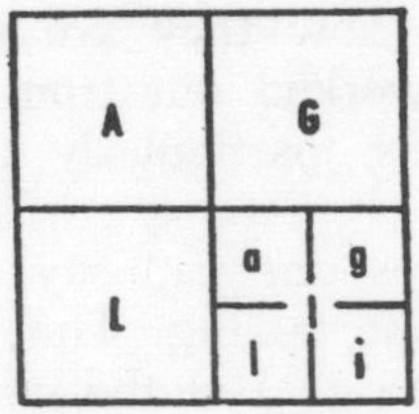

Let us call the macroscopic system of action and objects we are theorizing about a "world of events". Let the "world of events" be represented by the total figure. Let the phases of the total system or "world of events" be represented by the large quadrants, A, G, I, and L, with the phase meanings we have given them above. Let the "world of symbols" used in *interpersonal* communication within the system be represented by the small quadrants a, g, i, and l. These are all to be found in the large quadrant I. Let "a" be a symbol or cluster of them which refers to "A", let "g" have a similar relation to "G", and so on, so that each large quadrant is represented by a small quadrant with the same letter designation.

Now we may say that I, as constituted by the quadrants a, g, i, and l, is a *microcosm* of the *macrocosm* A, G, I, L. But at the same time, I, and so its constituent parts, is a *part* of the whole, A, G, I, L. This is the kind of relation we suppose interpersonal communication to bear to the more macroscopic systems of action in which it is embedded.

We desire to say that interaction or interpersonal communication is a microcosm in relation to some one or several more macroscopic systems. The organizational roles of each of the persons involved in the conversation is one set of more macroscopic systems. Their "total personalities" are a set of still more macroscopic systems. The system of roles which make up the small group interaction system is still another system point of reference, not necesarily more macrocosmic than the personality systems (in fact, presumably less so), but more macrocosmic than the act-to-act overt interchange of symbols. The system including the experimenter(s), if any, is still another. The content of the symbols interchanged (or presented) in the overt communication process can be analyzed in terms of its reference to any one or all of these systems. It will typically have reference to all of these systems, though the references are at times very obscure, and practically impossible for an external observer to pick up. It is very important to emphasize that we have systematic instruments for analyzing the content of this symbol interchange for only a fraction of the content it presumably carries. The number of techniques of content analysis which would potentially be possible is presumably infinite, and the number of those which would be practically useful in research is very great.

Bales' set of categories is only one set out of this potentially indefinitely large number of modes of analysis of symbol content.

It is designed to pick up the reference of the symbols to only one system—that bounded by the overt interaction of members present in their roles as group members through a time span bounded by the goals which they expect to realize within the limited period of interaction with each other. The goal state is typically realized only "symbolically", for example, by general agreement regarding suggestions which refer to some activity to be carried out only later. The agreement about suggestions is the goal state of *the system which is the point of reference,* for the technical observation purposes. With regard to the more macroscopic system references, such a state is probably best thought of as constituting part of the activity of an integrative phase, along the lines of the examples presented earlier.

Bales' interaction categories are categories of interpersonal communication. The period of communication itself is thought of as "integrative" in its type of significance for the system as a whole. (Note that we say its *type* of significance. It is not assumed that it necessarily produces a *higher degree* of integration—it may in fact produce just the opposite. Within each type of significance, or on each of the dimensions we have discussed, one must distinguish positive and negative directions of movement.) The macroscopic system to which the symbols may refer involves adaptive and goal attaining activities which are not necessarily acts of interpersonal communication. Communication is used during the integrative phase of this larger system to refer to these acts. Interaction involves the use of symbols which refer to acts of all sorts relevant to the system in all its phases. Thus the movement of the system through each of its phases is "reflected in", "symbolized by", as well as planned, controlled, accomplished, consolidated, and held latent through the manipulation of symbols. Because of this peculiar relation of acts of communication to the total system movement, we can use these acts, which are observable, to trace the movement and state of the referent system, parts of which are not observable.

It is on these sorts of assumptions that we give the findings about how people talk to each other in small groups the generalized significance that we do. The categories of interaction are particular cases of the types of movement we expect to find in action systems in the broadest sense. The diagrams which follow in Figure 4 are to be regarded now as an "enlargement" of the portion of the diagram marked "a, g, i, l" in the previous diagram.

Figure 4
Phases in the Use of Symbols in the Process of Interpersonal Communication

POSITIVE TYPES

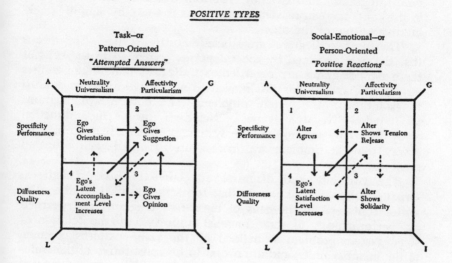

Task—or
Pattern-Oriented
"Attempted Answers"

Social-Emotional—or
Person-Oriented
"Positive Reactions"

NEGATIVE TYPES

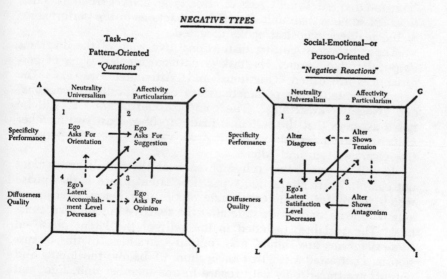

Task—or
Pattern-Oriented
"Questions"

Social-Emotional—or
Person-Oriented
"Negative Reactions"

We may note first that the Figure contains four smaller diagrams, each one of which contains four cells. Each cell is marked with a letter, A, G, I, or L, which are the short designations of the four system phases, or system problems, of Adaptation, Goal Gratification, Integration, and Latency. The four diagrams are exactly alike in this, and one can reassemble them, as it were, by simply "stacking one on top of the other".

The top two diagrams are labeled "Positive Types". This means that the acts classified by the categories contained in the cells of these two diagrams are regarded as indicators that some member unit of the system has just moved in a positive direction toward the solution of the system problems. The bottom two diagrams are labeled "Negative Types". "Negative" means in a direction away from the solution of the system problems, that is, in such a way, that the problems are more acute than had been indicated previously.

The two left-hand diagrams are labeled "Task or Pattern-Oriented Types". This means that the acts classified by the categories contained in the cells of these two diagrams are regarded as "performances" of some member addressed to the solution of some system problem as defined by the value patterns common to the member units, and are meant to be constitutive of that solution, or preparatory to it. The two right-hand diagrams are labeled "Person-Oriented Types". Acts of these types are regarded as "sanctions" of some system unit directed as reactions to the performance of the member who last spoke or acted.

These two cross-cutting distinctions give each of the diagrams its peculiar type name. The task or pattern oriented types of performances are called "Questions" and "Attempted Answers". The person oriented types of sanctions are called "Positive Reactions" and "Negative Reactions". The complete classification it will be noted assumes that the system is made up of at least two member units, who are referred to when it is necessary to keep the perspective clear, as Ego and Alter.

It will be noted that cell 4 on each of the sub-diagrams does not contain overt interaction types. The latent phase is that phase which stands for the inferred state of the unit before overt-interaction appears, and for its state after the reactive sanction has come back. The variables included in the cells of the latent phase on these diagrams are "input" and "output" variables. In this discussion as contrasted with that in Section VI below, the inputs and outputs are traced only with regard to one member unit, Ego, and would have to be traced with regard to each member unit if one wanted to speak of the inputs and outputs of the system as a whole. The two input-output variables shown are "accomplishment" and "satisfaction", which will be discussed in later sections of this paper.

The relations between the latent state, the performance, the sanction, and the resulting state can not be shown rigorously on a diagram of this sort, but by the arrows we mean to suggest roughly how the process is conceived to go. For example, let us start with Ego's latent state, as shown in cell 4 of the "Attempted Answers" diagram. If there is an increase of Ego's latent accomplishment level in the form of a perception, an insight, or the like, this is likely to be followed by an overt performance in which he gives an attempted answer to some problem facing the system. He makes a remark or a series of them classified by the observer as his "giving orientation", "giving opinion", or "giving suggestion". All of these three types are inferred to have arisen out of some change in Ego's latent state, and to be "headed for" system-goal gratification. Giving orientation proceeds by an emphasis on the adaptive problems of the system, giving opinion proceeds by an emphasis on the integrative problems and giving suggestion proceeds directly toward the goal state without adaptive or integrative detours.

We now switch to Alter, who receives the communication. We have not shown what happens to Alter's latent state on the diagram, because of the undue complication, but let us suppose that Ego's remark increases Alter's satisfaction level, and he responds with a positive reaction by agreeing, showing solidarity, or tension release. Any of these reactions received by Ego again are conceived to have reward value for him, and result in an increase in his latent satisfaction level. This increase of satisfaction, in turn is conceived to have further repercussions in that it rewards the performance which provoked Alter's favorable reaction. Ego's accomplishment is now confirmed, and furthermore, since he and Alter are parts of a solidary system, Alter is now committed to the task content of Ego's performance, and the accomplishment level of *the system of two*, and not simply that of ego, increases. Ego and Alter now have an additional item of "common culture", a common positive reaction to a set of symbols which can be perceived by the two in common, and which either or both can manipulate further to influence each other and to guide their common activity together as an operating unit. One or more of their "system problems", according to the type of act involved, has now progressed another step toward solution. The latent state of each has been changed, and the system is now prepared for another cycle, according to the potentials in the latent state.

We have illustrated in terms of a cycle of positive activity, but the same essential linkage of events can be traced through by the reader for negative, mixed, and other types of cycles. The reader is referred to Chapter 4 for empirical data on sequences of activity, and for a statistical model which will produce sequences approximately like those observed, distributed in approximately the observed way among members. Data are also presented there on the relation between sequences observed and satisfaction as measured after the meeting.

Let us now consider the definition of each category in terms of the pattern variables. The pattern variable designations are placed on each diagram just as they have been on the previous diagrams, except that we have listed them in such a way that the "opposites" such as "neutrality versus affectivity" have been listed directly opposite each other for easier reading of the distinction between categories. The combination of four, characterizing each cell is exactly as before.

It should be clearly recognized that we have no "absolute points" in terms of which "absolute neutrality" or "absolute affectivity" and the like could be defined, if indeed such absolute points even have theoretical meaning. They are relativistic like all of our concepts. One can say that one act is more affectively toned than some other or group of others, or less, and these judgments, we know from experience, can be made with sufficient reliability for research purposes. But the classification, which is here the basic operation of measurement, is made by comparison of the act with other acts.

In the operation of scoring actual behavior by this set of categories, not one, but a *series* of comparisons is made. This is not to say that the observer self-consciously goes through a numbered series of comparisons before he scores the act—rather he works rapidly and by a set of immediate and intuitive grasp of the "sense" of the activity. Nevertheless, something like the content of this intuitive grasp can be reduced to a series of logical operations.

First we may say that he determines whether the act is primarily a proaction—(a performance), or a reaction—(a sanction). Concretely, we know that all performances have a sanction element, and vice-versa, but the relative emphasis determines the classification. *In comparison to the reactions,* these acts with a *performance* emphasis tend toward the A pole as contrasted with the I pole, with an instrumental-adaptive task emphasis, and so have the characteristic pattern variable combination of the A phase. In the most general sense, the total group of *proactions* or *performances* tend toward Neutrality and Specificity of attitude, and a Universalistic–Performance orientation to the object *by comparison with* the total group of *reactions or sanctions* which tend toward Affectivity and Diffuseness of attitude and a Particularistic-Quality orientation to objects. This general "leaning" of the two halves of the category set toward A and I respectively is not indicated by pattern variable designations on the diagrams, but is implied in the assumption that reactions can act as sanctions—that they have a reward and punishment value by former association with goal states, (and hence by "expectation").

This first logical dichotomization is now followed by a second which is the determination as to whether the act is closer, as it were, to the solution of the Goal Gratification problem, or further away from it than the others it is being compared with. The comparison is made within the half of the categories the first choice has given. That is, if the comparison is being made *within the performance* set, it is determined whether the act is a *Question* or an *Attempted Answer*. On the other hand, if the comparison is being made within the *sanction set,* it is determined whether the act is a *Negative Reaction* or a *Positive Reaction.*

The act has now been located in one of four sets of three categories each. The next logical operation is to locate the act by comparison with the other acts which would also fall in this set. It will go in one of three categories. These three categories are specified by the pattern variable combinations of the A, G, and I cells on each of the four diagrams of Figure 4. Let us start with Attempted Answers.

If the act is an Attempted Answer we compare it with other acts of this type and ask . . . how does it compare with them as to attitude? If it is more neutral in affective tone, there is a presumption it should be classed as *giving orientation.* Then we ask . . . how does it compare with them as to the orientation to objects involved? If it is more universalistic, emphasizing cognitive standards this confirms the classification as one of giving orientation. In case of conflict, we give classificatory priority to the attitude. Any marked affective tone is enough to determine that the classification should not be that of giving orientation.

If the act is not one of giving orientation we now face a final choice, whether it is to be classified as giving opinion, or giving suggestion. We compare the act with others of these two types and ask: how does it compare with them as to attitude? If the attitudinal interest expressed is specific and sharply goal focused, the presumption is that the act should be classified as *giving suggestion.* Then we ask: how does it compare as to object orientation? If the objects are viewed in terms of their expected performance rather than terms of their diffuse qualities, then the classification is confirmed. In case of conflict, we give classificatory priority to the attitude. Any marked vagueness or lack of specificity leads to a decision to class the act as one of giving opinion rather than suggestion.

By comparison with other Attempted Answers then, *giving opinion* is marked by a Diffuse affective attitude toward the Qualitative aspect of the objects. These characteristics set it off from both giving suggestion and giving orientation, which have in common a specific interest in a focal goal state and an assessment of the object in terms of its performance relative to reaching that goal state. By a process of internal comparisons within the Attempted Answers section we arrive at the final classification of the act. Giving opinion is, by comparison with the others in its section, marked by a diffuse affective attitude toward objects in their qualitative particularistic relation to ego. But this is only by comparison with other Attempted Answers. As noted above, it still belongs to the performance half of the category set which is marked by a specific neutral interest in objects universalistically defined by their performance characteristics, as compared to the other half of the set dealing with reactive sanctions.

It is clear that we are in an awkward position with regard to the use of words. We begin to feel the need of a representational model more in the nature of a "space" in terms of which all the relations can be represented simultaneously instead of as the outcome of a series of dichotomous classifications. The fact that we have four dimensions to represent rather than three prevents us from constructing a satisfactory physical model, such as the "color solid", where there are only three dimensions to be represented. Perhaps mathematical representation is not only desirable but necessary for further technical progress in this direction.

Let us look now at the Positive Reactions. Suppose the first two classifications have led to the identification of the act as a Positive Reaction. The problem now is which of the three types of positive reaction is the proper one. The procedure is exactly as described above—a comparison of the act with others that fall in the same section. How does it compare as to attitude? If it is more neutral in affective tone there is a presumption it should be classified as an act of *agreement*. Then . . . how does it compare as to object orientation? If the object (usually the previous performance of the other) is assessed in terms of universalistic standards—in terms of its cognitive validity rather than its affective tone as the basis of the reaction or judgment,—then the classification of the act as agreement is confirmed. In case of conflict of these two criteria, we give the attitude criterion priority. Any marked affective tone is enough to shift the classification to one of the other two categories.

If the act is not one of agreement, the problem is whether it is showing tension release, or showing solidarity. Both of these types are affectively toned and stress a particularistic relation to objects. The cutting criterion is with regard to the sharpness of goal focus implied. The more "naked" and directly explosive is the expression of the affect:—gratification relief,—the greater the presumption of its classification as *shows tension release*. It is presumed that in the latent phase or state these affective tensions are held in check, "anchored" in a constellation of symbolic pathways which channel the affect to a series of other objects, giving them all a diffuse global quality by connections of affective association and instrumental generalization. When for any reason, the affective tension suddenly rises, it tends to "overflow its usual channels" and comes rushing out in a direct expressive flow, without instrumental or integrative detours, straight into the goal gratification state. It breaks over its diffuse anchorage and issues in a display of the more specific or "naked" affect. The object is that which by its present performance or immediate gratificatory significance has been able to stir the affect into its own specific performance or "acting out". Concretely the object is usually the preceding act of another person. In an act of showing tension release the object is viewed in its segmental significance. The person when stirred to sudden laughter, for example, sometimes exclaims: "What you just said!" or "What you did!" rather than: "You're so funny!" The emphasis is on the content of what was said or done (specific performance) rather than on the diffuse quality of the doer as a person. When the emphasis is on the latter, the act is classified as one of showing solidarity.

By comparison with the other Positive Reactions, then, *showing solidarity* is marked by a Diffuse affective attitude toward the Qualitative aspects of the object. The affect is "channeled" in the integrative direction rather than simply "bustin' out all over." The other person is praised or commended for what he *is*, the affect is fastened on him as a global being, a member of the collectivity, a part of the self in the extended sense. And in general, the affect is less marked, more controlled, more integrated with other interests and values—indeed in a real sense closer to latency and further from specific goal attainment than is direct tension release.

It is probably not necessary to discuss in detail the negative types. In general their pattern variable characteristics are exactly the same as their cognate positive types. The only difference is that they are indicators that the system has, at least for the preceding moment, moved farther from the positive solution of the A, G, and I system problems rather than closer.

The categories we have just been considering are appropriate to a very microscopic level of analysis of phase movement of member units within small groups. For many other sorts of analysis we require a more molar characterization of the activity taking place in longer time spans. The members of groups themselves "generalize" toward more molar time spans as they build their common culture. "Performances" and "sanctions" are very broad terms, particularly appropriate where there is a system of more generalized values defining the roles of member units. In the next section we turn to the problem of phase movement as it relates to the generalized values of the system as a framework within which the role performances and sanctions of member units in differentiated roles takes place.

V. *The Normative Control of Phase Movement*

In the preceding section we have outlined a classification of major types of overt social interaction in terms of the kinds of functional relation we suppose them to have to the actual movement of the system through its various phases. In this section we consider the fact that this movement is not simply "actual", but that it is to a considerable degree regulated and controlled by a structure of institutionalized values, or norms. These norms give a base line of "legitimate expectations" common to the member units, in terms of which "conformity" and "deviance" can be measured in a rough way.

Figure 5

Types of Performance Value appropriate to each Phase

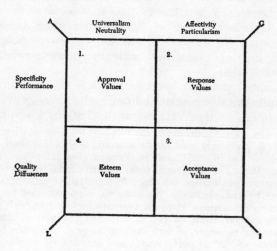

	Universalism Neutrality	Affectivity Particularism
Specificity Performance	1. Achievement Values	2. Appreciation Values
Quality Diffuseness	4. Ascriptive Values	3. Moral-Integrative Values

A ... G
L ... I

Types of Sanction Value appropriate to each Phase

	Universalism Neutrality	Affectivity Particularism
Specificity Performance	1. Approval Values	2. Response Values
Quality Diffuseness	4. Esteem Values	3. Acceptance Values

A ... G
L ... I

As specifications of what constitutes conformity in behavior and attitude, norms may be said to regulate the relations between performance and sanctions; they define the relations of appropriateness which are compatible with a given phase of the system, or change to new phases. The norms state the appropriate performance orbit of a unit through various phases and the appropriate sanctions for keeping it in that orbit. A classification of values by phases is presented in Figure 5.[10]

The performance aspect of the norm is a specification of how the member unit should act during the given phases: (the character of the attitude and orientation toward objects which other members have a right to expect of him), while the sanction aspect is a specification of the kind of reactions he in turn has a right to expect of them: (their attitudes and orientation toward him and his activities), according to his conformity or deviance. The norms of a system may be regarded as a cultural precipitate of the former cycles of performance and sanction in the system which have resulted in satisfaction and accomplishment. They are a product of learning, and a condition of a steady state.

It should be pointed out that in treating norms in relation to the control of action processes we are not confining our attention exclusively to the system as a point of reference, but we are dealing with the relation between the juncture of the system and the action processes of its units. . . . Norms are, as we interpret them, properties of the system. When the system is viewed as an object, the norms are principal aspects of its structure; they are its patterns of value-orientation. Viewed in relation to system process on the other hand, they are concerned with the dynamic relations of the units to each other.

The essential point to keep in mind is that the orbits of the different units are differentiated from each other—as we will show in more detail in Section VIII below—and at any given time, differ-

10 The reader should take note of the fact that this classification differs somewhat from those previously used by Parsons and Shils (cf. *Values, Motives* etc. Figures 3 and 4, pp. 249, 251, and by Parsons (*Social System,* Tables 2a, p. 102 and 2c, p. 108). The differences seem to derive from two principal sources: (1) in the earlier classification the object-categorization and attitudinal pattern variables were treated separately. We were not yet aware that they constituted a system of four dimensions. Here all four are included in each classification; (2) we were not yet aware of certain dynamic relations of these values to system-process and therefore, of both the continuity of transitions between them and the patterns of "fit" of performance and sanction types. We will not take space to explain just how the transition was made but only hope to save the reader confusion by making him aware of the change.

ent units may be found in different phases of their orbits. The primary function of norms is to keep these different phase movements of the units in harmony with each other and with the larger phase movement of the system as a whole. From the point of view of the system, then, their function is integrative. The values in question are thus always, in one aspect, moral-integrative values, but they are "applied" in each of the main functional contexts of the system.

Achievement values, for example, regulate the adaptive performances of any unit in the system from the point of view of their compatibility with the adaptive needs of the system as a whole, while approval-disapproval sanctions reinforce these values by rewarding a given performance or the reverse. It is the fact that these values are "held in common" by the members of the group, i.e. are institutionalized in the system, which makes them the focus of this regulatory process.

We may now review briefly the outstanding features of each of the four types of norm. This review may be brief because the description is essentially a repetition in normative terms of our earlier description of each phase. The first we may call "instrumental". This is the combination of the values of variables appropriate to the adaptive-instrumental achievement phase of action process. Its *achievement value* prescribes, on the one hand, performance that adheres to universalistic standards in the cognitive assessment of the relevant facts of the situation, on the other hand, the investment of adequate effort toward the attainment of the goal, because only in these terms can the performance maximize contribution to the adaptive functions of the system. The *"approval value"* on the other hand prescribes sanctions that preserve affective neutrality both in evaluation of situational exigencies as the basis for agreement or disagreement (i.e. objectivity), and specificity of orientation, in "keeping on the track" and not being diverted by other interests. It will be noted that the norms specify nothing about the integration of this process with other interests, except negatively in preventing interference by them.

The second type of norm we may call "norms legitimating specific unit-goal-states", or "permissive" norms. These govern action in the phase in which consummatory attainment is approached by the unit, and in which the problem of its integration with others in the system begins to intrude on gratification, unless gratification of specific goals is at least temporarily legitimated. The *appreciative values* of this phase have the function for the system of protecting sufficient gratification and tension release for later diversion to adaptive and integrative purposes. The *response values* on the other hand describe in normative terms the kind of reaction the actor has a right to expect of others when their free affective reaction is an integral component of his goals. The two values, of course, are motivationally congruent with each other, and tend to aid in the distribution of gratification among the member units by their direct interaction with each other in this phase.

In the third phase, we speak of moral-integrative norms. Here, the emphasis on performance has given way to an emphasis on an evaluation of the quality of objects. The attainment or direct enjoyment of a specific goal-state by the unit is no longer the major emphasis. The emphasis is rather on its congruence with other goals in the system and the solidarity of the member units with each other as a moral collectivity in which there is some generalized common adherence to a constellation of goals and values, ordered in some kind of congruent way. According to the *moral-integrative* values of this phase, performance should consist in the expression of values and manipulation of symbols which externalize and reinforce this desired congruence and solidarity. The appropriate sanction, according to the values of this phase, is *acceptance;* it is felt that ego's show of solidarity calls for reciprocation in diffuse-affective terms. The maintenance of relation between system-integration and the value-pattern systems of units is thus the crucial problem with which this norm deals.

Finally, in the fourth phase we speak of "ascriptive-qualitative" norms. Here the process of internalization or institutionalization of the new accomplishment is complete; the system can function as a unit on the new basis, and comes to be ready for a new instrumental performance phase. The crucial "performance" area (insofar as one can speak of performance in this phase) is the relation between the newly established patterns and the changing situation; the problem is the latent preservation and expression of these internalized or institutionalized patterns in a manner which does no violence to them and which also still allows the system to move into adjacent phases, when the situation calls for it. Ego is expected to manifest or exemplify the internalized cultural values which are *ascribed* to him. The crucial sanction area is that of the diffuse evaluation of the unit in the light of the institutionalized system pattern. Ego expects to be held in *esteem* for what he "is", rather than for what he "does".

The definition of these norms for a particular phase of the unit's orbit, also defines as we have said above, the appropriate activity for that phase. However, the changing flow of inputs which are extra-systematic in each phase, will set into movement changes toward other phases, and hence begin to activate other values. A new phase will be produced. There must, therefore, be a transition to the relevance of some other norm as the consequences of these input changes accumulate. Each phase has its own norms regulating the action of the unit in that phase and regulating also (either positively or negatively) the relations of that phase of the system and the other phases. For the system to be an orderly one in equilibrium, the value-pattern contained in the normative system of any phase must be relatively consistent (in pattern) and thus to a sufficient degree, empirically compatible with the value-patterns of subsidiary phases. The normative system of the paramount phase must either permit or facilitate a "smooth" transition to the next phase of the system. This possibility is expressed in our scheme by the sharing of certain pattern variables with the value-patterns of the adjacent phases. Thus both achievement values and appreciative values have in common a "specificity" of interest in the "performance" of objects.

This need for processes of transition between the predominance of different norms would seem to be a restatement in more formal terms of the fundamental proposition, strongly emphasized in *Values, Motives, and Systems of Action,* and in *The Social System* that no system of action can be perfectly integrated in value-pattern terms but that a plurality of such patterns must have a place in its control system. Indeed we would now maintain that all the major types of normative pattern appropriate to each phase must be represented in any system, but of course their relative prominence in the system as a whole as well as at different phases may vary greatly. Exactly how relative incidence is distributed in different types of system is a problem concerning structure which we will take up briefly in a later section.[11]

[11] There is another feature of the norms which is notable in the light of the history of the pattern variable scheme. In the earlier stages of its development, in *Values, Motives,* etc. we took pains to elaborate the same combinations of the four pattern variable components as those describing the phase movement. We did not, however, at that time succeed in grounding the significance of these combinations satisfactorily. Now these combinations have reappeared in a highly significant place in the conceptual scheme. Attention may be particularly called to the combinations involved in what are here called the instrumental and the system-integrative norms, which very closely characterize what in much socio-

Before embarking on this set of problems, however, it is necessary to go somewhat more deeply into the dynamic aspects of the
phases of process.

We have not yet adequately analyzed the balances of "input"
and "output" associated with the process, and hence the *conse-
sequences* of different orders of variation in the conditions imping-
ing on a system. Closely associated with these problems are others
we have so far altogether neglected: the analysis of process of
change in the symbolic content itself, with its relations to the
pattern aspect of symbolic systems. To these problems we must
now turn.

VI. Input and Output and the Relations Between Motivation And Symbol Formation

General Considerations about Motivation

Before entering upon a more detailed analysis of the problems
of input and output, it will be helpful briefly to recapitulate some
of our basic assumptions about motivational process. These have
already been expounded at length in our earlier writings, but it
will be pertinent to summarize those features which have a special
bearing on our present problem.

We may start with what may perhaps seem to be a radical
assumption about motivation, namely that, *for purposes of the
theory of action* motivation is best treated as "originally" undifferentiated with regard to the system in which it is used. According
to this conception, for the personality as a system, motivation consists in a single unitary "urge to gratification"; it is simply an urge to
"get something", to level the existing state of motivational tension.
The specification of goals, the *content* of what the actor wants, is
thereby assumed to derive, not from any inherent structure of the
motivational system as such, but from the "orientations" which
have developed in processes of action themselves. The specification
of a goal is a product of "learning". In short, motivation is conceived
as a "flow of energy" from the organism as a physiological system.
This flow of energy is organized, distributed and utilized in and
by the "personality" as a system of action, and through this, by
whatever system of social interaction is the point of reference
for the particular analysis. This "flow" may be traced in Figure 7.

logical literature have been thought of as polar types of institutional structure,
the best known version of which perhaps has been the *Gemeinschaft—Gesel-
lschaft* dichotomy of Toennies.

Now it is obvious that for the personality as a system a certain empirical specificity of action-goals is imposed by the needs of the organism. This biological element in the structure of the empirical goal-system will, however, here be treated as a set of points of reference for the organization of action by orientation. The relative empirical importance of a set of biologically organized elements in action, and of the components derived from the system of learned orientation may be left open at this point.

A second basic assumption is that this flow of motivational energy becomes differentiated into a "branching stream" through the learning processes in the course of which a system of orientation is developed. The learning process is represented in Figures 7 and 8. The allocation of motivational significance to objects in the situation, we refer to as "cathexis". Concomitantly there is the process of cognition of the object-world which on the action level is the primary focus of the mechanisms of adaptation to the situation. The system of orientation is built up by the learning of cathectic and cognitive orientations.

The relations between cognitions and cathexes are organized by the process of evaluation. The evaluative process establishes two sorts of connections. In relation to the *unit* of the action-system itself, say a particular need disposition in a personality, evaluation results in *commitment* of the motivational energy of the unit to the particular content of goal orientation which is constitutive of a concrete action process. At the same time evaluation enters into the determination of *relations* of the particular need disposition unit to other need disposition units in the system.

The fact that the goals which are empirically important for the theory of action are always "secondary" or learned goals presupposes the development of a system of symbolic patterns which govern the relationship of member units and objects in the consummatory phase. (We may suspect that in the most important cases at least the objects are "complex objects," in the sense discussed in Chapter 2, and that correspondingly the cathectic orientation is not merely an "elementary" or "primitive" cathexis but an "attitude" in the sense of an expressive-symbolic value pattern. Quite clearly gratification or satisfaction in effective achievement or in a love attachment to a human being belong in this category.) This specification of the consummatory goal state, in terms of a symbolically organized, cognitive and expressive "definition of the situation", is what we meant above by "commitment" to a goal. The primary or elementary "direction" of action process toward the state of goal-attainment cannot be empirically defined without an element of symbolically organized commitment, i.e. specification of goal-orientation.

Specification of the *goal-state* is however, only the first step in the statement of the four differentiated phases which must be taken into account in the analysis of motivational process. Next we must take account of two further elements. These are the two sets of *exigencies* of goal-attainment. The meeting of these sets of exigencies are the conditions of maintenance of a steady state of action-process in a system. Both involve problems arising from scarcity and hence the necessity of allocation. We shall call these the "exigencies of the task orientation area" and "exigencies of the social emotional area" of a system of action. More specifically they are the exigencies of *adaptation* and of *integration*.

The first of these sets of conditions—the solution of the adaptive problems of the task orientation area—arises from the fact that a goalstate is a state of relationship between the member units in the system and a set of situational objects. The stability of this relationship depends not only on the stability of the member units' motivational orientations, i.e. on their "commitment" to the goal, but also on the stability of the situational factors themselves in relation to the system. Since this relationship cannot be presumed to "stay put" without processes of control and/or adaptation on the part of one or more of the member units, a major *task* is imposed. In the interest of the maximization of gratification and satisfaction over time, then, there must be diversion of some energy from direct goal-gratification to manipulation of situational factors, that is, into "instrumental" activity. Maximization of goal-gratification, is then, other things being equal, a function of the balance between consummatory activity and instrumental activity. The "success" of this instrumental activity is then constituted by adequate adaptation to the exigencies of a changeable situation.

Seen in these terms, consummatory activity and instrumental activity have in common the feature that they treat the relevant need-dispositions of member units as oriented to certain specific goals. The need-dispositions in question are conceived at the time to be in control of some important part of the motor apparatus of the organism as well as of other facilities—a control which may be to some degree incompatible with other need-disposition units operating in it at the same time. Opportunities for need-dispositions to go into overt action constitute a scarce resource of the personality as a system; they are facilities which must be allocated. The phases, in which the performances occur, differ, however, in that in the consummatory phase the relation to the object is an "intrinsically" gratifying (or deprivational) one; in the instrumental phase, on the other hand, there is greater or less distance from such a goal-state and activity is directed to altering the system-object relationship in the goal-state direction. This involves "inhibition" of tendencies toward direct gratification or aversion in a double sense. The first is postponement of primary goal-consummation until a more favorable situation has been produced. The second is the passing-up of secondary opportunities—perhaps for gratification of other need-dispositions—along the way, the acceptance of which would interfere with the efficiency of the instrumental activity.

The second set of conditions of maintenance of a steady state consists in the meeting of those exigencies to which the gratification of a particular need-disposition is exposed as a result of the presence of other units in the same system. These are the exigencies of the social emotional area and constitute the integrative problem. The units in a system may be either other need-dispositions in the personality of ego or those in other personalities (alters) in a system of social interaction, or both. The problem here is closely analogous with that on the adaptive side. Given the expectation pattern of one member unit, there is no guarantee that the relations to other units on which the fulfillment of the expectation depends will "stay put". There will, therefore, be a necessity for processes of adjustment, either by positively controlling the relevant unit or by accommodation to it. This is perhaps easier to follow on the level of interpersonal communication than on the level of the interaction of need-dispositions within the personality, so let us change the system point of reference to that of the small group with persons as member units.

The modes of adaptation to new system situational exigencies consist in the cognitive understanding of cathected objects and in the instrumental manipulation of their relationships to each other and to the system. Adjustment to other member units, on the other hand, we conceive to operate through cognition also, but it involves preponderantly expressive communication, i.e. the obtaining and giving of emotionally significant positive sanctions, and the avoidance of negative ones from other member units. Whereas the adaptive processes operate through regulation of the situational non-system *consequences* of the investment of motivation in a given goal-attainment process under varying conditions, integrative processes operate through shifting the *allocation* of motivational energy as between alternative "channels" of its employment, i.e. as between the encouragement or discouragement of activity of given member units. A sanction consists in an "intentional" (in the sense of Chapter 2) manipulation by one member unit of expressive symbols which presents to some other member unit "secondary" objects of cathexis connecting with primary objects by paths of generalization. Such symbolic manipulation either "drains" energy by providing appropriate channels of cathexis or prevents its draining off in dysfunctional channels by withdrawing potential opportunities for cathexis, or other opportunities for energy expenditure.

(It should be recognized that the concrete unit of the action system is empirically an object both of adaptive and of integrative processes. It is an adaptive object so far as its motivational orientation is not subject to expressive influence but is responsive only to changes in situational conditions.)

The fourth focus of the differentiation of the action process concerns the problem of "tension". There is a common assumption that the term tension should be used only to refer to the organic state of the physiological system as defined in physiological terms; and while empirically this usage is highly important, for our theoretical purposes this use of the term is precluded by our assumption of the undifferentiated character of "original" action motivation. As a result of this assumption, our attention is more easily drawn to a fundamental set of problems which may be either altogether overlooked or seriously misunderstood. These essentially center about the fact that the unit of the action system, the need-disposition of the member of a social group, is, from a different vantage point, *itself a system* which has its own set of conditions of equilibrium. This conception is of fundamental importance in view of our claims for microscopic-macroscopic applicability of the theory of action. Most of the more elementary action problems involve two adjacent levels on this range. The unit is the "lower level," while the "system" is the higher of the two.[12]

Tension, as we should like to use the term, exists in so far as the actual "position" of one or more units in the system involves a discrepancy relative to the position, which in terms of necessities of their *own* equilibrium as systems they *ought* to occupy. Tension is thus a vague residual term designating the state of the motivational reservoir available for use or pressing for expression in the system under consideration. "Tension" is, of course, the result of mechanisms internal to the unit, as well as its direct reactions to the larger system of units of which it is a part. But the treatment of the unit as a unit and not as a system means that on that level of analysis we are concerned only with the *consequences* of the operation of these internal mechanisms, not with the mechanisms themselves. Hence the end result is taken as given and called "tension". To deal with the latter explicitly, it would be necessary precisely to shift the system reference so that what was formerly treated as a unit was now treated as a system.

One major source of difficulty in being methodical about system-references lies in the fact that the integration of a symbolic pattern system in fact, typically, extends beyond the sub-system which, at the time, is being treated as a unit. Thus in most problems of the process of social interaction it is difficult to deal explicitly with the personalities of the participating actors as distinct systems, and for many purposes it is unnecessary to do so. In such a case, a level of tension will be attributed to the *actor*, and not to some particular need-disposition which is involved as a role-expectation in this particular interaction process. It is assumed that the personality of the actor, is, in the relevant sense, sufficiently well integrated so that no serious error will result from failing to distinguish which of his need-dispositions in engaged. For other problems, on the other hand, such as those in which role-conflict is involved, such a distinction may be of the first importance.

If the unit is itself a system at the lower level of the range, then treating it as a "unit", analogous with the particle, means that it is treated as being itself an *integrated* system. In this context, we ascribe to it an integrated pattern which permeates all of its "references", its goal specification or commitment, the patterns of adaptive or integrative orientation. From this conception of a unit emerges our fourth dimension, that of "latency".

In terms of the theory of action this integrated pattern means the "qualities" of that unit as an object in all its relevant references in action process. This in turn consists, in fact, in the cultural or symbolic pattern-system of the unit, assuming that it is integrated, or "pattern-consistent". This is what we mean by the relevance of the latency dimension of the action system. A unit "tends" to attain the goal to which it is committed. It also "tends" to adapt to situa-

12 The self-vs. collectivity-orientation pattern-variable, which we have deliberately omitted from the combinations which play the principal part in this analysis, derives its chief significance in problems where it is necessary to consider explicitly still a third level "above" the level of the usual system-reference. The self-vs. collectivity-orientation pattern-variable is a function of the fact that the system in question in integrated in still a wider system, of which other comparable systems are also units.

tional and to integrative exigencies. But equally it "tends" to maintain and to "express" itself, that is both to remain stable and on occasion "act out" in terms of its own qualities, its own symbolic pattern of meaning-integration, not only in goal-gratification, but in other respects as well.

With the differentiation of a system of action into parts or member units, with a stabilized allocation of motivational energy, and a stabilized process of action and gratification, there develops a system of *expectations*. This concept refers simply to one major aspect of processes in a system in equilibrium, which is the presumption of their continuance unchanged. We will interpret what psychologists call "frustration" as a disturbance in the equilibrium of the system seen from the point of view of some particular need-disposition unit under consideration. Disequilibrium is the obstruction or deflection of the process of flow of energy in relation to performance and to gratification.

Under these assumptions, we can make an important inference as to the nature of reaction to frustration in this sense. The tendency in a system, the equilibrium of which has been disturbed, will, we assume, be to restore the equilibrium by eliminating the source of the disturbance. The frustration of any one unit will result from some change in its relation to cathected objects, including other units. The cathexis of the object or objects will tend to persist; only after a process of learning including extinction, i.e. reaching a new equilibrium, would it disappear. This continuing cathexis will produce a tendency to change the new relation to the object in the direction of a restoration of the old relationship, and to do so by controlling the relation to the object. At the same time, there will be an effort to reduce the cathexis of the older frustrating path of action. This is the basis in the analysis of system process for the generalization that the reaction to a frustrating experience is in the nature of the case *ambivalent* in structure.

The paradigm for the analysis of deviant behavior (*Social System*, Chapter 7) formulates, relative to any given pattern of expectation, the main logical possibilities of orientation in such a situation of frustration, with respect first to the primacy of the positive or the negative components of the frustrated and ambivalent motivational structure, and second to the mobilization of motivational energy into this particular need-disposition unit, or withdrawal of energy from it. This problem will be discussed more fully below.

General Considerations about Input and Output

The basic duality of the action frame of reference, between actor and situation, attitude and object etc. has underlain all of our analysis of systems of action and processes within them. We now wish to make this duality the starting point for a somewhat closer analysis than before of two major aspects of this system-process namely (1) the process of what happens to *motivation* or drive in the course of action and, on the other hand, (2) how objects change their *symbolic meanings* and this altered meaning comes to be built into the patterning of the action process or system structure itself.

In this connection it should be kept in mind that, as we have repeatedly pointed out, what we *mean by the* structure of action systems as social objects consists precisely in their patterning as systems of symbolic meanings. Therefore change in symbolic meaning is by definition change in the structure of the actor-situation system in its capacity as a system of objects.

It is convenient to approach these problems in terms of the conceptions of "input" and "output". By input we mean what goes into any given sector of the phase process of a system of action both from outside the system and from its antecedent state, variations in which will influence processes in the system; by output on the other hand we mean changes in the resulting state of the system or its situation, i.e. of other systems of action and of non-social objects, observable at the end of the period, which may be regarded as consequences of the system process. The input-output point of view thus is not an independent mode of analyzing system process, but rather a way of describing the differences between starting state and ending state of a cycle, by looking at the system from "outside", i.e. from the point of view of an observer, and attempting to assess the balances between what "goes in" at the beginning of a cycle and what "comes out" at the end including changes in the properties of the system itself as seen by an outside observer. We wish to hold rigorously to this point of view and never to speak of input or output as something happening within a system phase cycle, but only as something happening *between* the beginning of such a time segment of process and the end. However, we must remember that system-references are to point arbitrary and may be changed. Therefore what is the process of interaction between the units of a system on one level, i.e. analyzed as performance and sanction, may be treated as input-output balance of any given unit, when this is treated as a sub-system with its own phase period from an outside point of view. But when we speak this way it will always involve a shift of system-reference. In input-output analysis the focus is not on interaction process, but on the *consequences* involved in a given time sector of such process: on the one hand its "cost" in what has been "used up", on the other hand its outcome, or to continue the economic terminology, its product.

The concepts of input and output are inherently quantitative and their introduction constitutes, we hope, another step toward analysis of the quantitative aspects of action process. The fundamental base line for reference in this respect is an implication of the conception of equilibrium, of which we have made so much use. This is the proposition that, for the stable state, the inputs into a system must over time be balanced by the outputs or, put the other way around, that any excess or deficit in a category of input will necessitate changes in the state of the system which will, unless balanced out over time, be reflected in changes in one or more categories of its output. This proposition in turn we feel is derivable mainly from one of our four principles which were stated in Chapter 3, and repeated at the beginning of the present one, namely that of acceleration or effort. This essentially says that if "resources" are put into a system, what happens to them must be accounted for, either the situation or the state of the system, or both is changed as a consequence; and conversely for the case of withdrawal of resources. This aproach to the problem points to the underlying conception of some kind of principle of conservation; not in this case of energy, because of our conception of one-way process, but a conservation of inputs, in the sense that if we identify inputs, we must account for them; they do not just evaporate nor, in the relevant respects, does the system process simply "create" new things without reference to the "something" out of which they are made.

Our first problem, then is to define the major categories of input and output, because only then can we make an approach to definition and analysis of the "transformations" which occur in the course of a process of action. On the input side we must think first of the initial state of the system at the inception of an "accounting period" and then of inputs from outside the system—similarly in the output side there is the distinction between the terminal state of the system and that of the "outside" i.e. of the situation which is not itself defined as part of the system. In relating the two, the conception of equilibrium in the stable state is fundamental. Our basic postulate is that in the stable state inputs and outputs as a whole will balance through time and that change in one category will be "compensated" by an "equivalent" change in other categories.

When we come to consider the *kinds* of input and output it seems best to cross-cut the system-situation distinction and to speak of two most fundamental categories of each; namely (1) the input of motivational energy or drive and its output "products" and (2) the input of object properties and relations and their output consequences.

The Input-Output Economy of Motivational Energy

Motivational input from the antecedent state of the system must be thought of not as an absolute quantity but as a rate of flow which has both a total "volume" and an allocative distribution among whatever channels may have become established. Output as correspondingly measured in motivational terms must be conceived in terms of the question of whether this volume and distribution has changed over the period in question.

Using the rate of motivational energy flow as our point of reference is in accord with our conception of action from this point of view as a one-way process which consumes energy. This energy we conceive as converted into changes in the state of the system and of its situation *from what it would have been* had the input of energy not occurred. Part of this then goes to the *maintenance* of the system in a stable state, part to *alteration* of that state and the situation. Finally we have the question of the comparison of the rate of motivational input at the end of the period with that at the beginning.

In talking about the output of the motivational process we must therefore make a distinction between what has happened to the energy consumed, and what has happened to the rate of energy flow. The measure of the relation between energy consumed and output in maintenance or change of state of the system-situation complex we will call *satisfaction*. The measure of comparative motivational potential, i.e. rates of flow and distribution, at the two ends of a period we will call the level of *gratification* of the system. Both these concepts are in need of some elucidation.

Both must be related to the normative patterns of the system but in different ways. Satisfaction is essentially the relation between normatively defined expectations of performance—in the social system case role-expectations—and the actual outcome of a performance process as evaluated in terms of system norms. Gratification on the other hand is the motivational state of the units of the system—that of the system as a whole being their algebraic sum—as seen in terms of tension-level, which in turn we know to be a function of the balance between motivational input to the unit and its "consumption". In this connection we must keep clear that all process in a system of action is process of interaction between units—thus while our input-output analysis is concerned with the system as a whole the system does not "act", only units do that —hence all inputs are distributed to units and all outputs come from units.[13]

This brings us to a further set of considerations about motivational inputs and outputs. We may presume that at the beginning of an accounting period each unit of the system has a given motivational potential (i.e. rate of inflow) with a given set of "commitments" through value-patterns. But we assume that this can be added to or subtracted from through outside influences. Here we are concerned only with such influences coming from outside the system, but the fundamental mechanisms seem to the same whether the process be across the boundary or within it. Essentially this balancing operates through the shifting availability of and commitment to what we have called reward-objects. The presentation of a positively cathected reward-object tends to "pull" more motivational energy into a unit or system-process; its withdrawal or the presentation of a negatively cathected object to drive it out—to "raise tension" or to bring about transfer to another outlet. Then reward objects made available from outside the system constitute the second source of motivational inputs. This process we presume to include what we call expressive communication.

This process, however, seems to be subject to one fundamental constraint. We assume, that is, that all motivational energy originates in organisms. We see no reason to believe that *as motivation* (as contrasted with output of achievement or accomplishment) it can be transferred from one personality system (which is the action system of a single organism) to another. If this is correct then

[13] Our way of conceiving the relation between satisfaction and gratification gives a theoretical basis for Durkheim's famous empirical generalization that "happiness" cannot increase cumulatively over time. What we will analyze below as the outputs of achievement and accomplishment can lead to cumulative results, but satisfaction and gratification are ratios of rates relative to a stable-state base and both are bound to the potential of energy-output of the organism which is presumably only secondarily a function of action-process.

the effect of shifting availability of reward-objects is to shift the allocation of motivational energy between the need-disposition units of the same personality but not between personalities. In a system of social interaction then there is a very special kind of boundary-process continually going on which consists in the balancing of motivational inputs and outputs between the need-disposition system involved in the particular role participations of the members and the rest of their personalities. The regulation of these balances is, we presume, one of the most important aspects of the equilibrating process.

Object Qualities and Relations

The input of motivational energy and what happens to it in the course of system-process is only one aspect of the total input-output problem. The other is the balance between initial and terminal states of the system and of the situation in their capacities as objects to the observer but also to their component actors.

The system at any given moment in time is always an object which has properties as an object and relations to other objects, and which is divisible into parts—its units—which have both properties and relations to each other. These properties of the system as units at the initial point, however these be broken down, constitute one fundamental class of inputs into the system-process of the accounting period. The "help" or "hindrance" of the process attributable to objects in the situation at the same time constitute a second type of input. The first we will refer to as *system-capacities*, the second as *facilities*.

The utilization of objects in action we suggest takes place through two fundamental types of process, first that of the perception of objects and second that of their instrumental control. Perception, through the cognitive processes of the personality system, yields an output of information which is an alteration in system-capacity, i.e. one set of properties of the system.

It is also essential to realize that the processing of direct object-perception into information may be short-cut by cognitive communication. In this case the objects perceived are interpreted as symbols and their meanings incorporated into the system. Through this channel we may speak of an input of information into the system but this should be distinguished from the input of perception.

Instrumental control involves the "investment" of motivational energy beyond that necessary for perception or understanding of information in changing the *relation* of the object to the system (including changing its properties) in the direction we will define as either achievement or accomplishment.

Inputs of perception or information are transformed into outputs of "knowledge" as a system-property which may be "stored" in memory or externalized in symbolic form (e.g. by being "written down" and "filed"). In the latter case there is a communication process from self-to-self over time with creation of symbolic objects and their later perception as the intermediary steps.

Inputs of facilities are combined with information *and* the commitment of motivational energy to achieve instrumental control. The outcome of the process then will take some combination of two forms. One is valued change in the qualities of objects independently of their relations to the system—i.e. as evaluated in universalistic terms. This is what we mean by *accomplishment*. This change in the qualities of social objects is a particularly important type, and within this again we include change in the qualities of the action system which is the point of reference. Where it is only information which has been created we are dealing with meaning content—but where it is change in the pattern-structure of the system, we speak, if it is a personality, of internalization; if a social system of institutionalization. Only these latter patterns, we assume, can define and control the boundaries of a system of action.

The second basic type of output in object terms is the particularistically evaluated change in *relation to* objects. Such relations may be designated by the category of possession which in turn can be subdivided into facilities and reward-objects. These two together we will call *achievement* which then is the balance between valued relations of possession of objects attributable to the system at the end of the accounting period as compared with the beginning. The facilities aspect of achievement then concerns the performance capacity of the system—has it been augmented or diminished so far as facilities count? The reward aspect on the other hand concerns the stability of expectations of gratification—how does the balance of this in relation to expectations of performance compare at the end of the period with that of the beginning?

Figure 6 presents a tabular view of the basic input-output relations which have just been reviewed.

Figure 6

Tabular View of the Input-Output Process

	Initial State as Input	Intermediate Inputs—Outputs	Terminal State (Output)
Motivational Process	Volume and Rate of energy flow as distributed between units, Level of tension.	+ Acquisition of reward-objects and positive expressive communication — Loss of reward-objects and negative expressive communication.	Satisfaction balance, Relation of Achievement-Accomplishment to energy expenditure. Gratification balance Relation of flow and tension level to initial state.
Object-system Process	Initial object-qualities and relations including qualities of system now system and latter as possessions.	1. Perception and information through communication. 2. Gain and loss of possession of valued objects.	Accomplishment balance Gain or loss of valued qualities of objects including those of system itself. Achievement balance Gain or loss of valued possession of objects as facilities and future rewards.

Performance and Learning as System Processes

This account of the processes of input-output in relation to the stable state of a system of action enables us to gain a certain perspective on the relations of processes of performance and learning, as they are called in psychological terminology, and such cognate concepts as socialization and social change.

Both types of process are formulated in terms of what happens to a system-situation complex in its aspect as a system of objects which, we remember, is a patterned system of symbol-meaning relationships. Both are concerned with the ways in which a system of objects comes to be organized *in relation to* a process of motivational flow and to processes of change in that mode of organization.

Very simply we may speak empirically of performance processes as those in which the change from the point of view of system values in the object world and the system's relation to it exceeds the change in the qualities of the system itself as object. A learning process on the other hand is one in which the significant change in the system exceeds that in the situation. This way of looking at it makes it quite clear that performance and learning are, in our view, two aspects of the same process, both are continually going on in all systems of action; thus the distinction is to be looked at either as analytical or as a matter of quantitative balances.

Nevertheless the analytical distinction and its relation to the quantitative balance points to a fundamental implication of the duality of the action frame of reference from which this discussion took its departure. This is essentially a derivative duality of directions of the action process relative to the phase pattern.

We may say that given specification of goal-orientation for the system (and hence its units) the direct "drive" of the flow of motivational energy is to bring about the goal state which by definition is a *relation* of the system to situational objects, it is therefore a drive to change the situation relative to the system. The phase periodicity of the process then is attributable to the fact that these changes have consequences *internal* to the system which we refer to as affecting its states of integration and of tension (i.e. generalization), and that only in a limiting case can these two processes completely "cancel each other out" so that goal attainment proceeds uninterrupted in one direction for a long period. Indeed any regularized stabilization of this performance process requires not only what we have called goal specification but also a stabilized pattern with regard to the processes of adaptation, of system-integration, and of latent pattern maintenance and tension management. This total pattern complex is what we mean by the internalized "character structure" of a personality or the institutionalized "value system" of a social system.

But this symbol-meaning pattern structure is not merely a static "given", except for specific purposes. It is caught up in the action process itself and changes as a function of its variables. This change is, if it supposes a particular phase-cycle, the process of learning. It means that motivation is not merely expended on gratification in relation to cathected goal-objects and utilized in instrumental

Figure 7
Phases of Modification of the Motivational State of a System

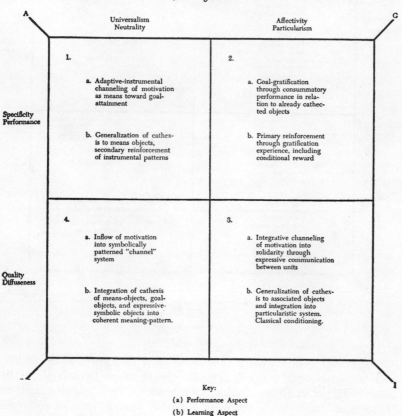

Key:

(a) Performance Aspect

(b) Learning Aspect

control but cathexis is generalized from previous goal-objects to associated objects, instrumental or otherwise, so these objects acquire new meanings which become organized and stabilized.

Figure 8
Phases of Modification of the Symbolic-Associative Patterning of an Action-Situation System

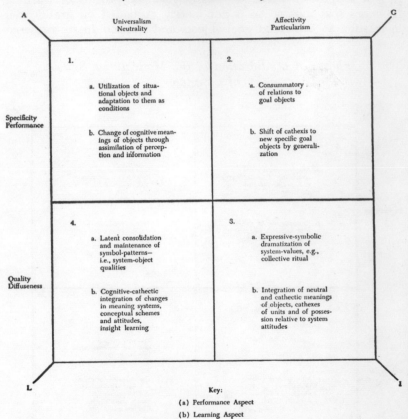

A

Universalism
Neutrality

Affectivity
Particularism

G

Specificity
Performance

1.

a. Utilization of situational objects and adaptation to them as conditions

b. Change of cognitive meanings of objects through assimilation of perception and information

2.

a. Consummatory of relations to goal objects

b. Shift of cathexis to new specific goal objects by generalization

Quality
Diffuseness

4.

a. Latent consolidation and maintenance of symbol-patterns— i.e., system-object qualities

b. Cognitive-cathectic integration of changes in meaning systems, conceptual schemes and attitudes, insight learning

3.

a. Expressive-symbolic dramatization of system-values, e.g., collective ritual

b. Integration of neutral and cathectic meanings of objects, cathexes of units and of possession relative to system attitudes

L

I

Key:
(a) Performance Aspect
(b) Learning Aspect

Figures 7 and 8 give a schematic view of motivational process and object-system process respectively in ways which show the obverse directionalities of their performance and learning aspects. If we take the Latency phase in Figure 7 as our point of reference for analyzing performance, we may conceive a stabilized inflow of motivational energy which is "distributed" in the established channels. This *may* proceed in any one or combination of three ways, (1) "directly through" by "acting out" to a consummatory phase which if the primary goal object relation has not been established must be "symbolic", or by one or both of the "detours" via (2) instrumental or (3) integrative-expressive performance. We presume that it is normal, given a system-goal, for the instrumental to predominate until the consummatory phase is reached, and for the system then to shift to integrative activities.

During this process, which we remind the reader, is a "model", we think of the expenditure of energy as gradually being balanced by satisfaction in achievement and accomplishment. However we also assume that the deflection of the phase process from a "straight line" is reflected in a changing balance of roughly the following structure: The impetus for movement out of the latency into the adaptive phase is given by "mounting tension" which means a diminution of gratification levels. This is balanced by a combination of increase of satisfaction levels (mainly through achievement) and the prospect of gratification output. As the consummatory phase is approached, the gratification level rises temporarily above the equilibrium point.

Satisfaction with the attainment of this gratification level, however is dependent on the degree to which both the system-state and the situation-state are in accord with the "values" of the system. Since the adaptive phase has, in a fairly well integrated system, brought the situation *more* into accord with these values (expectations) than before, the deficit is most likely to lie in the internal state of the system, to the "repair" of which the process then turns. When this, which we may presume consumes the previous surplus of gratification, is complete, the satisfaction level is high enough to restore equilibrium and make it possible for the system to enter into latency. This, from the motivational point of view, then remains stable until the motivational inflow again raises tension levels.

This is a highly idealized model but it illustrates the way in which our broad categorization of motivational inputs and outputs can be applied to the different phases of a system cycle. Above all it abstracts from learning processes, from changes in facilities and from "intermediate" inputs and outputs through rewards and punishments.

It is precisely here that the learning aspect of the process becomes relevant, for in one sense this is a process of disturbance of the phase-equilibrium of the performance process. In motivational terms we accept the generalization of learning theory that on some level consummatory gratification is the source of the motivation for all learning. In this sense learning is the experience that simply "taking" this gratification is "not enough", that gratification-satisfaction output can be increased by *shifting* cathexes, i.e. by "generalizing" them from original or "primary" goal-objects. This is to say that objects "associated with" the primary goal object can come to some degree to be cathected.

Our paradigm then tells us that this association may become selectively determined by its "significance" or *meaning* in either of two directions. One of these is in terms of the instrumental-adaptive significance of the object in the situation leading up to consummation. This will lead to selection in terms of relevance to the specific goal-interest and to performance, either of the *object* in providing rewards or of ego in utilizing it. This in turn leads over into stress on the universalistically evaluated properties or capacities of the object as a basis of its selection. Only as a result of such a selection process is the cathexis of the new, previously indifferent, object reinforced. This is what is meant by "instrumental" conditioning in stimulus-response learning theory.

The second direction of generalization of cathexis leads from a primary gratification experience to selection in terms of the criteria of common belongingness of the new object with the primary object in a *system* defined in relation to ego. If this belongingness, e.g. by common agency, has priority over the specificity of inherent cathexis, then the selective process builds the new object into a diffusely cathected complex, which in turn must be continuous in its cathectic meaning with the solidary relations of the units of the system to each other as constituting a system. We thus get something intrinsically unrelated to the goal-object coming to "stand for" it, i.e. to be conditioned to it, and the connection "standing up" so long as the "complex" as a whole is reinforced. This is the pattern of "classical conditioning".[14]

It seems to be in the nature of systems of action that both types of generalization of primary cathexes are proceeding at the same time though one is more prominent in one phase, the adaptive, the other, in another, the integrative. But in any case their consequences cannot simply remain at "loose-ends" but must somehow be integrated in the course of system processes. Essentially this means that first the specificity of instrumentally significant objects

[14] Cf. Hilgard and Marquis, *Conditioning and Learning* for an authoritative discussion of the distinction between these types of conditioning.

must find a place in the total meaning complex of the action system, they must be fitted into a diffusely cathected system. Secondly, the affective significance of particularistically associated objects must be accommodated to other than the consummatory phases, must find its place by being inhibited the requisite part of the time, thereby acquiring the attributes of a neutral object when occasion requires.

Thus tracing the process to the latency cell helps us analyze the integration of the more specific cathexes of objects as they shift in the process of learning into a more integrated cathectic orientation system, the "attitudes" of the system.

We may sum up the relation between the two aspects of motivational process as follows: Performance is the process by which *given* the structure of the action system as object the situation is utilized and changed to bring about a gratification-satisfaction balance both with respect to quantitative relations between initial and terminal states and with respect to distribution at the terminal state, relative to the "value-system". Learning on the other hand is the process by which elements of instability in the relations between system and objects lead to redistribution of cathexis between available objects, and thus to the modification of goal-specifications and of the adaptive and integrative patternings of cathectic meanings "radiating" from this reference point, and culminating in the integrative restructuring of the total cathectic attitude pattern of the system as a system.

There is a corresponding duality of direction in the symbolic patterning aspect of the system process as shown in Figure 8. In the performance process, seen in ideal type terms, the system-structure itself as object remains unchanged. Situational objects, however, are acquired as possessions (a form of achievement) utilized as facilities and thereby possibly "consumed"; enjoyed as goal objects and again possibly consumed, and created or changed in accord with system values, an output of accomplishment. The essential problem is what happens to the situational object system including the system's relation to it, in the course of the cycle of action process.

The learning aspect of the process on the other hand concerns the processes of change in the symbol-meaning pattern structure of the system itself. In direct contact with the external object world this must mean the shifts of cathexis to new objects discussed above and changes in their cognitive meaning through the assimilation into the system of new perception and information inputs. But then a dual integrative process internal to the system must take place. On the one hand the cognitive meanings of particular objects must be organized in a more or less coherent system in the relations between adaptive and latency aspects of the system. On the other hand the new cathectic meanings must be integrated into a system of possessions and assimilated to the integrative patterns of the system. Finally, both types of integration of discrete meanings meet in the latency cell to form a single cognitive-cathectic orientation structure. In its significance as regulating the orientations of the system throughout the phase process we speak of this as the "value system". It is internalized or institutionalized in so far as there is "commitment" to conformity with its norms so that performance tends to modify the situation in conformity with these norms. In so far as on the other hand discrepancy between situation and system values tends to lead to modification of the system in conformity with the situation, i.e. to learning processes, we would speak of the value patterns as not strongly internalized or institutionalized.[15]

The Pattern Variables Again

When we consider the formal structure of the processes we have just reviewed our attention is called again to the significance of the combinations of pattern-variable components across the attitude-object line. Besides those which constitute the dimensions themselves we called attention above to the four combinations which are built into Figure 2 and thus our analysis of the phase process. These are, going around clockwise and taking the attitudinal component first, specificity-performance, affectivity-particularism, diffuseness-quality, and neutrality-universalism.

These combinations clearly have to do with the patterns of generalization and integration of meanings which we have just reviewed. Thus specificity-performance define the coincidence of the paths of the instrumental generalization of cathexis and the lending of ultimate gratificatory significance to instrumental knowledge. Thus it is here that essential components of patterning relative to the *combination* of adaptive and goal-gratification factors are brought together.

[15] We recognize that this statement is open to the interpretation that rigidity defines the maximum of institutionalization. This is not meant. Rigidity is the case where unduly specific, hence usually "symbolic" patterns are the focus of resistance to change. High levels of control of the situation are only feasible with a considerable degree of adaptive flexibility.

Secondly, affectivity-particularism defines the coincidence of the paths of associative generalization of cathexis in an integrative direction and of the cognitive recognition of objects as belonging together in a cathectic system. This concerns relations between essential components of the goal-gratification and the integrative aspects of the system. Similarly diffuseness-quality concerns relations between the integration of system units with each other and their relation to the common culture of the system. Finally, neutrality-universalism concerns the relations between the qualities of the system as an object and the situation as a set of objects.

We may generalize these formal statements by saying that (1) if performance is to serve a specific gratification-interest, the corresponding motivational commitment must be attitudinally specific or conversely, if a particular instrumental means-object is to be cathected, i.e. its use motivated, it must be conditioned to a specific process of consummatory performance. (2) If objects are to be integrated in a particularistic, i.e. "solidary" system, they must be associated by generalization of cathexis from primary gratification-experiences or, conversely, if generalization of cathexis to associated objects is to "stick" in other than instrumental ways, then objects must be integrated in a particularistic system. (3) The attitudinal counterpart of this particularistic integration, a diffuse attitude toward the complex as a whole, must be congruent with quality patterns which can be ascribed to the complex as a whole—and conversely, if diffuse cathexes of such "complex objects" are to be stabilized, there must be a cognitive categorization of the object in terms of ascertainable qualities. Finally, (4) an integrated quality pattern cannot be oriented only to the specifications of goal states and direct expressive symbolization but must, through neutral attitudes and universalistic standards, be integrated with the cognition of the total object world as a system. Conversely any particular expressive or cognitive "input" must be evaluated in accord with this integrated standard-system.

These four paths of generalization and integration we may thus regard as structural links between the object-categorization and the attitudinal aspects of the symbol-meaning system. They go beyond the dimensions in that they state directions of process which are related to conditions of equilibrium in action systems. In recognizing their significance we have taken a step toward the formulation of substantive generalizations about system process.

Symbols as Situational Objects

We may now recall that in Chapter 2 we maintained that a symbol is *always* a situational object. Symbols *as such* then must be capable of being classified in terms of the object-categorization schema. This schema, as formulated in terms of the pattern-variables, classifies symbols according to their relevance to action from the *performance* point of view, that is from the point of view of the type of "objective" input-output which they *mean*, i.e. constitute. Thus the combination universalism-performance *means* either an achieved change in the object-situation or a facility which can be utilized in an achievement process. Similarly the combination performance-particularism means a reward-object, either an object of immediate gratification produced by ego's action, or a reward-object placed at his disposal by alter. Quality-particularism means an object of expressive appreciation, i.e. if it is an output of action process, an accomplishment, and universalism-quality one which represents a universalistically assessed accomplishment.

This way of looking at the organization of symbolic content makes it clear that objects as symbols relative to action are organized in terms of the type of *value* which they have for the action system. The meaning of an object for an actor is thus *defined* by its value to him in the process of action—by what it enables him to "do" in the broadest meaning of that term. This explains why we have found it justifiable to use the *same* fundamental classification for the ordering of four kinds of entities which, to common sense, do not seem to belong together, namely, (1) types of object generally, (2) types of symbol, (3) types of performance, and (4) types of value-pattern so far as object-categorization is concerned.

There are of course other valid bases for the classification of symbols—such as the particular classes of objects to which they refer or their own common attributes as objects. But it is the classification in terms of the object-categorization pattern-variables which gives us the *patterning* of the symbol system as a system which is integral to the structure of the system of action itself. It is this which enables us to treat system-structure and situational objects in directly homologous terms.

The attitudinal pattern-variable combinations on the other hand classify, not symbolic objects as objects, but the cathectic or motivational *meanings* of these objects. These meanings in turn are based on the inputs and outputs of motivation and gratification-satisfaction in the course of system-process.

Thus we have had objects classified, i.e. orientations to them ordered, in terms of their meanings, i.e. their functional significance in the action process, and we have had attitudes toward these same objects classified in terms of a *complementary* set of meanings. In what sense are these two sets of meanings complementary? *In that they are measured in the same or interchangeable units along the same dimensions.*

It must be kept clear that these meanings are by definition symbolic—they are, in Durkheim's terms "superimposed" on the intrinsic properties of the object. Only in one of four dimensions, the adaptive, are the "intrinsic" characteristics of objects crucial— including of course those of actors who perform and have attitudes. But the values of the other three dimension, i.e. the properties of social objects described in terms of these dimensions, all constitute "accomplishments" of the process of action itself. Their relation to "reality" outside the system is creative, not adaptive.

The congruence of object-categorization and attitudinal meanings then becomes the "surrogate" in three dimensions for the stability of the external object-world. Or put a little differently, this congruence *is the definition of the conditions for the stable state of an action system.* This is the meaning on a new level of the familiar proposition that a common value system is indispensable as the core of a common culture for the functioning of a system of action.

The four paths of generalization and integration we discussed above then formulate the principal modes of articulation of symbol-meaning relationships in terms of their organization *across* the object-attitude duality which in interaction, as we know, becomes the performance-sanction duality. Thus specificity-performance links the specificity of attitude—i.e. of cathectic investment, and the motivation of action performance in both instrumental and consummatory activity. In the adaptive phase, however, this link is combined with neutrality-universalism, integrating instrumental performance with universalistic cognitive standards and inhibiting premature or distracting consummation. In the consummatory phase, on the other hand, it is linked with affectivity-particularism, making some of the motivational energy released in the consummatory phase available for cathexis of associated objects in addition to the specific goal-object.

We discussed above four types of norm, each of which could be thought of as "made up" of an object-categorization or performance type of value-pattern and an attitudinal or sanction type. We can now see that the "pairing" of the two patterns involved in each norm may be considered to be made up of two sub-pairs each of generalized significance in the action system. Thus when we say that approval is the sanction-type appropriate to instrumental performance in accord with achievement values we stress the fact that it *both* maintains the specificity of the relevant goal-interest and at the same time the neutrality necessary to avoid premature tension release or consummation—it yields an increment of satisfaction, not gratification. These relationships stand at the very heart of the equilibrating processes of the system of action.

In conclusion of this section we may again call attention to Bales' finding in Chapter 4 that positive reactions predominate heavily over negative in the normal interactive process. In the light of the treatment of input-output problems just completed we may take this to be empirical evidence in favor of our postulate that, motivationally considered, action is a one-way process which *consumes* energy. In general, we have argued, negative sanctions have the effect of slowing down the processes of action. If the "problem" of systems of action were only or predominantly to maintain static equilibrium there would, it would seem, be much more emphasis on preventing deviance. The preponderance of positive sanctions suggests emphasis on task-performance—on the production of a substantial output of satisfaction and gratification to balance the consumption of motivational input.[16]

VII. *The Equilibrating Process and the Mechanisms of Social Control*

On the basis of the considerations analyzed in the preceding section we can now proceed to give a considerably more precise and technical account of the process of interaction in its relations to system-equilibrium than before.

We assume that, at any given point in process which is chosen as an "initial state", the system will have a "structure". It will be composed of a plurality of units differentiated both with respect to the "configuration" of their orbits and with respect to their phase at the moment. There will be a common culture of symbolic meanings and their patterns, especially their value-patterns. These meanings will include both object-qualities and attitudes. By virtue of the latter, the system will operate at some level of integration

16 It may be that some part is payed here by the particular types of task-oriented groups studies by Bales. We do not, however, believe that the significance of this finding is confined to one rather narrowly defined class of system.

which will be manifested in the solidarity of the members—their mutual acceptance of each other in their respective roles.

Let us then assume that a task-orientation process is initiated by a member performing one or a series of acts of orientation. This, as shown in Figure 4 tends to increase the adaptive (A) components in his behavior while reducing certain components characteristic of each of the other three phases. It introduces a strain in the direction of neutrality and universalism, thus decreasing his state of integration with his system members because it minimizes the affectivity and particularism which are characteristic of system integrative behavior. At the same time his demand for a reaction of agreement is increased since the input of motivation into the system, coming through his act of orientation, has not yet been balanced by an output of gratification or satisfaction.

At the same time that ego has changed the orbit of his phase movement and thus precipitated at least momentarily the beginning of a state of system-disequilibrium, a corresponding change has occurred for alter. First, alter's situation has been changed by ego's action—he is presented with a cognitive or informational problem of understanding what has happened, of evaluation, and of what to do overtly. Second the motivational meaning of the situation has been changed and he is presented with an attitudinal problem —he must react.

Alter's reaction will, we are aware, have both instrumental and expressive-symbolic significance, but he can vary the relative emphases.

He may respond with an act of agreement or disagreement which would also be an application of the sanction of approval-disapproval. The effect would be to accelerate ego's action in the direction initiated by changing ego's satisfaction level or to slow it down, or in the case of sharp disagreement perhaps to halt it altogether.

Positive agreement by alter presumably would lead to leaving the initiative with ego for further acts of orientation, opinion or suggestion. Disagreement by alter on the other hand would tend to shift the initiative to alter or a third person (while increasing ego's tension level in response to the sanction) with the probability of resorting to opinion to justify the disagreement.

Alter's reaction might, however, take another form, namely that of continuation in the same direction.[17] In that case he might ex-

[17] To represent alter's behavior in the task area another similar figure would be necessary in which "ego" and "alter" on the present figure would be reversed.

press his implicit agreement with ego by a positive contributory act, following ego's lead, which would probably be recorded as an act of orientation or suggestion, or possibly a favorable opinion forestalling anticipated disagreements. But we may suggest that contributory acts following the lead of an initiator should usually be considered to include at least a component of agreement.

On the other hand, if alter's reaction is in the negative direction with an act which blocks ego's initiated line the act is equivalent to an act of disagreement, and is so scored in Bales' method as defined at present. The question now is which line of action best meets the normative requirements of the adaptive phase. The disagreement could stimulate ego to strengthen or resume the previously initiated act of orientation, or if the tension level has risen to the point where task orientation can no longer be maintained it could be submitted to the "arbitration" of opinion, or antagonism leading to a vicious circle could set in.

It would take too much space to attempt to follow this type of analysis through all the phases, and it would be unnecessary.[18] We can go directly to certain general considerations. The first is that every act in an interaction process unless it is completely "discounted" and falls exactly on a stable state line, presents the other actors with "problems" in *both* the cognitive and the cathectic senses. The existence of a problem in this sense means that for the various alters in the system there is an unresolved imbalance of the input-output factors in question, and unless "reactions" tending to the resolution of this imbalance appear, the system will not regain its former equilibrium state. Conversely the consequences for ego of alter's reaction influences his own input-output balance through the channels we have analyzed.

Every "action" which does not fall exactly on the stable state line, or within the range of permitted variation on either side of that line, constitutes to varying degrees a case of deviance; it involves a slight departure in some direction from the balance required for equilibrium and is analyzable in terms of the three dimensions of deviance we discussed above, activity-passivity, conformity-alienation and pattern-emphasis vs. social-object or cathectic emphasis. In each case, in whatever phase the unit happens to be situated in its orbit, this deviance will be definable in terms of an excess or deficit in one or more of these three categories of conformity with the expectation constitutive of the

18 This is what Bales is attempting to do systematically with his probability models, which are described in Chapter 4 above.

stable state. The function of reactions as sanctions, then, is to reinforce internalized patterns oriented towards conformity with expectations, and where these internalized patterns do not exist or are insufficient, to counteract this deviant component and restore the balance. If there is an excessive input of motivation, allocated in a given direction, i.e. if the deviance is in terms of "activity", the sanction should take away some motivation allocated in the disturbing direction, which, as we have seen, disapproval of instrumental actions does. If there is an insufficient input of motivation, i.e. the deviance is passive, it should add motivation, through encouragement or through facilitating cooperation.

If the deviant tendency is in the direction of alienation, i.e. towards an excessive input of negative types of expressive communication, then the sanction-reaction should add to the incentive to conformity. If, for example, when the system is in the instrumental phase, the alienated individual tends to premature gratification to the neglect of adaptive considerations, alter's disapproval, operating through disagreement and possibly unfavorable opinion will, in the normal case, deprive ego of satisfaction in his consummatory performance. Hence, any gain in gratification is overbalanced by a loss of satisfaction. If, on the other hand, the deviance is in the direction of complusive conformity to achievement standards then agreement, encouragement, showing solidarity or provoking tension release may aid in righting the balance, i.e. by enabling ego to renounce overly strong cathexis on certain standards such as "exaggerated scruples" in favor of more venturesome goal-directed performance.

Similarly with deviance in terms of the balance between pattern-emphasis and person-emphasis. We might say that the pattern-oriented deviant is overly sensitive to what he believes are alter's performance demands or expectations of him—whereas the person-oriented deviant is over sensitive to alter's reactive sanctions of agreement-disagreement solidarity-antagonism etc. The balance in the first case might be restored by alter's increasing his rate of positive reactions and decreasing his rate of task oriented activity and negative sanctions,—and in the other case, by decreasing his rate of all types of sanctions and increasing his rate of task oriented activity.

In essence, this equilibration process in cases where serious deviance does not exist is analyzed empirically by Bales in Chapter 4 above. It will above all be noted that the equilibrating process as analyzed is compatible with both performance and learning processes going on continually in the system. The only condition is that the changes brought about by these processes should be relatively gradual so as not to exceed the capacities of the system to continue self-equilibration through these "normal" adaptive-adjustive mechanisms.

A further set of problems arises, however, in connection with tendencies to the development of "vicious circles" of deviance and the mechanisms which may control these. The latter are the "mechanisms of social control".

Only a brief statement of the vicious circle problem is necessary since this has been discussed at length in Chapter 7 of the *Social System*. We may center our brief statement on the concept of expectations. Frustration we defined earlier as the "normal" reaction to non-fulfillment of expectations. We further maintained that the reaction to a frustrating event necessarily has an ambivalent structure. On the one hand there is the tendency to restore the state which would have existed had there not been such a departure from expectations, on the other hand there is the tendency to react deviantly in response to the strain imposed by the frustration. The deviance, depending on the state of the system, might be active or passive, alienative or conformative, with pattern-emphasis or person-emphasis, or some resultant of these three.

The further consequence is connected with the quantitative balance of inputs and outputs. Inertia gives us the presumption of continuance of the unit in the same direction. But the stable state of the system is, as we have seen, dependent for its continuance not only on the energy and pattern-direction of the unit itself, but on continuing inputs from other units in the system, inputs of motivation through expressive communication such as encouragement and contributory performance, of information and of normative control through opinion. These inputs may be in deficit or they may be excessive. What we have defined as a frustration is thus *either* a deficit *or* an excess in one or more of the classes of inputs on which the process of a unit at the relevant phase of its orbit is dependent. It is *most* important to be clear that departure from expectation in *either* direction is frustrating, not only insufficient reward or encouragement, but excessive reward or encouragement as well. This was a fundamental insight perhaps first clearly formulated by Durkheim in his interpretation of anomic suicide.

Equilibration requires the relatively prompt and correctly proportioned righting of the imbalances of these deficits or excesses, either by alter's sanctioning activity or through the mobilization of resources from other parts of ego's personality system or the system of objects external to personality or social system. If this balancing does not occur within some limits which must be empirically determined, ego's deviance will tend to become cumulative, with two sets of consequences. In the first place it "carries over" from the phase in which the initial frustrating event occurred, and begins to permeate subsequent phases. Thus inadequate encouragement, or still more, illegitimate but unmistakable discouragement in the adaptive-instrumental phase will tend to increase tensions and increase the motivation to direct goal-consummation or tension release, to the neglect of adaptive considerations. In the consummatory phase this will have the tendency to cut down the degree of integration of ego's own goals with those of other units in the system; his suggestions will give undue emphasis to obtaining acceptance of his "personal point of view"; at the same time his need for response-rewards grows. Then, in the system-integrative phase, he will make excessive demands for solidarity and be excessively sensitive to acceptance. By this path an initial frustration in the instrumental performance sphere may develop into the inevitable frustration of a need for acceptance which will be unrealistic because in terms of the common culture it will be illegitimate. The normal manifestation of solidarity may thus turn into antagonism.

The second order of consequences derives from the impact of ego's deviance on alter's expectations. In some sense a deviant actor always places excessive demands on others; he makes it more difficult for them to react in such a way that their reaction will be an equilibrating sanction. Hence unless alter is able to mobilize extra resources of patience, and tolerance coupled with willingness to deny ego's demands, alter's sanctioning reactions will grow less and less adequate for re-equilibration. The vicious circle in social interaction becomes most conspicuous when there is an outbreak of mutual antagonism. The end result can be the complete disruption of the group.

Thus we see that unless balanced, the deviance arising from frustration tends to ramify through the system in two directions, in ego's cumulative deviance throughout the phases of action of the particular unit, and in deviant reaction on the part of alter which makes sanctions less rather than more effective. In this latter case it should be kept in mind that a sanction which would have been effective in response to that minor deviance which we think of as "normal," will cease to be effective at a more advanced stage, indeed it may come to have exactly the opposite effect. This is when the *real* vicious circle stage is reached.

The essential explanation of this phenomenon lies in the ambivalent structure of all reactions to frustrating experiences. This ambivalence, if cumulative, results in chronically high tension levels —of which anxiety is a manifestation in the personality. Then progressively, as the tension level mounts, tension-release comes to have priority over other alternative paths of action. The actor becomes progressively more insensitive to the normal stimuli of adaptive and integrative processes, indeed even of opportunities for goal-gratification. He tends to impose his own idiosyncratic expressive-symbolic meanings on situations, and perhaps above all on social objects, thus distorting the "definition cf the situation" which is part of the common culture of the system. There is, then, the increasing tendency for action to become a violent process of oscillation between sheer "acting out" of tension in personalized symbolic form rather than system-goal-gratification form and, on the other hand, motivated by anxiety, sheer inhibition of what otherwise would be normal activity.[19]

We are now in a position to interpret considerably more precisely than was possible in Chapter 3, the significance of Parsons' paradigm of the processes of social control (cf. *Social System*, Chapter 7). This, it will be remembered, was originally stated in terms of the process of psychotherapy, and then generalized to other processes of social control. The paradigm consisted, it will be remembered, of the four categories of permissiveness, support, denial of reciprocity and manipulation of rewards.

The interpretation of this paradigm is facilitated by bearing in mind the difference between it and the normal equilibrating processes we have reviewed above. It becomes applicable when the vicious circle process is well advanced and the normal sanctioning process is no longer effective. The social control paradigm

[19] The well-known psychoanalyst, Dr. Grete Bibring (in an oral discussion) has stated three principal criteria of "mental health" which can be used to judge stages of therapeutic progress, namely capacity to work, capacity to love, and capacity to enjoy. It is striking how closely this fits our analysis. Capacity to work may be interpreted as normal adaptive patterns in phase 1, capacity to love, normal integrative patterns in phase 3 and capacity to enjoy, normal patterns of goal-gratification in phase 2. Important deficiencies in all three directions seem to mean the concentration of action in phase 4; the oscillation between forced inhibitory latency, and inappropriate tension-releasing "acting out."

is relevant in the analysis of responses to systematic deviance in which not only one particular type of action in a particular situation shows the marks of deviance, but in which there is generalized deviance permeating several phases and several action-reaction relationships in interaction or at least large areas of them. In our analysis we will continue to utilize the therapeutic process as an example because the relationships are easiest to see here.

We begin with *permissiveness*. We suggested above that cumulative deviance narrows the range of action by exaggerating the alternation between latent tension build up and tension-release in the latency phase. We may deduce first that the patient's incapacities in other phases have become so great and his need for tension release so high that blocking this outlet to the extent that is normal in equilibrated social interaction would be deleterious; it would missive must be "able to take it"; he must somehow control his own simply reinforce the vicious circle. But the therapist in being per- reactions which would otherwise be normal in response to this tension-releasing activity. He must also keep this tension release on the symbolic-expressive level by refraining from what would otherwise be "appropriate" reactions. Essentially permissiveness, then, is the way of allowing the patient to express himself in areas close to his major conflicts and difficulties in the ways in which he is able most easily to do this.

The second major component of the pattern is *support*. Its significance derives from the aspect of the progressive development of the vicious circle process we just mentioned, namely, that the frustration of alter's expectations which deviance inevitably involves, leads to the undermining of ego's solidarity with others. From the point of view of capacity to behave normally this is the "bottom" of the vicious circle because of the strategic significance in the personality system of the need for acceptance or for security. The therapist, then, must be able to tolerate the excessive demands of the patient and "accept" him as a human being; he must form a solidary collectivity with him, in spite of the fact that the patient behaves in ways which in ordinary social relationships would undermine this acceptance. Here we see one of the most important functions of the definition of illness as an institutionalized role; if a person is sick, certain behavior will not, it is true, be fully legitimized, but it can be "excused" as "understandable" in the light of the illness.

The focus of these two aspects of social control in the social-emotional area of action is highly suggestive. The mechanisms of control take hold of one aspect of the vicious circle by, as it were, cutting down drastically the price the patient has to pay for his deviance. He is not punished for deviant tension-releasing expressions which otherwise would incur punishment, and at the same time he is given a supportive solidarity which otherwise his behavior would destroy. But if this were all there were to the process, it is highly probable that it would not be effective.

The third component of the process is the *denial of reciprocity*. By this we mean, essentially, the refusal of the therapist to allow expressive-symbolic tension-releasing productions or "acting out" to constitute the cognitive element in the common culture of the doctor-patient relationship as a social system. It must be remembered here that what a social object *is* as an object is *itself* the product of the process of action. The patient's tension-releasing activity is never *only* that, it is also an effort to gain acceptance of his definition of the situation. If his bid is accepted, then by the standards of the larger social system, therapist and patient become to that extent "partners in deviance," they begin to establish a deviant sub-culture over against the larger culture. Hence we see the importance of the therapist's resistance to the "counter-transference" which would establish the reciprocity which the patient seeks.

The desire for acceptance of deviant definitions may take place in *any one* of the three major directions we have discussed, limited only by the intrinsic circumstances of the therapeutic situation. Thus, the patient may seek approval for his distorted rationalization of his instrumental failures: "It really was all the fault of that terrible boss I had, wasn't it?" Or it may be the attempt to obtain legitimation for a deviant goal-gratification outlet, such as a sexual perversion, or finally it may be, and very generally is, an attempt to define the therapist's solidarity with the patient in a deviant manner; either to undermine his support by open antagonism which is expected to be reciprocated in kind, or to make a bid for a familial type of solidarity relationship, when only a "professional" relationship is in fact legitimate.

Finally, within the framework given by these other three features of social control, the therapist acts as a "normal" agent of the learning process *through his manipulation of rewards*. The ways he can operate are sharply circumscribed by these other features of his role. He must not give either rewards or punishments which would be distorted so as to undermine his role in any of these other three respects. But within these limits he can approve and disapprove or perform any of the appropriate sanctions. A particularly important part is played by the sanctions of approval and esteem, because of the professional character of the relationship.

The possibility that therapist and patient should come to constitute a deviant sub-collectivity in which they mutually reinforce each other in patterns of orientation at variance with those of the larger society, underlines the importance of the institutionalization of the therapist's role and of the complementary role of the patient. It is this institutionalization which provides the basis of *leverage* for the change of vicious-circle deviance back into normally equilibrated social interaction. The therapist legitimizes his refusals to reciprocate the patient's expectation, not only with his own "personal influence", but with *institutional authority*. It is because *both* occupy institutionalized statuses that therapy can work. The articulation of the structure of these statuses with the dynamics of the interaction process should be clear in this case.

It may help to connect this relatively concrete account of the therapeutic process as a prototype of the process of social control, with the more technical conceptual scheme we have been expounding if we attempt to follow it through in terms of Figures 2 and 4.

Because of the central significance of the tension aspect of cumulative or vicious-circle deviance (which, with the requisite qualifications, in the personality system, we equate with "mental disturbance") we start with the assumption of high tension in the L cell, with the patient as ego.

The first phase of the therapist-patient relationship has a paramount emphasis on permissiveness. Permissiveness (passivity—letting the patient talk—withholding of sanctions) on the part of alter (the therapist) complements ego's (the patient's) greatest performance-need, namely tension-release. Such activity, we infer by the logic of balance between action and reaction directly increases ego's need for reactive sanctions of some kind and in combination with it, his sensitivity to alter's evaluative opinions. The patient begins to build up a strong need for an affective, particularistic relation with the therapist—i.e. transference begins to be established, and the focus of concern of the patient begins to shift to the I dimension or cell.

The fact that movement in the A dimension is here minimized and that in the I dimension is maximized is significant. One major problem of the patient is the legitimation of ego's goal-gratification orientations, which are clearly affected by alter's opinions. Alter's permissiveness towards ego's tension release must be associated

in the therapeutic control paradigm with the raising of two fundamental questions for ego, namely (1) the basis of his solidarity
with alter, the agent of this crucial benefit and (2) his status in
the light of alter's opinions.

We are now concerned with the I cell in which the maximization of the integrative phase corresponds to the supportive relationship. Here we assume that, in terms appropriate to the institutional
definition of the relationship, alter will, within limits broader than
are "normally" customary, support ego. This support suggests to
ego that he and alter are bound to common moral integrative
standards, as persons in a solidary collectivity typically are, so
the fact that alter does not give way to illegitimate suggestions
or to disagreement—or illicit agreement—raises the question in turn
of the evaluative status of the suggestions for which ego expects
alter's acceptance.

Thus we see that with respect to input-output balance in these
two respects ego gains—by tension release and by security, but
at a price in the raising of "uncomfortable" questions with respect
to (1) the relations between alter's permissiveness and his support,
which cannot *both* be motivated by alter's simply "going along"
with ego's wishes; (2) the relation between alter's solidarity and
permissiveness and the status of ego's suggestions.

In the light of ego's guilt and/or shame about his tension-release
and illegitimate suggestions, and the *absence* of antagonism and
condemnatory opinion, ego's concern begins to turn to the content
and normative justification of his suggestions.

Turning now to the G cell, the primary focus of the role of
alter, the therapist, is on the *denial of reciprocity*, i.e. for ego's
suggestions, so far as they are defined as deviant. It should be noted
that in the *first* instance this is denial of response-reward, including
we suggest, gratification in being duly punished for an aggressive
act. Here the price for the benefits of permissiveness and support
really begins to be felt. The "illogical" expectations favored by these
attitudes come to frustration. The patient, in a word, is "trapped".
He cannot justify his deviant suggestions because his therapist has
not been non-permissive or non-supportive; still they are not grati-
fied, and tension, instead of being permanently reduced, is built
up again.

Somewhere along here in a phase-process, there occurs an optimal opportunity for learning processes to take hold. Here the
role of the therapist is to manipulate rewards—as a process of rein-
forcing "reality oriented" adaptive instrumental performance of ego

to bring about alteration of ego's quality pattern (his "personality") and through this of the character of the therapeutic relationship *as a social system.*

From the paradigm we may infer that approval for genuinely valued achievement—in ego's handling of his "problems"—is the focal reward which brings not only favorable opinion but *agreement,* i.e. a positive reaction in recognition of progress. But the specificity and neutrality of this agreement, which is appropriate to the professional relationship, stand in sharp contrast to the diffuse affective legitimation and acceptance formerly expected by ego in reaction to his *illegitimate* suggestions. The second most critical sanction manipulated by the therapist is, we suggest, esteem which is the condition of solidarity on the new basis that ego is "recovering" and can be judged by the full standard of the wider common culture and not merely as "ill." Alter's opinions are no longer favorable in a permissive sense only, but in a positive sense.

Thus we see that in the initial phases the therapeutic relationship is *in fact* a conditionally legitimated deviant sub-culture. The therapist's role is originally oriented to the norms of the sick role but then comes progressively to be oriented to the norms of the wider culture. It is, however, as we noted above, this anchorage in the wider value-system which gives the therapist's role its power. It is, in a sense which we will discuss in the next section, a *representative* role. For this reason it is crucial that, in the wider system, of which the therapist-patient collectivity is a subsystem, it should be a *collectivity-oriented* role.[20]

It would be easy to go on from here to show how the above analysis of the therapeutic role can be generalized to cover all the main features of the mechanisms of social control so far as they are relevant to breaking the vicious circles of cumulative deviance. Space, however, is lacking so the reader may be referred to the examples brought forward in the last section of Chapter 7 of *The Social System* to carry out his own analysis. These were, it will be remembered, the youth culture in our society, funeral ceremonies, and the situations leading to cumulative alienation from a political regime.

As compared with previous treatments of the process of therapy, and hence of operations of the mechanisms of social control more generally, there are two new features of the above account namely, first, the connection of the four components of the paradigm with

[20] The therapeutic relationship is analyzed not only in Chapter 7 of *The Social System* but more fully in Chapter 10.

the succession of phases of an interaction process *in time*, and secondly, the insight that this connection could be worked out if the order of succession of phases were the reverse of that on which we have originally fixed our attention, and which Bales has found to be typical of task performance processes with the small group. This order of phases in terms of our paradigm, starts with latency, then moves to the system-integrative phase, then to the system-goal attainment phase, and finally to the adaptive.

Once this insight had been attained, it fitted logically with. the fact on which we have laid emphasis above, that there is an oppositeness of directionality involved in performance processes and in learning processes; after all, reversal of the vicious circles of deviance does involve learning processes. But once having established this connection we began looking for other cases of learning processes to which this analysis might apply. We will illustrate here with one further striking example, namely that of the pattern of the principal phases of the socialization of the child especially as that has become standardized in thinking influenced by psychoanalysis.

The earliest phase might, following psychoanalytic terminology but without attempting to account for the more refined distinctions, be called "oral dependency". In it the child plays a passive role and his activity is primarily of a tension-releasing character, if gratification of his hunger needs etc. may be regarded in this way. The role of the parent becomes primarily that of taking *care of* the child in the sense of acting as agent of these tension-releasing processes.

With a certain stabilization of gratification levels in this respect and hence of expectations with respect to periodicity, to agency, etc. there occurs a gradual transition from dependency on the mother's care *of* the child to dependency on her care *for* him, in the sense of a reciprocal love relationship between them. The child has come to be incorporated into a solidary collectivity with the mother in which the primary activity is system-integrative through the mutual show of affection, i.e. solidarity. For purposes of this brief sketch, we may skip over the "anal" phase, though it does seem to fit as a transition between the two types of dependency.

The interactive system established between mother and child has, however, certain elements of instability which are related to the consequences of the child's own process of maturation, to the role of the father, and to the mother's own expectations of what a child who is "growing up" should do. In any case the oedipal crisis seems to arise at the point of transition between this system-integrative phase where the solidary relation with the mother is the primary focus of the child's orientation system, and the next phase. Here, notably, his affection for his mother, including its erotic component, must be subordinated to the demands of participation in system-goal attainment, which we may interpret to mean the function of the family as a system including in the first instance the father and secondarily the siblings. Essentially we may speak of the positive aspect of this new phase as responsible participation in an interactive system with reference to system goals, and of its negative aspect, as the "latency" of the earlier system-integrative need system with its erotic component. This then is the latency phase in the Freudian sense.

Finally, there is the gradual process of emancipation from the family of orientation which culminates in adolescence where autonomy of adaptive orientations becomes the primary criterion of "adequacy", i.e. of the stable state of interaction. Here we may say that the child has become autonomously adapted to the same extrafamilial social environment to which the family itself has had to be adapted in the larger society.

The simplicity of the phase pattern thus outlined is, we are well aware, cross-cut by various complicating considerations. The most important of these lies in the fact that the social, i.e. interactive, system-participation of the child does not remain constant throughout the process, but there is a progression from the predominance first of the mother-child sub-system to the conjugal family as a whole, and finally to participation in the wider society. But even with this complication the correspondence of our phase pattern (in reverse) with such a well-established account of the process of child development is so striking that we wish to call attention to it as a starting point for analysis of the complications we are sure are present.

VIII. Differentation of Role Structure

Earlier in this chapter we assumed that as far as action was concerned, motivation was to be treated as originally undifferentiated. This means that differentiation must be treated as a problem. The structure of motivation must not be assumed as given from the nature of the biological structure of the organism. We assume that in the foregoing analysis of system-function and system- and unit-phases, of the equilibrated balance of a plurality of unit orbits in a system, and in our account of the learning process, we have at hand the conceptual materials for constructing a coherent account of the nature and processes of the structural differentiation of systems.

Even though they are both constituted by the same elements, unit phase-differentiation must be clearly distinguished from the structural differentiation of the system. An orbit pattern of a unit does not go through all possible points and does not pass through all the phases at the same rate. Two units may have different orbit-patterns i.e. be structurally differentiated and at any given moment, they may be in different phases. Two units which occupy structurally different roles in the system will have different orbit patterns. A structurally differentiated system is a constellation of system phase areas and points where there are relative concentrations of activity as compared with other system phase areas and points. Each system phase area or point entails units in a variety of unit-phase areas. The fact that we are dealing with systems undergoing one-way process which are made up of a plurality of units precludes, except as a limiting case, under very simple conditions, that these units should be undifferentiated.

Among other things, a system in which units were uniform would presume that goal-attainment phases had the same content for all units. But the motivational and learning inputs of units differ to begin with, and the nature of system problems in the task-oriented and the social-emotional areas imposes inter-unit and correlatively system differentiation in any system. Internal differentiation of a system is a condition of its continued structural existence as a system. It is for this reason that we argue that in human action systems there is an extremely wide range of possible concrete goal-states.

These *become* goal-states by the processes of learning—by the generalization of cathexis from original consummatory experiences to associated objects, and by the selective legitimation of these cathexes through their integration, in the first instance, into instrumental or particularistic—solidary meaning patterns. The first path leads to the cathexis of means-objects which in turn can become cathected as goals; the second to "substitution" of new goal-objects or more importantly, to the building up of "complex objects" which as such, become diffusely cathected objects of an independent gratification-need.

The evidence from the study of conditioning suggests that the range of objects which can be cathected by generalization through association is extremely wide. This in turn suggests the paramount importance, in the *structuring* of specific goal-states, of the selective factors in the learning process to which we have called attention, above all in instrumental and particularistic generalization. It also indicates the importance of the two modes of integration, the diffuse-quality and the neutral-universalistic, of which we have already spoken.

This means that the primary principle of selection of cathexes lies in the *value* for the action-unit, of the cathected object, i.e. of the object in relation to the action unit. Here certain complications must be taken into account. First, reward objects are scarce relative to motivational input, and facilities are not only scarce but their use involves commitments to certain goal-states. Further, the consummatory phase of a unit *as a subsystem* cannot be indefinitely prolonged, in view of the nature of the unit as a subsystem with problems of its own and as a component of a system with system problems. For the unit alone then the maximization of gratification involves *balancing* the output of gratification in the consummatory phase with the other inputs and outputs of the total orbit. Thus there is no presumption that what, in the narrow sense, is the "most gratifying" object cathexis will survive in favor of others which maximize different gratifications and satisfactions relative to input.

These exigencies of the limited duration of goal-states and of the necessary balancing of gratifications, inputs and outputs are in turn accentuated and of course in part determined, by the direct exigencies arising from integration with the plurality of other units *in the same system*. Here there seems to be a "natural" tendency to inter-unit goal-differentiation not only because of the differentiated motivational and learning inputs, but because of the tendency of systems to reduce strain. Since a system is constituted by a plurality of units, competing, actually or potentially, both for the same goal-objects and for the same facilities, lack of differentiation tends to maximize both the adaptive strain resulting from the scarcity of facilities and the integrative strain involved in competition for the same reward-objects. The differentiation of unit-goal objects alleviates these strains within the system.[21]

Hence, if generalization of cathexis by association is relatively free, we would expect this differentiation to be facilitated. To carry further the analysis of the bearing of system exigencies on this process and its consequences, we must first recall that both unit

[21] This proposition was clearly stated by Durkheim in the *Division of Labor*.

and system-exigencies *force* a given unit to move in phases other than the consummatory. This fact underlies the possibility of "exacting a price" for gratification—the "price" is the performance of "services", not only toward the unit's own gratification interest, but on behalf of the system, i.e. of other units as parts of the system.

This consideration states the main basis for explaining the coincidence of the *direction* of goal-differentiation and the functional needs of the system. The unit-gratification interest—including its instrumental and integrative investments—can thus be harnessed to the needs of the system. This is essentially the basis of what, for social systems, (*Social System,* Chapter 2) has been called the theorem of "the institutional integration of motivation". "The institutional integration of motivation" is in the present context an aspect of equilibrium, stating a condition of the balance of inputs and outputs.[22]

We have taken differentiation of goal-specifications as the point of departure for this analysis. This is justified by the specially "ultimate" status of goal-gratification as the motivational "end-product" of the action process. But it is in the nature of *systems* of action that such a process of differentiation, wherever it starts, should comprehend all the phases of system-process and structure. Merely pointing to the nature of the interdependence involved in our conception of system is sufficient to justify this statement.

Thus far in this argument we have asserted three propositions: (1) that the discrimination of differentiated unit object-cathexes and hence differentiation of consummatory unit goal-states within the orbits of the respective units is an inevitable *tendency* in action systems; (2) that the consequences of such goal-differentiation will ramify through the structure of the phase-orbits of the units in the system and; (3) that the pattern of this differentiation, if it is to become stabilized in terms of the conditions of equilibrium of the system, must conform with the functional prerequisites of the system (a simple application of the principle of system integration.)

Let us now turn to the problem of the interpretation of the findings of Bales on the subject of role differentiation in small groups stated near the end of Chapter 4 above. The essence of these findings can be summarized in the following propositions: (1) Small groups of the task-oriented types observed by Bales and his collaborators tend to produce differentiated roles, with the absolute amount and qualitative emphasis of participation of differ-

[22] It is thus another statement of the principle of system-integration which explains the "natural selection" of goal-orientations.

ent members being the criteria of differentiation. Broadly the larger the group the greater the differentiation of participation. (2) In their post-meeting evaluations group members differentiate between what Bales calls the "instrumental leadership function" ("who had the best ideas?" and/or "who did most to keep the group moving?") and that of the "socio metric star" ("whom did you *like* best?"). The "top man" in participation terms was unaccountably low in rating as best liked, and some other, usually the second in participation, was unaccountably high. (3) In answer to the question, "whom did you *dislike* most?" the "top man"—the instrumental leader—was unaccountably high, as was the man with least participation, who was thus a "scapegoat."

We interpret these findings to mean first that groups tend to become quickly differentiated internally in the exercise of initiative. The units quickly begin to move through different orbits. Whatever may be the role of personality or unit-properties, in the *allocation* of persons to roles, the emergence of the roles themselves is clearly related to uniformities of system exigency. The system as the situation of action of the constituent units imposes a set of orbits which must be accepted by a unit if the system is to go on functioning.

Second, the differentiation between the instrumental and the expressive leader suggests that even in small, short-lived groups there is an early differentiation of roles with respect to the distinction between the task-oriented and the social-emotional areas of the group's activities. Specialization in the maintenance of solidarities and in the facilitation of tension release seems directly to complement that in proceeding with the solution of the situationally imposed group task.

Third, the fact that the "top man" is not best liked, and in some cases accumulates more than his share of dislikes is, in terms of the phase process, evidence that pressure in the system task-orientation direction generates tensions within the system, which on the one hand are channelled towards antagonism toward the instrumental leader and toward a bottom "scapegoat", but which it is *also* the function of expressive leadership—and other roles differentiated in this direction—to mitigate or resolve. Thus we see how unit orbit differentiation is correlative with system-structural differentiation and how this in turn is a product of system-exigency or the functional prerequisites of systems.

We may add that Bales also presents evidence that the role of the task-oriented leader tends to be differentiated further into two sub-roles: the initiator of orientations and suggestions regarding the substantive steps towards the solution of the task and the role of guiding the group smoothly and efficiently toward solution of the group task. The former is, in an embryonic differentiation, the role of the technical expert, the latter the role of the executive.

Role Differentation and Goal Specification

In the situation which is analyzed in the foregoing pages, the emergence of differentiated roles went hand in hand with an effort on the part of the actors to find roles in which they could fit or to create the roles they needed to act in or to interact with. One part of the process of finding and creating the necessary roles is a competitive struggle for role status. In the early stages of the interaction of a group, the members of which are not previously known to each other, there is a process of "jockeying for position" and otherwise settling questions of relative status. The initial allocations of specific roles to specific persons are dependent on the willingness of individuals initially to take them or permit others to do so. If, however, a structure of the group is once established on a stable basis, it tends to be increasingly accepted by most of the members as the situation of their action. The units or members of the group adapt their goals to what is achievable within the limitations imposed by the situation, and major situational reconstructions are not likely to be undertaken. Then the primary *functional content* of the role as an element in the system (as it is described in terms of our analysis of systems) becomes the primary *goal-specification* content of the role of the individual member. To take only the elementary differentiation between the instrumental leader and the sociometric star, in the one case the primary personal goal-specification of the unit comes to be attached to instrumental performance; solution of the group task comes to be the primary *personal* goal of this individual. The sociometric star, on the other hand, accepts as a given feature of the situation the performances of the leader and he certainly contributes to instrumental function, especially perhaps through agreement, but his *primary* personal gratification derives from success in his role as promoter of solidarity and provider of opportunities for tension release; he may in part be the "funny man" who tells timely jokes as a way of facilitating tension release.

That instrumental performances should play an important part in the role of the instrumental leader goes without saying. But in the case of the leader in the social-emotional area, or sociometric star, differentiation leads to a type of "instrumental" performance different from that predominant in the contributions of the instrumental leader. The "instrumental" performance of the social-emotional leader consists in the exercise of skill in furthering solidarity and tension release. He becomes, we may say, skilled in the management of "human relations"[23] as distinguished from the more "impersonal"[23] subject-matter of the task leader's instrumental performances. The manifestation of solidarity on the part of others, his "being liked" by them is then not only the fulfillment of a system-requirement but a unit goal-gratification which parallels the instrumental leader's gratification in achievement of the externally imposed group task. The process of intra-unit differentiation ramifies into all the phases of the role-orbits of both parties.

Despite our emphasis on intra-unit differentiation, unit orbit differentiation, and its distinction from inter-unit or system differentiation, there can be coincidences at particular moments, but it will be necessary to keep system-references clear. One refers to the differentiation of functional content of goal-states, instrumental performance, expressive-integrative action and latency *from the point of view of the interactive system as a system.* The other refers to the differentiation of the corresponding, theoretically formulated, entities *from the point of view of the system-unit in that system considered as a sub-system.* What in the larger system is one phase will very often coincide with different phases of the units or subsystems. Thus what is instrumental performance for the larger system may be a consummatory goal-state for one unit, while what is expressive-integrative in function for the larger system is a consummatory goal-state for another unit. Moreover, the several units in the system must of necessity have their own unit consummatory phases in *different* functional phases of the larger system. The phases of the different units must in the sense of having determinate relations at a series of points in time, be synchronized and articulated at each system-phase. (If they were identical, this would be the negation of the concept of structural differentiation of the system.)

In what, then does this synchronization and articulation consist? It is simply the equilibrating process, described in terms of the balancing of inputs and outputs and the mechanisms of social control, as we have discussed it in the preceding sections. Here we need only to call attention to certain implications of our earlier discussion.

[23] These terms will be defined in a technical sense below.

First, what we have called the institutionalized-internalized value-pattern is essentially the definition of the internal conditions of the stable state of the system, the articulation of performance values and sanction values. The value-pattern defines the situation and gives the appropriate expectations for *all* the phases *both* of the system-process, *and* of each unit-process.

This is the essential structural significance of the composition of norms from both a performance and a sanction value pattern. The "common value system" thus may include, among others, a primary obligation of a group to accomplish a task set for them rather than merely to "enjoy themselves". This essentially means proliferation of activity in one of the phases and a consequent adjustment of the volume and type of activity in the other phases.

The stable state for the phase-movements of a particular unit is generally identical with what we refer to as the "institutionalized pattern of the role." When we say that a role is institutionalized and that its pattern accordingly *derives* from the common value system we mean essentially that the incumbent of this role as a unit in a system performs certain types of interaction, in characteristic sequences, so that his phase movements have a determinate pattern and that this *role* or phase pattern is integrated with others which together with it constitute both a differentiated and an integrated system. In its social structural aspect, integration is the articulation of the actions of ego and alters in accordance with these requirements. In its cultural aspect, integration is the legitimation of the value pattern of a specific role by conformity with the common value pattern.

Ultimately, synchronization of unit phases and system phases hinges on the balancing of inputs and outputs through performances and sanctions. The legitimation of a differentiated role is "permission" granted in accordance with the common value pattern by alter or alters for ego to act *differently* from the way they do; for example when alter is in a stage of instrumental performance, ego's role which is primarily solidarity-promoting and which may be in a stage of latency will be legitimated if this is in accordance with the common value pattern and if alters approve or permit it. Legitimation might also involve a set of obligations, either to perform when others are not required to do so, or to refrain from performance expected of others. These permissions (or rights) and obligations to act in different phases of sub-system process are legitimated on the ground that both contribute to the system functions in different ways.

There is an apparent paradox in the fact that different roles, different rights and privileges, different obligations can be equally legitimate in a particular system, and that the legitimation is derived from a common value system. The solution of the paradox lies quite simply in the nature of a social system. These divers rights are legitimated by their bearing on the "interests" of the system as a system. They are indeed differentiations of certain general roles, rights, privileges and obligations, differentiations made with respect to the different problems, internal and external, confronted by social systems. The system requires differentiation for the performance of the functions necessitated by the problems of the system, and its common value pattern approves those roles which contribute to its fulfillment or which at least are consistent with it. A permissive common value pattern will require less positive sanctioning with respect to system-interest and will legitimate wider ranges of variation from a differentiated role pattern than would a more prescriptive, more prohibitive common value system. But both will require and approve a wide variety of roles. The role pattern is, to use an emanationist simile, the "unfolding" of the common value system, but *in its application* to the *fulfillment of the system-functions* in a wide variety of concrete situations, taking due account of the "needs" of the units as well as their contributions, i.e. their input and output capacities.

In the foregoing discussion, we have talked about the *roles* of ego and alter as differentiated units in a system. Though it is a sociological commonplace, it must never be forgotten that it is the role and not the personality of an actor which is the unit of a system of social interaction. The personality is itself a complex system of action of which the actions making up a particular role form *only one sub-system.*[24] Naturally this subsystem is subject to the integrative exigencies of its relations to the other sub-systems of ego's personality, as well as those of the interaction system, but theoretically it must never be identified with ego's personality as a system, even though for many empirical purposes its interdependence with the rest of the personality need not be specifically analyzed.

We have stated that the fundamental key to the analysis of structural differentiation of action systems lies in the relationship of system and sub-system. In aproaching the analysis of social structure on the more macroscopic levels, we find that it is essential

[24] Some implications of this fact will be noted below in connection with discussion of family structure.

Working Papers in the Theory of Action

to extend this analysis beyond the treatment of two adjacent levels
to include three or more such levels. It is here that the pattern
variable of self- vs. collectivity-orientation becomes relevant as well
as the concept which we mentioned above, of "representative role."

The Occupational System

Instead of developing the uses of these concepts in purely
abstract terms, we will attempt to sketch briefly the analysis of
two major structural complexes in our own society, as they have
proved relevant to the current study in the field of social mobility,
to which reference was made in the Preface of this publication.

The aim of that study is to contribute to the understanding
of the determination of the allocation of personnel to roles in the
occupational system. It seeks to discover what factors apart from
the status of the family of orientation (as indicated by father's
occupation, both parents' education, type of residential community,
etc.) determine the distribution of boys in their adult occupational
careers, i.e., the "level" of occupational status they achieve and
the qualitative type of role they enter. It is obvious that family
status is a heavily determining factor—though the mechanisms by
which this operates are only fragmentarily understood—and so is
the ability of the boy, as roughly measured by intelligence tests.
However, empirical evidence for a large sample from high schools
of a metropolitian area clearly demonstrates that when these two
factors have been taken into account the residual variance is substantial. According to indices constructed by Stouffer, relative to
an index of probable occupational level, the multiple correlation
with family status index and I.Q. is .54.

It is not possible here to enter into the various ramifications of
these problems. But certain phases of the work provide appropriate
illustrations for our approach to the analysis of social structure. It
has proved necessary in the research to attempt to carry systematic
structural analysis of the occupational role system much farther
than other studies in the literature have done, and to do so in a
way which could be directly articulated with the analysis of the
role-structure of the family—as well as school and peer group,
though we will not discuss the last two here.

We have found it necessary in the first instance to treat the
system of occupational roles in the context of American society
as a system. The whole occupational system constitutes a sub-system
of the total society which is functionally differentiated from other

sub-systems such as the kinship system, the structure of local communities, the political system, the religious system, and the cultural system. The occupational system is essentially the institutionalized differentiation of the adaptive aspect of the task-orientation area of the social system. It is structurally the most central part of what is generally called the "economy." It is that part which defines the major pattern of *roles* in this area. The position of the occupational sub-system in the total social system will be influenced, within limits, by the common value system. For example, the economy and its occupational role-system occupy a particularly crucial place in American society because the paramount or common value system gives primacy to the functions institutionalized in this area. Hence the primary functions and hence common value system of any occupational sub-system here coincide with and are particularly strongly reinforced by the common value system of the society as a whole.

The central point for present purposes, however, is that the primary functions of the occupational role system for the larger society are adaptive; they center in understanding and control of the situational factors. The performance of the system goal-attainment, integrative and expressive functions of the total society are *not* primary functions of the occupational system as a sub-system.

In interpreting this approach, it must be kept clearly in mind that every sub-system of the society is subject to the same tendencies toward structural differentiation as is every other, and that, for example, internal differentiations of the political system may articulate in specific ways with internal differentiations of the occupational system; thus we speak correctly of "jobs" in the political system. It is therefore likely that structurally identical role-types will appear in more than one sub-system of a complex society. It is, however, essential to start with reference to a carefully defined system and then refer separately to each additional articulation with other systems.

The primary function of the occupational subsystem then is adaptive. As a system, however, it has its own orbit in which the adaptive phase is preponderantly important. It has naturally its other phases as well. Its adaptive phase, though synchronized with the adaptive phase of the total social system, is not necessarily coincidental with it.

A function of a subsystem may be analyzed in terms of outputs of that subsystem which in turn constitute inputs for the other units of the total system. The outcome of successful adaptive processes is, we have come to realize, a changed relation of the system to objects external to itself—which may include creation of new objects, changes in the properties of objects and changes in their relations to actors. In our classification of outputs, this falls primarily in the category of achievements as distinguished from accomplishments.

The primary output "passed on" to the other subsystems by the occupational subsystem then is valued possessions, which in turn we may subdivide into facilities and rewards. The relevance of this distinction in the present context touches the uses to which the possession is put—hence its functional significance for the recipient subsystem. If it is a facility, it serves primarily adaptive functions for the recipient subsystem, thus strengthening the adaptive phase of its orbit and, hence, of the system as a whole. Thus the "economy," in its monetary aspect, produces income part of which goes to units of government in the form of taxes to facilitate *their* adaptive processes. If the occupational output on the other hand is a reward it goes to serve a nonadaptive function of the recipient subsystem, e.g., family "consumption." It may be a consummatory goal-object or an integrative or otherwise expressive symbol.

This functional significance of occupational output across the "disposal" lines for the recipient subsystem or unit of it provides us with one major axis of our classification of occupational roles. If the output is significant as a facility, we speak of an instrumentally oriented role; if as a reward, of an expressively oriented one. The distinction is independent of whether the recipient unit is or is not another subunit of the occupational system or belongs in another subsystem of the society.

It follows from our argument above that the common value system of the occupational subsystem, like that of the larger society, gives primacy to universalistic-achievement or performance values. This then gives us from another point of view the content of the primary goal-specification of occupational roles, which is that "success" in occupational achievement is the primary source of goal-gratification for this class of roles in the larger social system as distinguished from other major subsystems. The "success" goal in this sense we define in achievement terms as we have just explained this. Furthermore, it is equally applicable whether the unit in the occupational subsystem be a collectivity, i.e. an "organization" or the role of an individual. In the latter case it should be remembered the question of how far the success goal dominates his personality system-goal-orientation is left completely open at this point. It is a question of the place of this subsystem goal in the total system of the personality.

The occupational system differs from other subsystems of the total society in that *their* common value-systems must be different from that of the occupational subsystem. Thus the functions of the political subsystem center in the areas of system goal-attainment and *system*-integration. This subsystem, considered as itself a system, becomes differentiated like any other. This involves a differentiation between its "occupational" and its "political" subsystems.[25] In the latter, occupational success can be the dominant subsystem goal, just as in the general occupational system. But there is a difference, namely with respect to the common value-system and its relation to the value-pattern of the differentiated role. In the case of a sub-role of the occupational system, the success goal is as it were "compounded." It is the success goal of a unit as a contribution to the "adaptive" goal of the subsystem of which it is a unit. In the case of an occupational role within the political system, on the other hand, the success goal of the occupational role contributes to the "integrative" goal of the political system. This is the basis of both the common factors and the differences.

The occupational subsystem of the society is, like all subsystems, in turn composed of further subsystems. Just how it is divided up into units and how many steps will be distinguished will of course depend on the purpose of the analysis. One of the commonest and, for purposes of economic analysis, most important is that into "industries," where the criterion of differentiation of units is the class of possessions which constitute the output of the subsystem, e.g., the coal industry or the women's clothing industry. For our purposes, however, it is possible to by-pass certain of those intermediate bases of differentiation.

Our primary interest at this stage is in the classification of the occupational roles of individuals in a highly differentiated occupational system like our own. The individual actor's occupational role may be a subsystem of a subsystem and so on through a large number of steps. But since our interest is in structural types, we may concentrate on one fundamental criterion, namely that where the role enters directly into input-output relations with other units (e.g., in the exchange process) and that where it is

[25] If there is danger of confusion, we could speak of the "primary" occupational subsystem and of several "secondary" occupational subsystems.

a role in an organization which is the unit of input-output relations.

The distinguishing criterion is the authorship of the "product" or achievement-object which crosses the disposal line. The distinction depends upon the extent to which the "product" or achievement is, as such, the contribution of an individual or of an organization to the two primary functions of the occupational system as a system, the provision of facilities or of reward objects to the other units.

Whatever the action-unit at this disposal line, whether it be the role of an individual or of a collectivity, two problems in addition to that of the function of the output for the recipient unit arise concerning the pattern of the orientation of this unit to its "exchange partner" across the line. The first is whether with respect to the specific content of the relationship, the two should be treated as fellow-members of a solidary collectivity, or in this respect, are not bound by the obligations of such common membership. The second concerns the nature of the process by which, if the partners to the transaction are not members of a solidary relationship, the terms of disposal are settled, and agreement is reached. Here the problem is whether ego, who performs the occupational function, acts vis-a-vis alter primarily through providing information and manipulating the situation in which alter must act, but leaves the "decisions" entirely to alter, or whether, on the other hand, ego performs his function through attempting to influence alter's decisions through helping him to "make up his mind" by expressive communication and expressive sanctions, i.e. by producing some of the elements of a solidary relationship.

In the first of the above problems, the self-vs. collectivity-orientation pattern-variable becomes relevant. Thus in the doctor-patient relationship which we have cited above, though in one sense the physician is "selling his services" to the patient, i.e. there is a transaction across the disposal line, in another they constitute together a solidary collectivity; i.e. a sub-system of the social system; this is indeed a fundamental condition of the support which plays such an important part in the psychotherapeutic processs.[26] In the case of the ordinary commercial market relationship, on the other hand, self-orientation is institutionalized. Here it is permissible,

[26] One of the clearest indices of this characteristic of the relationship is the taboo on "shopping around," i.e. a patient's "bargaining" with several doctors to obtain the best service and most favorable conditions. A patient either is or is not a member of the collectivity which is signalized by being "Dr. X's patient." He must either accept the obligations of membership or "resign".

indeed obligatory, to shop for the best conditions subject only to the regulative restrictions of the "rules of the game." Here also it is permissible to attempt to "win" *against* the exchange partner in a conflict of interest, within limits of legitimate action or rules of fairness. Even that range of permissiveness would be strictly tabooed in the collectivity-oriented case. Put a little differently, in the collectivity-oriented case those on both sides of the disposal line are subject to a prescriptive, not merely regulative, common value system with respect to the specific subject-matter of their relationship. In the self-oriented case this is not true; they are free to seek their own goals.

The second problem concerns the nature of the process, in either the self- or the collectivity-oriented case, by which ego plays a part in bringing about alter's decisions across the disposal line. The first type, that in which ego confines himself—or gives primacy—to providing information and manipulating situational objects, we have called in a special sense "impersonal". (This corresponds to the impersonal, competitive market of economic theory.) The second type in which ego attempts to influence alter's decisions through playing on the balance of his motivational system, we call a "human relationship" type, again in a special sense. Though concretely there is a continuous shading, one of the more conspicuous fields of the "human relationship" type is in salesmanship.

To illustrate the dynamics of this problem we may say a word on this. We have seen throughout our analysis that expressive communication is intimately bound up with the integrative problems of the system of action. Commercial market relationships, in a predominantly self-oriented context, tend to shade over from impersonality into the area of human relations, creating particularly difficult problems of adjustment. The capacity and the need to influence alter's decisions raises in an acute form the question of ego's intentions toward alter: does he try to promote alter's genuine welfare or is he trying to exploit him?[27]

[27] This is a situation of strain in which there is a tendency for the salesman to oscillate between an effusive friendliness, which only the cynic would call a "false front," and a toughness in bargaining. This seems to be one of the main foci of what Merton has called "pseudo-gemeinschaft" in American society. In the case of the psychiatrist, however, who manipulates human relations on a much deeper level, the same order of problem is less likely to arise, because the relationship to his patient is institutionalized in accordance with a collectivity-oriented pattern. The same is true of an elementary school teacher who manipulates the balance of the child's motivational system within a collectivity oriented context.

The above distinctions deal with the distinction of primary occupational function and the types of orientation across the disposal line. There remains the question of the relation of the role of the individual to the structure of the collectivity of which he is a part, where he is not alone in relation to the market structure but is a member of a "producing" organization.

At least one major component of his occupational role will derive from the fact that his organization itself is a sub-system of the occupational sub-system. As an occupational organization, it will give prominence to the adaptive functions of the organization. A church, on the other hand, with a different functional problem will differ in its role structure from a business firm or, in another part of the cultural sub-system, a scientific laboratory.

Each of the major sub-systems is differentially concentrated on some one system task or on some aspects of one or more system tasks. The political sub-system is largely concentrated on internal system integration over a defined territory and most of its more differentiated activities are derived from its orientation to that system function. The cultural sub-system is differentially concentrated on the construction of patterns of cognitive orientations of various degrees of generality (science, information) and in the creation or reformulation of patterns of expressive-integrative orientation (art, music, ethics). Except for certain marginal roles (and excluding of course the adaptive roles within the cultural sub-system) cultural roles are very seldom directed towards the fulfillment of adaptive or instrumental system-functions.[28]

Since the primacy in function of the occupational sub-system rests on the universalistically oriented adaptive performance of the organization itself, besides the technical functions within the organization, the most important are those centering on responsibility for the conduct of the affairs of the organization as such, (i.e.

[28] The generalized patterns of cognitive orientation which are produced in the cultural system, even though they can often be articulated into adaptive roles within the occupational system, are not ordinarily produced in the prosecution of the activities constituting adaptive roles. The producers of these orientations perform some minor incidental adaptive functions in the course of their incumbency in roles in the cultural sub-system but this is secondary to their primary function. The skills which they develop there are often applicable in adaptive roles in the occupational sub-system and inter-sub-system role. Shifts of personnel are neither impossible nor infrequent. Indeed certain of the sub-systems (i.e. universities) communicate and create for some of their members the knowledge (in a general form) which will enable them to fill adaptive roles in the occupational sub-system and roles with adaptive functions in the political sub-system.

those centering on responsibility for system-goal-attainment.) The primary differentiation within the organization is between those roles oriented to technically specific functions entailing primarily the manipulation of facilities, and those oriented to diffuse responsibility for the organization or for sub-organizations within it. Further sub-differentiations with reference to the reward system and the management of tensions are also possible, but with reference to this type of collectivity, the main axis of internal role-differentiation distinguishes between the technical and the executive roles. Here the specificity and diffuseness of responsibility respectively stands out as the differentiating criterion.

There is a second conceptual distinction which is pertinent in dealing with collectivities as "producing" units, namely the distinction between "internal" and representative roles—or role-components. The internal role is that aspect of the total role in which ego is acting vis-a-vis other members of the organization, while the representative role is that in which he acts on behalf of the organization vis-a-vis non-members. Internal roles in organizations are *always* collectivity-oriented, they presume loyalty to the organization within the defined limits, and the alternative of cooperation or resignation. This, for example is a fundamental feature of holding a job, and hence of the organization of incentives for work, and of the institutionalization of authority in economic or occupational organizations.

In representative roles, on the other hand, the orientation to alter may be self- or collectivity-oriented according to the system-reference. It might be self-oriented towards alter but ego must still act within obligations defined by his relation to the collectivity he represents. This explains in part what to some seems a paradox, namely that it may be a positive obligation to pursue "self-interest." It is therefore necessary to distinguish the two contexts in which the role must be analyzed. Thus the treasurer of a university is certainly bound, like any other officer of an organization, to promote the welfare of the organization, an obligation perhaps underlined by the fact that in this case it is a non-profit organization. But in his dealings on the security markets he is, in a representative role, certainly oriented to "profit" which is usually defined in self-interested terms. In this case the relevant "self" is not himself as a personality but the collectivity which he represents. He is not in the same sense obliged to promote the interests of those from whom he buys securities as he is to promote that of the university. It should be clear that this fundamental distinction is entirely independent of the character of the organization. The nature of a married man's relation to the labor market is fundamentally similar when it is considered in terms of his representative role vis-a-vis his family.

Finally we must say a word about the fact that the role of an individual in such a sub-system as the occupational is inevitably *itself* a differentiated sub-system, differentiated according to the same principles as are other systems. What we characterize as the role-type describes the paramount value-pattern, and hence the primary obligation of functional performance and personal goal-specification in this role. But this has the same order of primacy in his role, e.g. a technical specialist's role, as does what we have defined as the function and hence paramount value pattern of the occupational sub-system as a whole. But as in the case of the latter there must be subsidiary functions. Essentially this is because *any* role is imbedded in what (cf. *Social System*, Chapter 3) we have called a "relational context". Even the narrowest technical specialist must at some points deal with others in relation to the disposal of his services, in relation to procurement of facilities, and generally he must have cooperative relations with some others. He must be oriented at some points to *their* goal-gratification problems, to the conditions of solidarity with them, and to their tension-management problems. He may manage these aspects of his role well or badly, but it is impossible to avoid involvement in them entirely.

We have seen that the main structure of the occupational role system is derived from two sources. The first is the application of our fundamental system paradigm with its distinction of functional system and sub-system problems, as used in its elementary two-level sense. The second is the repetition of this application for a series of interlocking system-references. It may be useful to recapitulate the latter series. We started with the total American social system and located the occupational system as a sub-system within it. Then we distinguished two fundamental types of orientation for occupational roles, first, to the provision of facilities for the recipient units, second, provision of reward-objects for them. Then cross-cutting this distinction, we introduced a further system distinction relative to the "disposal line" according to whether the relations across this line were characteristic of memberships in a common sub-system or were only "ecological" relations to another sub-system. Then we added the distinction of expressive-integrative or "human relationship" focus in the relations to alter as distinguished from the "impersonal" focus. Then we raised the problems concerned with the case where the role of the individual is part of a collective sub-system or an organization. Finally we raised the questions of the internal differentiation of the *role* of the individual considered as itself a sub-system.

The series of distinctions thus arrived at is inevitably complex. But considering the enormous empirical complexity of the field it does not seem to be unduly so, and it seems to us notable that it has proved possible to reduce what are for us the essential problems to such a relatively simple scheme which can be systematically derived without any *ad hoc* assumptions which are not integral to the general theoretical scheme. Finally, it should be mentioned that this scheme of occupational classification has been formulated in close connection with empirical work. The criteria and indices have been worked out in the course of classifying a sample of occupations from designations available on questionnaires (the occupations of their fathers as described by high school boys). The scheme has in turn been used as the basis for securing new data on a more refined level, which are in course of analysis.

The following outline of this scheme of classification may be helpful to the reader.

The Occupational Subsystem

(As differentiated from other subsystems of the society by primacy of adaptive functions)

A unit of this subsystem, (role of individual or collectivity) then, will be classified as:

I. *Instrumental*—if its primary output to other subsystems or units consists in what *to them* are facilities.

II. *Expressive*—if its primary output consists of *rewards* to the receiving unit.

Whether instrumental or expressive in function for the receiving unit, a role will be classified as:

A. *Specific*—if its function for the collectivity of which it is a unit is primarily adaptive, or

B. *Diffuse*—if its function for the collectivity is primarily oriented to responsibility for system goal-attainment and/or integration. (If the relevant output is produced by the role of an isolated individual, this distinction does not apply.)

Whether instrumental or expressive, specific or diffuse, a role will be classified as:

1. *Impersonal*—if terms of exchange are settled primarily by manipulating the objective situation and access to information of alter.

2. *Human Relations* oriented—if terms of exchange are settled primarily by "persuading" alter through influencing his attitudes.

Finally, whatever its classification in the above respects, a role will be classified as:

a) *Collectivity-oriented*—if, across the exchange line, ego and alter in the relevant respects belong together in a solidary collectivity.

b) *Self-oriented*—if their relation is only "ecological" and pursuit of self-interest is limited only by regulative norms.

The Family

The family presents a very different set of problems for structural analysis than does the occupational system. This is particularly true of the modern American urban family, of which we wish mainly to speak, because of the high degree of general structural differentiation of American society. Whereas our occupational structure forms an immensely elaborate network of highly differentiated roles, in one sense the direction of development of kinship in our society has been one of "de-differentiation", in that more and more what are sometimes called "extended" kinship relations have become attenuated and have left a residuum of relatively isolated conjugal family units with relatively loose kinship relations to each other, while at the same time many functions have been transferred from the family to other agencies. Moreover in terms of "gross" structure, i.e. the total familial roles of their members, these conjugal units are extremely simple, the main basis of differentiation being of course by generation between parents and children and by sex, between husband and wife, sons and daughters. Some would say that even these bases are biological so that sociologically considered the family is *only* a collection of "interacting personalities," it is not really a social system at all.

We believe indeed that the distinctive features of the family as a subsystem of the society are most intimately connected with its special relation to and functions for personality, but that far from negating the importance of its character as a social system, this provides a particularly crucial case of the fruitfulness of analysis on the level of the social system, including the structural aspect which is the present focus of attention.

We may start with the observation that the meeting of certain needs of its constituent personalities constitutes one of the most fundamental classes of functional prerequisites of the stable functioning of any society as a system. These prerequisites in turn fall into the two basic classes of the "stabilization" of the adult personality in its relations to role-performance, and the process of socialization by which the child comes to be integrated into the social system and thus in time capable of assuming a normal adult complex of roles. It is the coincidence of this double functional significance in relation to personalities as essential to societies which constitutes the primary point of reference for the analysis of the family. The American urban family is a particularly good example for our purposes precisely because its functional differentiation from other subsystems in this direction as well as others has gone farther in the American social system than in most other societies.

We may approach the problem from a different point of reference by pointing out that by comparison with other family types our family in the direct sense seems to be particularly "functionless". It does not *as a unit* make very significant contributions to the "economic production" of the society; it does not as a unit take political responsibility, though its members "as individuals" may do so, and it does not perform many system-integrative functions. From these considerations we may infer that its functions for the wider society are mainly *latent*—through its indirect influence on the other subsystems which do perform these functions. Since the conjugal family is so small as itself to be differentiated only into a few roles, the *systems* on behalf of which these functions are directly performed must, to a very important extent, be the personalities of the members. It is through these that influence on other subsystems of the society in which these individuals have roles is exerted.

This is particularly true of our society because of the unusually high degree to which the extra-familial roles of family members are autonomous as distinguished from representative, i.e., status in the relevant interaction system is variable independently either of the individual's status *in* the family or of the status *of* his family. This, however, is, we must grant, only one part of the picture. There are other subsystems of the social system of which the conjugal family as a unit is directly itself a unit. These are what Parsons (*Social System,* Chapter 5) has called the "diffuse solidarities" of kinship (beyond the conjugal family), community, ethnic group and class. In the ideal type structure of our society, the most important of these are community and class, although, of course, the other two are far from negligible. The relation between these diffuse solidarities in which the family is embedded and the predominance of representative roles on the part of its members is quite clear. We may say further that in so far as these structures have the character of systems composed of conjugal families as units, the latter will tend to have *more* than latent functions in relation to them. In other words, the latency of family function may be regarded as a rough index of the relatively secondary importance of these diffuse solidarities in our society.

Before discussing the relation between the internal role structure of the family and the extrafamilial roles of its members, a few further considerations about the significance of the latency of family function need to be mentioned. If we are correct about this shift of primary functional significance of the family in the direction of personality systems, then this provides us with an important point of departure for the type of analysis of structure in which we are interested. The important point is that the individual member's role in the family system must be regarded as itself a subsystem of the personality system of the family member. There must, therefore, be *systematic* relations between the bases of structural differentiation of roles *in the family* and the structural differentiation of personality types so far as these are important to the social system. This is particularly evident in view of the importance of the family as an agency of socialization.

We will attempt briefly to follow up this theme but we must note still one further starting point. The family in our type of society is a subsystem highly differentiated from other subsystems in structural type. If we are right that it has peculiarly important functions for personality, then these must be associated with its special features as a differentiated subsystem which, as we have seen, center precisely on its "latency." Ignoring the socialization function, we may say that this centers in "pattern-maintenance" and "tension-management"—to repeat the characterization given above of the latency phase. Then by the principles of structural differentiation outlined earlier in this section, the primary subsystem goal of the family must be to facilitate this pattern-maintenance and the tension-management of its members as personalities.

This immediately gives us the basis for characterizing the dominant type of subsystem norm for the family; it is the "ascriptive" type, with the pattern-variable combinations of quality, neutrality, universalism and diffuseness, or, put a little differently, the primary performance values are of the ascriptive-qualitative pattern and the primary sanction values, those of esteem.

Essentially, this is to say that the essential focus of the family system is, relative to others, ascriptive-expressive. The individual is treated in *status* terms, first as a family member and second in terms of the diffuse quality patterns of his "social personality" of which age and sex are the primary foci. Furthermore, in all these respects there is a paramount significance of what we may call style-of-life symbolism. Part of this focuses on the family as a whole as shown in the character of the home, its location, its furnishings, and the common patterns of life of the members. Part of it is differentiated by role in regard to dress, manners, etc.

But this latency function of the family gives us only the base point for the analysis of the relation of its structure to its functions for personality. Next we must consider the fact that the family itself has certain functional problems as a system and these have to be articulated with the personality systems of the members in roles other than the familial. This problem is particularly well illustrated by the role of the husband-father in our family system.

Successful adaptation of the family as a system above all depends on the availability of the facilities for maintenance of its style-of-life patterns which in our monetary economy means adequate income. The primary source, of course, is the adult male's occupational role. In addition this role is, through its prestige status, itself an important symbol of the family's "style", i.e., its "position" in the community. Certainly, in our society no index of family community status could ignore the occupation of the father as a major component.

Because of the crucial importance of this adaptive function for the *family* as a system—apart from the functions of occupational roles for other systems—broadly the husband-father may be regarded as the primary "task leader" of the system. In this connection, it is significant that immature children are largely disqualified from important contribution in this sphere.

The composition and small size of the conjugal family mean that there is only one possibility of differentiation of a major role relative to this axis, namely, that of the wife-mother. There are then two primary aspects of this differentiation. The first is that the commitments of the husband-father outside the family circle of interaction—an important part of which have functions for the family—precludes his taking certain responsibilities inside the circle, especially, of course, for child care. The second is that a primary condition of meeting the system-goal of the family as a system is skillful management of the emotional problems of the members; there is thus a peculiarly urgent need in the social-emotional area, with special reference to system-integration, tension management and style-patterning, i.e., expressive symbolism. This is obviously the primary traditional focus of the feminine role.

Thus we may speak of the major division of labor as that between responsibility *for* the family in the adaptive sense, and responsibility *in* the family. This internal structural differentiation clearly has a close resemblance to that found by Bales (without biological differentiation by sex) in small groups between the task leader and the "sociometric star." It also has much to do with the differentiation of the sex-roles in their extrafamilial sectors. In our society, the occupational system and the man's anchorage in it clearly demand a high degree of autonomy of his occupational role relative to the familial. The dependence of the family on him in adaptive connections strengthen this. On the other hand, the greater absorption of the woman's personality in the family makes it more difficult for her to develop autonomous roles to an extent comparable with her husband. This fact is in turn closely connected with her greater emphasis on *quality* style-symbolism, e.g., in dress and personal appearance and her tendency to play representative roles on behalf of her family. With respect to style symbolism and unit-to-unit integrative adjustments, the feminine role is in our society the primary focus of the diffuse solidarities in which the conjugal family is centrally involved—notably, community and class.

The above is a mere sketch of some considerations about the role structure of the urban American family—both internally and in its articulation with the rest of the social structure and with personality. Among many topics of great interst above all it abstracts almost entirely from variability of type, confining itself to a single highly schematic ideal type characterization, and it fails altogether to take up the exceedingly important problems of socialization. Both of these problem areas are major centers of attention in the research on social mobility mentioned above and in later publications on that problem it is hoped to carry out a considerably more advanced analysis of them. The purpose of the present brief sketch has been only to illustrate the use of our conceptual scheme in the analysis of social structure in a field radically different from that of occupational structure and close to the motivational dynamics of social process.